SOFTWARE ARCHITECTURE

PERSPECTIVES ON AN EMERGING DISCIPLINE

SOFTWARE ARCHITECTURE

PERSPECTIVES ON AN EMERGING DISCIPLINE

MARY SHAW
Carnegie Mellon University

DAVID GARLAN
Carnegie Mellon University

An Alan R. Apt Book

Prentice Hall, Upper Saddle River, New Jersey 07458

Library of Congress Cataloging-in-Publication Data

Shaw, Mary
    Software architecture: perspectives on an emerging discipline /
Mary Shaw, David Garlan
      p.   cm.
    Includes bibliographical references and index.
    ISBN 0–13–182957-2 (paper)
    1. Computer software. 2. Computer architecture. I. Garlan,
David. II. Title.
QA76.754.S48 1996
005.1'1—dc20

                                          95–49957
                                          CIP

Publisher: Alan Apt
Production Editor: Mona Pompili
Cover Designer: Bruce Kenselaar
Copy Editor: Nick Murray
Manufacturing Buyer: Donna Sullivan
Editorial Assistant: Shirley McGuire

© 1996 by Prentice-Hall, Inc.
Simon & Schuster / A Viacom Company
Upper Saddle River, New Jersey 07458

Printed in the United States of America

20 19 18 17 16 15 14 13 12

ISBN   0-13-182957-2

PRENTICE-HALL INTERNATIONAL (UK) Limited, *London*
PRENTICE-HALL OF AUSTRALIA PTY. LIMITED, *Sydney*
PRENTICE-HALL CANADA INC., *Toronto*
PRENTICE-HALL HISPANOAMERICANA, S.A., *Mexico*
PRENTICE-HALL OF INDIA PRIVATE LIMITED, *New Delhi*
PRENTICE-HALL OF JAPAN, INC., *Tokyo*
SIMON & SCHUSTER ASIA PTE. LTD., *Singapore*
EDITORA PRENTICE-HALL DO BRASIL, LTDA., *Rio de Janeiro*

To our families.

FOREWORD

USER: "I need a software system that will help me manage my factory" (or my hospital, product distribution system, satellite system, etc.)

SOFTWARE ENGINEER: "Well, let's see. I can put together components that do sorting, searching, stacks, queues, and so forth."

USER: "Hmm, that's interesting. But how would those fit into my system?"

SOFTWARE ENGINEER: "Actually, at a pretty low level. We'll have to spend some time figuring out what you need at a higher level, and how it would all fit together."

Conversations such as the above illustrate one of the biggest problems in software engineering today: the shortage of intermediate abstractions that connect the characteristics of systems users need to the characteristics of systems that software engineers can build.

This kind of problem can usually be handled in other engineering fields. For example, if a user wants a bridge built, a civil engineer can ask the user a number of questions about the bridge's function, traffic loads, setting, and environmental factors. Based on the answers, the engineer can identify the most appropriate architectural style for the bridge: suspension, cantilever, arch, truss, etc. This intermediate abstraction then enables the engineer to capitalize on codified principles and experience to specify, analyze, plan, and monitor the construction of this style of bridge, with high levels of efficiency and confidence.

Not only are such intermediate abstractions scarce in the software field, but also we need to cope with a proliferation of architectural claims such as:

- "Our Web language will enable your applications to operate on Unix, Macintosh, OS/2, and Windows platforms."
- "Our product is CORBA-compatible, and thus will fully interoperate."

- "Our system's balanced architecture ensures fast response time across all client-server configurations."

In Chapter 1 of this book, Mary Shaw and David Garlan show that these kinds of problems generally characterize a field that is trying to progress from a craft to an engineering discipline. In the remaining chapters, they lay the foundations and provide initial concepts and techniques for one of the critical needs of an engineering discipline: product architecting.

In particular, they provide several classes of intermediate abstractions to help bridge the gap between software needs and solutions. A key gap-filler is the classification and analysis of architectural styles for software, analogous to those for bridges. Shaw and Garlan provide definitions and discussions of major current software architectural styles: pipes and filters; data abstraction and object-orientation; event-based; layered; repository; and process control. They also apply the styles to some representative software applications, to show the differences among the resulting design solutions, and their comparative advantages and disadvantages.

Other key architectural gap-fillers provided in the book are domain specific software architectures (DSSAs), architecture definition languages, and architecture-based tools. DSSAs provide a set of intermediate abstractions particular to a given product domain, such as factory, hospital, product distribution, or satellite control domains. These domains may share some abstractions, such as functions for data acquisition, monitoring, control, and decision support. But they will have some further domain-specific differences, depending on characteristics of their typical users, environments, and quality requirements such as safety and information security.

Architecture definition languages provide more precision in representing the architecture of a system than do the usual software box-and-arrow drawings. Shaw and Garlan's treatment of architecture definition languages also emphasizes an important insight about software architecting: getting the connectors (interface assumptions, protocols, etc.) right is at least as important as getting the components (algorithms, data structures, etc.) right. Architecture definition languages also provide the basis for a stronger next generation of tools for defining a software architecture, and for reasoning about the properties of systems which would be built to that architecture.

Architecture definition languages and tools enable this to be done at the early architecting stage, rather than finding out about these properties after implementation, when the cost and freedom to change the architecture is often prohibitive.

Thus, software architectures provide the software engineering field with more than a set of gap-filling abstractions. They provide the basis for the most important milestone in the software life cycle process: the milestone that determines whether your proposed or default architecture has the strength to cope with current and future workloads; the flexibility to adapt to changing technology and requirements; and the affordability and risk-freedom to be developed within its planned budget and schedule. If you pass this milestone successfully, you have a confident basis for committing major resources to develop and sustain the software system. If not, the de facto architecture you marry in haste will be there for you to repent at leisure.

My favorite chapter in the book is Chapter 5, which begins to provide guidelines on how to determine an architecture which best fits a set of software system requirements. For a class of user interface software, it establishes a "design space" of functional dimensions (required portability, customizability, external event handling, basic user interface mode, etc.) and structural dimensions (abstraction level of the application program interface, control thread mechanism, communication mechanisms, etc.). It then provides guidelines for matching structural dimension choices to functional dimension characteristics, and for reconciling structural design choices with each other. This provides the beginning of an engineering discipline which can be taught to students and applied across increasing ranges of software projects.

Another good feature of the book is its guidance on organizing and teaching a course on software architecture, based on several years' experience in teaching such a course at Carnegie Mellon University. At USC, we are beginning to offer a course on software architecture for our MS program in software engineering, and are finding that the book provides a good set of organizing concepts and material for the course. A final bit of expectations management: this book is a first cut at codifying a just-emerging field. It has some rough spots, and it doesn't provide all the answers. It won't provide you with fully mature industry-consensus architecting languages and terminology; surefire cookbook architecting solutions; or tools that automate the analysis of complex tradeoffs among functionality, performance, cost, and various desired software qualities. On the other hand, it provides the best general framework and set of techniques for dealing with software architectures that is available today. And it conveys the excitement of being able to look at the software field in new ways, and of experiencing a new branch of software engineering in the process of being developed and applied.

BARRY BOEHM
TRW Professor of Software Engineering, USC

PREFACE

ARCHITECTURE FOR SOFTWARE SYSTEMS

"Good Heavens! For more than forty years I have been speaking prose without knowing it!"

Molière, *Le Bourgeois Gentilhomme*, Act II, sc. iv

So it is with architectures for software systems. Ever since the first program was divided into modules, software systems have had architectures, and programmers have been responsible for the interactions among the modules and the global properties of the assemblage. Historically, architectures have been implicit—accidents of implementation, or legacies of systems past. Good software developers have often adopted one or several architectural patterns as strategies for system organization, but they use these patterns informally and have no means to make them explicit in the resulting system.

We got interested in architectures for software systems while investigating better ways to support software development. We were struck by the evidence of patterns for system organization that software developers use purposefully but nearly unconsciously. Informal traces in system descriptions reveal a substantial folklore of system design, used with little consistency or precision. Here—waiting to be exposed and organized—is a rich language of system description. Its vocabulary includes constructs and patterns not supported by current models, notations, or tools. The clear utility of the architectural concepts, evidenced by practical use even in the absence of crisp definitions or tools, persuaded us to tackle the problem of closing the gap between the useful abstractions of system design and the notations and tools. This book is one of the results.

We present here an introduction to the field of software architecture. Our purpose is to illustrate the current state of the discipline and examine the ways in which architectural design can affect software design. Naturally, a short volume such as this can only highlight the main features of the terrain; indeed, the terrain is even now in the process of being mapped. Our selection emphasizes informal descriptions, touching lightly on formal notations and specifications, and on tools to support them. We hope, nonetheless, that this will serve to illuminate the nature and significance of this emerging field.

AUDIENCE

The book serves two groups. First, professional software developers looking for new ideas about system organization will find discussions of familiar (and perhaps unfamiliar) patterns for system organization. By identifying useful patterns clearly, giving examples, comparing them, and evaluating their utility in various settings, the book will sharpen their understanding and broaden their options. Second, students with interests in software system organization will find fresh ideas here. They will be able to develop a repertoire of useful techniques that allows them to approach systems from an architectural point of view and that goes beyond the single-mindedness of current fads.

EDUCATION IN SOFTWARE ARCHITECTURE

Software architectures now receive little or no systematic treatment in most existing software engineering curricula, either undergraduate or graduate. At best, students are exposed to one or two specific application architectures (such as a compiler or parts of an operating system) and may hear about a few other architectural paradigms. No courses seriously attempt to develop comprehensive skills for understanding existing architectures, developing new ones, or selecting one to match a given problem. This results in a serious gap in current curricula: students are expected to learn how to design complex systems without the requisite intellectual tools for doing so effectively.

The software component of the typical undergraduate curriculum emphasizes algorithms and data structures. Although courses on compilers, operating systems, or databases are usually offered, there is no systematic treatment of the organization of modules into systems, or of the concepts and techniques at an architectural level of software design. Thus, system issues are seriously underrepresented in current undergraduate programs. Further, students now face a large gap between lower-level courses, in which they learn programming techniques, and upper-level project courses, in which they are expected to design more significant systems. Without knowing the alternatives and criteria that distinguish good architectural choices, the already challenging task of defining an appropriate architecture becomes formidable.

We have developed a course, *Architectures for Software Systems*, to bridge this gap. Largely using the materials of this book, the course brings together the emerging models for software architectures and the best of current practice.

Specifically, the course does the following:

- Teaches how to understand and evaluate designs of existing software systems from an architectural perspective
- Provides the intellectual building blocks for designing new systems in principled ways, using well-understood architectural paradigms

- Shows how formal notations and models can be used to characterize and reason about a system design
- Presents concrete examples of actual system architectures that can serve as models for new designs

This book can be used, together with supplemental readings, as a text for a such a course. (Chapter 9 describes the course in more detail.) Equally well—and perhaps more practical for many—the book can be used as a supplemental text for courses in software engineering or software design.

ACKNOWLEDGMENTS

This volume integrates the results of several years of research that depended critically on the contributions of our collaborators. Most significantly, our collaborators on results incorporated here are godparents to the current work. We particularly appreciate the willingness of Tom Lane, Toru Asada, Roy F. Swonger, Nadine Bounds, Paul Duerig, and Marco Schumacher to allow us to include their papers on design guidance [Lan90a, ASBD92, S+94]. Thanks go to our co-authors on other work: The formalization of instrumentation systems represents joint work with Norman Delisle and others from Tektronix. The formalization of implicit invocation systems represents collaborative work with David Notkin and Kevin Sullivan. Our collection of sample architectural problems was developed in collaboration with Rob Allen, Daniel Klein, John Ockerbloom, Curtis Scott, and Marco Schumacher. The formalization of software architecture was joint work with Rob Allen and Gregory Abowd. The implementation of implicit invocation was done in collaboration with Curtis Scott. The UniCon language and tool were developed jointly with Rob DeLine, Daniel Klein, Theodore Ross, David Young, and Gregory Zelesnik. The Aesop System was developed with the help of Rob Allen, John Ockerbloom, Ralph Melton, and Bob Monroe as well as numerous undergraduates. The report on initial experience with a course reports a joint offering with Chris Okaski, Curtis Scott, and Roy Swonger.

These, of course, are not the only ones who helped. Many colleagues have contributed to the development of the ideas by helping with examples, challenging our ideas, insisting that we be rigorous, providing constructive comments on drafts, and in untold other ways. So, thanks again to James Alstad, Pepe Galmes, Lorin Grubb, Chris Okasaki, Curtis Scott, and Roy Swonger for their help in developing our course on this material; David Notkin, Kevin Sullivan, and Gail Kaiser for their contributions to understanding event-based systems; Rob Allen for help in developing a rigorous understanding of the pipe-and-filter style; the oscilloscope development team at Tektronix for their part in demonstrating the value of domain-specific architectural styles in an industrial context; Eldon Shaw for fostering Mary's appreciation for engineering; Roy Weil for providing engineering sensibilities and tolerating the vagaries of authorhood; Angle Jordan for arranging the opportunity to study the history of engineering; Bill Wulf and Ralph London for the long-term collaboration that taught us the need to choose different architectures for different problems; colleagues at Fisher Controls, for the opportunity to learn about control software; Marc Graham, for arranging discussions with most of the DARPA Domain-Specific Software Architecture groups; Will Tracz, for presenting an architecture for avionics whose essential core was essentially a feedback loop, thereby provoking another look at process control; Allen Newell, for inspiring the analysis of shared information systems; David 'Steier for discussions about Soar/IBDE; Daniel Jackson and Jeannette Wing for their help in clarifying the benefits and limitations of formal approaches to software architecture; Lynette Garlan for letting David come to Pittsburgh to pursue research in software architecture; David Notkin, Kevin Sullivan, and Rob Allen for their collaborative efforts in developing a scientific basis for implicit invocation; Raj Rajkumar, for helping us incorporate real-time analysis in UniCon; Robert DeLine, Daniel Klein, Fuchun Jiang, and Gregory Zelesnik, for contributions to the UniCon implementation; Michael Baumann, Chanakya C. Damarla, Steven Fink, Doron Gan, Andrew Kompanek, Curtis Scott, Ralph Melton, Bob Monroe, Brian Solganick, Peter Su, and Steve Zdancewic for contributions to the Aesop implementation; Gregory Abowd, Rob Allen, Mario Barbacci, Rob DeLine, Stu Feldman, Marc Graham, Kevin Jeffay, Dan Klein, Eliot Moss, John Ockerbloom, Reid Simmons, Pamela Zave, José Galmes, and Greg Zelesnik for participating as guest lecturers in our course.

We also thank Barry Boehm, Rob DeLine, Larry Druffel, Frank Friedman, Norm Gibbs, Bill Griswold, Ralph Johnson, Nancy Mead, Eliot Moss, Allen Newell, David Notkin, Gene Rollins, Robert Schwanke, Dilip Soni, Will Tracz, Roy Weil, Jeannette Wing, members of CMU's Software Architecture Reading Group, and numerous anonymous referees for their constructive comments on drafts of various parts of the work.

Research can't be done without support, and we appreciate the interest and support of numerous government, academic, and industrial sponsors. The work was funded variously by the Department of Defense Advanced Research Project Agency under grant MDA972-92-J-1002; the Wright Laboratory, Aeronautical Systems Center, Air Force Materiel Command, USAF, and the Advanced Research Projects Agency (ARPA) under grant F33615-93-1-1330; the U.S. Federal Government under Contract Number F19628-90-C-0003 with Carnegie Mellon University for the operation of the Software Engineering Institute, a Federally Funded Research and Development Center; Mobay Corporation; National Science Foundation Grants CCR-9109469, CCR-9112880, and CCR-9357792; Siemens Corporate Research; Digital Equipment Corporation's Graduate Engineering Education Program (for support for collaborators); and the Carnegie Mellon University School of Computer Science and Software Engineering Institute (which is sponsored by the U.S. Department of Defense).

The views and conclusions here are our own. They should not be interpreted as representing the official policies, either expressed or implied, of the U.S. Government, the U.S. Department of Defense, the National Science Foundation, Wright Laboratory, Siemens Corporation, Mobay Corporation, or Carnegie Mellon University.

Much of the material in this book is derived from work we have published in other forums. We have relied principally on the following.

- Chapter 1: "Prospects for an engineering discipline of software" [Sha90].
- Chapter 2: "An introduction to software architecture" [GS93b], "Beyond Objects: A software design paradigm based on process control" [Sha95].
- Chapter 3: "An introduction to software architecture" [GS93b], "Beyond objects: A software design paradigm based on process control" [Sha95], "Candidate model problems in software architecture" [S+94].

- Chapter 4: "Software architectures for shared information systems" [Sha93b].
- Chapter 5: "Studying software architecture through design spaces and rules" [Lan90a], "The quantified design space—A tool for the quantitative analysis of Designs" [ASBD92].
- Chapter 6: "Formal approaches to software architecture" [Gar93].
- Chapter 7: "Characteristics of higher-level languages for software architecture" [SG94], "Procedure calls are the assembly language of system interconnection: Connectors deserve first-class status" [Sha93a], "Adding implicit invocation to traditional programming languages" [GS93a].
- Chapter 8: "Abstractions for software architecture and tools to support them" [SDK+95], "Exploiting style in architectural design environments" [GAO94], "Beyond definition/use: architectural interconnection" [AG94a].
- Chapter 9: "Experience with a course on architectures for software systems" [GSO+92].

We also wish to thank the authors and publishers of several of the figures for granting permission to reprint them here.

Figure 1.1 is reproduced with permission of the McGraw-Hill Companies from *Computer Structures* by G. Bell and A. Newell, McGraw-Hill 1971.

Figures 3.16, 3.17, 4.8, 4.9, 4.11, 4.18 are reprinted with permission of IEEE from Grady Booch's "Object-oriented development" which appeared in *IEEE Transactions on Software Engineering* in February 1986, Won Kim and Jungysun Seo's "Classifying schematic and data heterogeneity in multidatabase systems" which appeared in *IEEE Computer* in December 1991, Rafi Ahmet et al.'s "Pegasus heterogeneous multidatabase system" which appeared in *IEEE Computer* in December 1991, Minder Chen and Ronald Norman's "Framework for integrated CASE" which appeared in *IEEE Software* in March 1992, and Gio Wiederhold's "Mediators in the architecture of future information systems" which appeared in *IEEE Computer* in March 1992; all © IEEE.

Figures 3.22 and 3.23 are reprinted from PROVOX product literature with permission from Fisher-Rosemount Systems, Inc.

Figure 3.25 is reprinted with permission of the Association for Computing Machinery from Frederick Hayes-Roth's "Rule-based systems" which appeared in *Communications of the ACM* in September 1985.

Figure 3.27 is reprinted with permission of the American Association for Artificial Intelligence from H. Penny Nii's "Blackboard systems" which appeared in *AI Magazine* volume 7 numbers 3 and 4, (c) American Association for Artificial Intelligence.

Figures 4.1, 4.2, 4.4, and 4.5 are reprinted by permission of John Wiley and Sons from Laurence J. Best's *Application Architecture* © 1990 John Wiley and Sons.

CONTENTS

1

INTRODUCTION

SOFTWARE ARCHITECTURE IS EMERGING as an important discipline for engineers of software. But it did not simply appear, well-formed and clearly articulated, as a new concern for software systems. Rather, it has emerged over time as a natural evolution of design abstractions, as engineers have searched for better ways to understand their software and new ways to build larger, more complex software systems.

    In this chapter we trace this evolution. We begin by identifying the engineering issues of architectural design and how those issues relate to other software design levels. Next we consider the nature of software engineering and its evolution over the past few decades. With this background we outline the current status of software architecture and its relationship to other aspects of software engineering.

1.1 WHAT IS SOFTWARE ARCHITECTURE?

As the size and complexity of software systems increase, the design and specification of overall system structure become more significant issues than the choice of algorithms and data structures of computation. Structural issues include the organization of a system as a composition of components; global control structures; the protocols for communication, synchronization, and data access; the assignment of functionality to design elements; the composition of design elements; physical distribution; scaling and performance; dimensions of evolution; and selection among design alternatives. This is the *software architecture* level of design.

    Abstractly, software architecture involves the description of elements from which systems are built, interactions among those elements, patterns that guide their composition, and constraints on these patterns. In general, a particular system is defined in terms of a collection of components and interactions among those components. Such a system may in turn be used as a (composite) element in a larger system design.

While it has long been recognized that finding an appropriate architectural design for a system is a key element of its long-term success, current practice for describing architectures is typically informal and idiosyncratic. Architectural structures are often described in terms of idiomatic patterns that have emerged informally over time. Usually, architectures are represented abstractly as box-and-line diagrams, together with accompanying prose that explains the meanings behind the symbols and provides some rationale for the specific choice of components and interactions. For example, typical descriptions of software architectures include statements such as these (italics ours):

- "Camelot is based on the *client-server model* and uses *remote procedure calls* both locally and remotely to provide communication among applications and servers" [S+87].
- "*Abstraction layering* and system decomposition provide the appearance of system uniformity to clients, yet allow Helix to accommodate a diversity of autonomous devices. The architecture encourages a *client-server model* for the structuring of applications" [FO85].
- "We have chosen a *distributed, object-oriented approach* to managing information" [Lin87].
- "The easiest way to make the canonical sequential compiler into a concurrent compiler is to *pipeline* the execution of the compiler phases over a number of processors. ...A more effective way [is to] split the source code into many segments, which are concurrently processed through the various phases of compilation [by multiple compiler processes] before a final, merging pass recombines the object code into a single program" [Ses88].

Such descriptions are common. It is striking that they communicate so effectively despite being almost completely informal. Labeling of individual components is idiosyncratic to the system being described, and even the generalizations such as architectural patterns are defined casually—and differently by different authors.

The relative informality and high level of abstraction of current practice in describing architectures might at first glance suggest that architectural descriptions have little substantive value for software engineers. But there are two reasons why this is not the case. First, engineers have evolved over time a collection of idioms, patterns, and styles of software system organization that serves as a shared, semantically rich vocabulary. For example, by identifying a system as an instance of a pipe-filter architectural style an engineer communicates the facts that the system is primarily involved in stream transformation, that the functional behavior of the system can be derived compositionally from the behaviors of the constituent filters, and that issues of system latency and throughput can be addressed in relatively straightforward ways. Thus, although this shared vocabulary is largely informal, it conveys considerable semantic content among software engineers.

The second reason is that although architectural structures are abstract in relation to details of the actual computations of the elements, those structures provide a natural framework for understanding broader, system-level concerns, such as global rates of flow, patterns of communication, execution control structure, scalability, and intended paths of system evolution. Thus, architectural descriptions serve as a skeleton around which system properties can be fleshed out, and thereby serve a vital role in exposing the ability of a system to meet its gross system requirements.

This is, of course, not to say that more formal notations for architectural description and rigorous techniques of analysis are unnecessary. Indeed, much could be gained if the current practice of architectural design could be supported with better notations, theories, and analytical techniques. In later chapters we explore specification issues in software architecture, with particular attention to the way improvements in the formulation of architectural issues set the stage for better formalization.

There is a considerable (and growing) body of work on this topic, including module interconnection languages, templates and frameworks for systems that serve the needs of specific domains, and formal models of component integration mechanisms. However, there is not currently a consistent terminology with which to characterize the common elements of these fields.

We are still far from having a well-accepted taxonomy of such architectural paradigms, let alone a fully developed theory of software architecture. But we can now clearly identify a number of the basic ingredients of architectural description. Moreover, we can also identify a set of architectural patterns, or styles, that currently form the basic repertoire of a software architect. (This basic repertoire is illustrated in the quotations above and is the subject matter of Chapter 3.)

The *architecture of a software system* defines that system in terms of computational components and interactions among those components. Components are such things as clients and servers, databases, filters, and layers in a hierarchical system. Interactions among components at this level of design can be simple and familiar, such as procedure call and shared variable access. But they can also be complex and semantically rich, such as client-server protocols, database-accessing protocols, asynchronous event multicast, and piped streams.

In addition to specifying the structure and topology of the system, the architecture shows the correspondence between the system requirements and elements of the constructed system, thereby providing some rationale for the design decisions. At the architectural level, relevant system-level issues typically include properties such as capacity, throughput, consistency, and component compatibility.

More generally, architectural models clarify structural and semantic differences among components and interactions. These architectural models can often be composed to define larger systems. Ideally, individual elements of the architectural descriptions are defined independently, so that they can be reused in different contexts. The architecture establishes specifications for these individual elements, which may themselves be refined as architectural subsystems, or implemented in a conventional programming language.

The informal documentation of architectures currently produced by software designers suggests that their applied body of architectural knowledge is not well-served by existing tools and notations. To establish the reasons for treating it explicitly, we now examine the significance of design levels in computer systems. Following that, we will assess the development of an engineering discipline for software and the way improved architectural techniques will serve the maturation of software engineering.

1.1.1   SOFTWARE DESIGN LEVELS

System design takes place at many levels. It is useful to make precise distinctions among those levels, for each level appropriately deals with different design concerns. At each level we find *components*, both primitive and composite; *rules of composition* that allow the construction of nonprimitive components, or systems; and *rules of behavior* that provide semantics for the system (BN71, New82, New90). Since these differ from one level to another, we also find different notations, design problems, and analysis techniques at each level. As a result, design at each level can proceed substantially autonomously. But levels are also related, in that elements at the base of each level correspond to—are implemented by—constructs of the level below.

The hierarchy of levels for computer hardware systems is familiar and appears in Figure 1.1 (BN71, p. 3). Note first that each level deals with different content. Different kinds of structures guide design with different sets of components. Different notations, analysis techniques, and design issues accompany the differences of content matter. Note also that each level admits of substructure: abstraction and composition take place within each level, in terms of the components and structures of that level. In addition, there is an established transformation from the primitive components at the bottom of each level to (probably nonprimitive) components of the level below.

Software, too, has its design levels. We can identify at least three:

1. *Architecture*, where the design issues involve overall association of system capability with components; components are modules, and interconnections among modules are handled in a variety of ways; operators guide the composition of systems from subsystems.

2. *Code*, where the design issues involve algorithms and data structures; the components are programming language primitives such as numbers, characters, pointers, and threads of control; primitive operators are the arithmetic and data-manipulation primitives of the language; composition mechanisms include records, arrays, and procedures.

3. *Executable*, where the design issues involve memory maps, data layouts, call stacks, and register allocations; the components are bit patterns supported by hardware, and the operations and compositions are described in machine code.

These roughly track the higher levels of hardware design. From the 1960s through the 1980s software developers concentrated on the programming level. The executable and code levels for software are now well understood. However, the architecture level is currently understood mostly at the level of intuition, anecdote, and folklore. It is common for a description of a software system to include a few paragraphs of text and a box-and-line diagram, but there are neither uniform syntax nor uniform semantics for interpreting the prose and the diagrams. Our concern here is to improve understanding and precision at the software architecture level. At this level the components are programs, modules, or systems; a rich collection of interchange representations and protocols connects the components; and system patterns often guide the compositions.

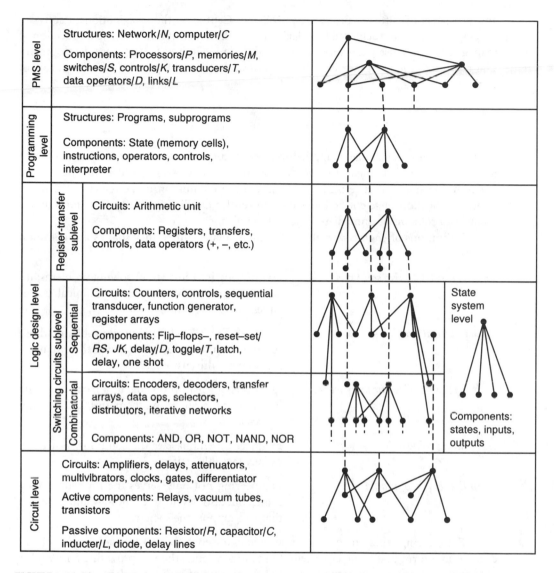

PMS level	Structures: Network/N, computer/C Components: Processors/P, memories/M, switches/S, controls/K, transducers/T, data operators/D, links/L	
Programming level	Structures: Programs, subprograms Components: State (memory cells), instructions, operators, controls, interpreter	
Logic design level — Register-transfer sublevel	Circuits: Arithmetic unit Components: Registers, transfers, controls, data operators (+, −, etc.)	
Switching circuits sublevel — Sequential	Circuits: Counters, controls, sequential transducer, function generator, register arrays Components: Flip–flops–, reset–set/ RS, JK, delay/D, toggle/T, latch, delay, one shot	State system level
Switching circuits sublevel — Combinatorial	Circuits: Encoders, decoders, transfer arrays, data ops, selectors, distributors, iterative networks Components: AND, OR, NOT, NAND, NOR	Components: states, inputs, outputs
Circuit level	Circuits: Amplifiers, delays, attenuators, multivibrators, clocks, gates, differentiator Active components: Relays, vacuum tubes, transistors Passive components: Resistor/R, capacitor/C, inducter/L, diode, delay lines	

FIGURE 1.1   Computer Hardware Design Levels. (Reproduced with permission of the McGraw-Hill Companies from *Computer Structures* by G. Bell and A. Newell, McGraw-Hill 1971.)

1.2   AN ENGINEERING DISCIPLINE FOR SOFTWARE

Explicit recognition of the architectural issues in software design is part of the maturation of the field. It contributes to establishing an engineering basis for software. It will provide useful context to examine the emergence of software engineering as an engineering discipline.

The phrase *software engineering* was coined in 1968 as a statement of aspiration—a sort of rallying cry. That year NATO convened a workshop by that name to assess the state and prospects of software production [NAT69]. Capturing the imagination of software developers, the phrase achieved popularity during the 1970s. It now refers to a collection of management processes, software tooling, and design activities for software development. The resulting practice, however, differs significantly from the practice of older forms of engineering.

1.2.1   WHAT IS ENGINEERING?

Software engineering is a label applied to a set of current practices for software development. Using the word *engineering* to describe this activity takes considerable liberty with the common use of that term. In contrast, the more common usage refers to the disciplined application of scientific knowledge to resolve conflicting constraints and requirements for problems of immediate, practical significance.

Definitions of engineering abound. Though details differ, they share some common clauses:

Creating cost-effective solutions…	Engineering isn't just about solving problems; it's about solving problems with economical use of all resources, including money.
… to practical problems…	Engineering deals with practical problems whose solutions matter to people outside the engineering domain: the customers.
… by applying scientific knowledge…	Engineering solves problems in a particular way: by applying science, mathematics, and design analysis.
… building things…	Engineering emphasizes the solutions, which are usually tangible artifacts.
… in the service of mankind	Engineering not only serves the immediate customer, but also develops technology and expertise that will support the society.

Engineering relies on codifying scientific knowledge about a technological problem domain in a form that is directly useful to the practitioner, thereby providing answers for questions that commonly occur in practice. Engineers of ordinary talent can then apply this knowledge to solve problems far faster than they otherwise could. In this way, engineering shares prior solutions rather than relying always on virtuoso problem solving.

Engineering practice enables ordinary practitioners to create sophisticated systems that work—unspectacularly, perhaps, but reliably. The history of software development is marked by both successes and failures. The successes have often been virtuoso performances or the result of diligence and hard work. The failures have often reflected poor understanding of the problem to be solved, a mismatching of solution to problem, or inadequate follow-through from design to implementation. Some failed by never working, others by overrunning cost and schedule budgets.

In current software practice, knowledge about techniques that work is not shared effectively with workers on later projects, nor is there a large body of software development knowledge organized for ready reference. Computer science has contributed some relevant theory, but practice proceeds largely independently of this organized knowledge. Given this track record, there are fundamental problems with the use of the term *software engineer.*

ROUTINE AND INNOVATIVE DESIGN

Engineering design tasks are of several kinds; one of the most significant distinctions among them separates routine from innovative design. Routine design involves solving familiar problems, reusing large portions of prior solutions. Innovative design, on the other hand, involves finding novel solutions to unfamiliar problems. Original designs are much more rarely needed than routine designs, so the latter are the bread and butter of engineering.

Most engineering disciplines capture, organize, and share design knowledge in order to make routine design simpler. Handbooks and manuals are often the carriers of this organized information [Mar87, P+84]. But current notations for software designs are not adequate for the task of both recording and communicating designs, so they fail to provide a suitable representation for such handbooks.

Software in most application domains is treated more often as original than routine—certainly more so than would be necessary if we captured and organized what we already know. One path to increased productivity is identifying applications that could be routine and developing appropriate support. The current emphasis on reuse focuses on capturing and organizing existing knowledge of a particular kind: knowledge expressed in the form of code. Indeed, subroutine libraries—especially of system calls and general-purpose mathematical routines—have been a staple of programming for decades. But this knowledge cannot be useful if programmers don't know about it or aren't encouraged to use it; further, library components require more care in design, implementation, and documentation than similar components that are simply embedded in systems.

Practitioners recognize the need for ways to share experience with good designs. This quotation appeared on a Software Engineering news group (Stephen V. Boyle unpublished communication on network newsgroup comp.software.eng, 1987):

> In Chem E, when I needed to design a heat exchanger, I used a set of references that told me what the constants were... and the standard design equations ...

> In general, unless I, or someone else in my engineering group, has read or remembers and makes known a solution to a past problem, I'm doomed to recreate the solution.... I guess... the critical difference is the ability to put together little pieces of the problem that are relatively well known, without having to generate a custom solution for every application ...

> I want to make it clear that I am aware of algorithm and code libraries, but they are incomplete solutions to what I am describing. (There is no Perry's Handbook for Software Engineering.)

This former chemical engineer is complaining that software lacks the institutionalized mechanisms of a mature engineering discipline for recording and disseminating demonstrably good designs and procedures for choosing among design alternatives. Perry's Handbook is the standard design handbook for chemical engineering; it's about 4 inches thick × 8½″ × 11″, printed in tiny type on tissue paper [P+84].

A MODEL FOR THE EVOLUTION OF AN ENGINEERING DISCIPLINE

Historically, engineering has emerged from ad hoc practice in two stages. First, management and production techniques enable routine production. Later, the problems of routine production stimulate the development of a supporting science; the mature science eventually merges with established practice to yield professional engineering practice. This model is depicted in Figure 1.2. The lower lines track the technology, and the upper lines show how the entry of production skills and scientific knowledge contribute new capability to the engineering practice.

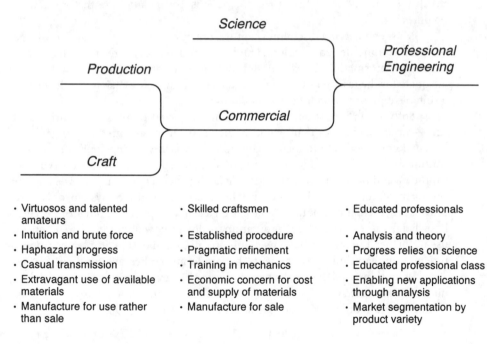

• Virtuosos and talented amateurs	• Skilled craftsmen	• Educated professionals
• Intuition and brute force	• Established procedure	• Analysis and theory
• Haphazard progress	• Pragmatic refinement	• Progress relies on science
• Casual transmission	• Training in mechanics	• Educated professional class
• Extravagant use of available materials	• Economic concern for cost and supply of materials	• Enabling new applications through analysis
• Manufacture for use rather than sale	• Manufacture for sale	• Market segmentation by product variety

FIGURE 1.2   Evolution of an Engineering Discipline

Exploitation of a technology begins with craftsmanship: a set of problems must be solved, and they get solved any which way. They're solved by talented amateurs and by virtuosos, but no distinct professional class is dedicated to problems of this particular kind. Intuition and brute force are the primary movers in design and construction. Progress is haphazard, particularly before the advent of good communication; hence, solutions are invented and reinvented. The transmission of knowledge between craftsmen is slow, in part because of underdeveloped communications, but also because the talented amateurs often do not recognize any special need to communicate. Nevertheless, ad hoc practice eventually moves into the folklore. This craft stage of development sees extravagant use of available materials. Construction or manufacture is often for personal or local use or for barter, but there is little or no large-scale production in anticipation of resale. Community barn raisings are an example of this stage; so is software written by application experts for their own ends.

At some point, the product being produced becomes widely accepted, and demand exceeds supply. At that point, attempts are made to define the resources necessary for systematic commercial manufacture and to marshal the expertise for exploiting these resources. Capital is needed in advance to buy raw materials, so financial skills become important, and the operating scale increases over time. As commercial practice flourishes, skilled practitioners are required for continuity and for consistency of effort. They are trained pragmatically in established procedures. Management may not know why these procedures work, but they know the procedures do work and how to teach people to execute them. The procedures are refined, but the refinement is driven pragmatically: a modification is tried to see if it works, and then incorporated in standard procedure if it is successful. Economic considerations lead to concerns for the efficiency of procedures and the use of materials. People begin to explore ways for production facilities to exploit the technology base; economic issues often point out problems in commercial practice. Management strategies for controlling software development fit at this point of the model.

The problems of current practice often stimulate the development of a corresponding science. A strong productive interaction often arises between commercial practice and the emerging science. At some point the science becomes sufficiently mature to be a significant contributor to the commercial practice. This marks the emergence of engineering practice in the sense that we know it today—sufficient scientific basis to enable a core of educated professionals to apply the theory to analysis of problems and synthesis of solutions.

The emergence of an engineering discipline allows technological development to pass limits previously imposed by relying on intuition; progress frequently becomes dependent on science as a forcing function. A scientific basis is needed to drive analysis, which enables new applications and even market segmentation via product variety. Attempts are made to gain enough control over design to target specific products on demand.

Thus, engineering emerges from the commercial exploitation that supplants craft; modern engineering relies critically on adding scientific foundations to craft and commercialization. Exploiting technology depends not only on scientific engineering but also on management and marshaling of resources. Engineering and science support each other: engineering generates good problems for science, and science, after finding good problems in the needs of practice, returns workable solutions. Science is often not driven by the immediate needs of engineering; however, good scientific problems often follow from an understanding of the problems that the engineering side of the field is coping with.

The engineering practice of software has recently come under criticism [Dij89, Par90]. Although current software practice does not match the usual expectations of an engineering discipline, the model described here suggests that vigorous pursuit of applicable science and the reduction of that science to practice can lead to a sound engineering discipline of software.

1.2.2   THE CURRENT STATE OF SOFTWARE TECHNOLOGY

We turn now to software. We begin by establishing that the problem is appropriately viewed as an engineering problem: creating cost-effective solutions to practical problems... building things in the service of mankind. We then address the question of whether software developers do or ever can do this by applying scientific knowledge. In the process we position software engineering in the evolutionary model described earlier.

SCIENTIFIC BASIS FOR ENGINEERING PRACTICE

Engineering practice emerges from commercial practice by exploiting the results of a companion science. The scientific results must be mature and rich enough to model practical problems; they must also be organized in a form that is useful to practitioners. Computer science has a few models and theories that are ready to support practice, but the packaging of these results for operational use is lacking.

Maturity of Supporting Science. Despite the criticism sometimes made by software producers that computer science is irrelevant to practical software, good models and theories have been developed in areas in which there has been enough time for the theories to mature. For example, in the early 1960s, algorithms and data structures were simply created as part of each program. Some folklore grew up about good ways to do certain sorts of things, and it was transmitted informally; by the mid-1960s good programmers shared the intuition that if you get the data structures right, the rest of the program is much simpler. In the late 1960s algorithms and data structures began to be abstracted from individual programs, and their essential properties were described and analyzed. The 1970s saw substantial progress in supporting theories, including performance analysis as well as correctness. Concurrently, the programming implications of these abstractions were explored; research on abstract data types dealt with such issues as the following:

- *Specifications* (abstract models, algebraic axioms)
- *Software structure* (bundling representation with algorithms)
- *Language issues* (modules, scope, user-defined types)
- *Information hiding* (protecting integrity of information not in specification)
- *Integrity constraints* (invariants of data structures)
- *Rules for composition* (declarations)

Both sound theory and language support were available by the early 1980s, and routine good practice now depends on this support.

Compiler construction is another good example. In 1960 simply writing a compiler at all was a major achievement; it isn't clear that we really understood what a higher-level language was. Formal syntax was first used systematically for Algol 60, and tools for processing it automatically (then called compiler-compilers, but now called parser generators) were first developed in the mid-1960s and made practical in the 1970s. Also in the 1970s we started developing theories of semantics and types, and the 1980s have brought significant progress toward the automation of compiler construction.

Both of these examples have roots in the problems of the 1960s and became genuinely practical in the 1980s. It takes a good twenty years from the time that work starts on a theory until it provides serious assistance to routine practice. Development periods of comparable length have also preceded the widespread use of systematic methods and technologies such as structured programming and object-oriented design. But the whole field of computing is only about forty years old, and many theories are emerging in the research pipeline.

Interaction between Science and Engineering. The development of good models within the software domain follows the pattern of Figure 1.3. We begin by solving problems in any way we can manage. After some time we distinguish in those ad hoc solutions things that usually work and things that don't usually work. The ones that work enter the folklore: people tell each other about them informally. As the folklore becomes more and more systematic, we codify it as written heuristics and rules of procedure. Eventually that codification becomes crisp enough to support models and theories, together with the associated mathematics. These can then help to improve practice, and experience from that practice can sharpen the theories. Further, the improvement in practice enables us to think about harder problems—which we first solve ad hoc; then we find heuristics, eventually develop new models and theories, and so on. The models and theories do not have to be fully fleshed out for this process to assist practice: the initial codification of folklore may be useful in and of itself.

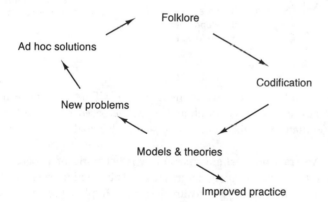

FIGURE 1.3 Codification Cycle for Science and Engineering

This progression is illustrated in the use of machine language for control flow in the 1960s. In the late 1950s and the early 1960s, we did not have crisp notions about what an iteration or a conditional was, so we laid down special-purpose code, building each structure individually out of test-and-branch instructions. Eventually a small set of patterns emerged as generally useful, generally easy to get right, and generally at least as good as the alternatives. Designers of higher-level languages explicitly identified the most useful ones and codified them by producing special-purpose syntax. A formal result about the completeness of the structured constructs provided additional reassurance. Now, almost nobody believes that new kinds of loops should be invented as a routine practice. A few kinds of iterations and a few kinds of conditionals are captured in the languages. They are taught as control concepts that go with the language; people use them routinely, without concern for the underlying machine code. Further experience led to verifiable formal specifications of the semantics of these statements and of programs that used them. Experience with the formalization in turn refined the statements supported in programming languages. In this way ad hoc practice entered a period of folklore and eventually matured to have conventional syntax and semantic theories that explain it.

Where, then, does current software practice lie on the path to engineering? As Figure 1.4 suggests, it is still in some cases craft and in some cases commercial practice. A science is beginning to contribute results, and for isolated examples it is possible to argue that professional engineering is taking place. That is not, however, the common case.

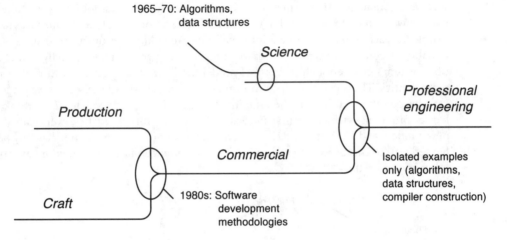

FIGURE 1.4   Evolution of Software Engineering

There are good grounds to expect that eventually there will be an engineering discipline of software. Its nature will be technical, and it will be based in computer science. Though we have not yet matured to that state, it is an achievable goal.

Codification through Abstraction Mechanisms.   One characteristic of progress in programming languages and tools has been regular increases in abstraction level—or the conceptual size of the building blocks used by software designers. To place the field of software architecture into perspective, let us begin by looking at the historical development of abstraction techniques in computer science.

When digital computers emerged in the 1950s, software was written in machine language; programmers placed instructions and data individually and explicitly in the computer's memory. Inserting a new instruction in a program might require manual checking of the entire program to update references to data and instructions that moved as a result of the insertion. Eventually it was recognized that the memory layout and update of references could be automated, and also that symbolic names could be used for operation codes and memory addresses. Symbolic assemblers were the result. They were soon followed by macro processors, which allowed a single symbol to stand for a commonly used sequence of instructions. The substitution of simple symbols for machine operation codes, machine addresses yet to be defined, and sequences of instructions was perhaps the earliest form of abstraction in software.

In the latter part of the 1950s, it became clear that certain patterns of execution were commonly useful—indeed, they were so well understood that it was possible to create them automatically from a notation more like mathematics than machine language. The earliest of these patterns were for evaluation of arithmetic expressions, for procedure invocation, and for loops and conditional statements. These insights were captured in a series of early high-level languages, of which Fortran was the main survivor.

Higher-level languages allowed more sophisticated programs to be developed, and patterns in the use of data emerged. Whereas in Fortran data types served primarily as cues for selecting the proper machine instructions, data types in Algol and its successors serve to state the programmer's intentions about how data should be used. The compilers for these languages could build on experience with Fortran and tackle more sophisticated compilation problems. Among other things, they checked adherence to these intentions, thereby providing incentives for the programmers to use the type mechanism. Progress in language design continued with the introduction of modules to provide protection for related procedures and data structures, with the separation of a module's specification from its implementation, and with the introduction of abstract data types.

In the late 1960s, good programmers shared an intuition about software development: If you get the data structures right, the effort will make development of the rest of the program much easier. The work on abstract data types of the 1970s can be viewed as a development effort that converted this intuition into a real theory. The conversion from an intuition to a theory involved understanding the following:

- *The software structure* (which included a representation packaged with its primitive operators)
- *Specifications* (mathematically expressed as abstract models or algebraic axioms)
- *Language issues* (modules, scope, user-defined types)
- *Integrity of the result* (invariants of data structures and protection from other manipulation)
- *Rules for combining types* (declarations)
- *Information hiding* (protection of properties not explicitly included in specifications)

The effect of this work was to raise the design level of certain elements of software systems, namely abstract data types, above the level of programming-language statements or individual algorithms. This form of abstraction led to the understanding that a good organization for an entire module that serves one particular purpose involved combining representations, algorithms, specifications, and functional interfaces in uniform ways. Certain support was required from the programming language, of course, but the abstract data type paradigm allowed some parts of systems to be developed from a vocabulary of data types rather than from a vocabulary of programming-language constructs.

Just as good programmers recognized useful data structures in the late 1960s, good software system designers now recognize useful system organizations. One of these is based on the theory of abstract data types. But this is not the only way to organize a software system.

The need for a notation to describe how subsystems written in typical programming languages connect to form larger systems, however, is not a new concern. In 1975, DeRemer and Kron [DK76] argued that creating program modules and connecting them to form larger structures were distinct design efforts; they created the first module interconnection language (MIL) to support the connection effort. In an MIL notation, modules import and export resources, which are named programming-language elements such as type definitions, constants, variables, and functions. A compiler for an MIL ensures system integrity with intermodule type checking: such compilers verify that if one module uses a resource that another provides, the types of the resources match; that if a module declares that it provides a resource, it actually does; that if a module uses a resource, it has access to that resource; and so on. Since DeRemer and Kron's MIL, MILs have been developed for specific languages, like Mesa [M+79] and Ada [CE78], and have provided a base from which to support software construction [Tho76], version control [Coo79], and system families [Par79, Tic79]. Enough examples are available to develop models of the design space [Per87, PDN86].

Current module interface languages, formalisms, and analysis techniques only support simple interconnection between programming modules through procedure calls and data sharing. Higher-level forms of structuring are now encoded only implicitly. Moreover, existing module interconnection systems typically require considerable prior agreement between the developers of different modules. For example, they assume that simple name matching can be used to infer intermodule interaction, that all modules are written in the same language, that all modules are available during system construction, and that module interfaces describe the other modules with which they interact.

To build truly composable systems, we must allow flexible, high-level connections between existing systems in ways not foreseen by their original developers. Essentially independently, developers of "open" software products have designed interchange representations such as PICT, RTF, SYLK, and MIF to allow distinct products to interact by data interchange. Although these were originally static, newer developments such as CORBA [Cor91] support dynamic sharing.

Large software systems require decompositional mechanisms in order to make them tractable. Breaking a system into pieces makes it possible to reason about overall properties by understanding the properties of each of the parts. Traditionally, module interconnection languages (MILs) and interface definition languages (IDLs) have played this role by providing notations for describing (1) computational units with well-defined interfaces, and (2) compositional mechanisms for gluing the pieces together.

A key issue in the design of an MIL/IDL is the nature of that glue. Currently the predominant form of composition is based on definition/use bindings [PDN86]. In this model each module *defines* or *provides* a set of facilities that are available to other modules, and *uses* or *requires* facilities provided by other modules. The purpose of the glue is to resolve the definition/use relationships by indicating for each use of a facility where its corresponding definition is provided.

This scheme has a number of benefits. It maps well to current programming languages, since the kinds of facilities that are used or defined can be chosen to be precisely those that the underlying programming language supports. (Typically these facilities support procedure calls and data sharing.) It is good for the compiler, since name resolution is an integral part of producing an executable system. It supports both automated checks (e.g., type checking) and formal reasoning (e.g., in terms of pre- and post-conditions).

Indeed, the benefits are so transparent that few question the basic tenets of the approach. However current MIL/IDLs based on definition/use have some serious drawbacks. As we will explain in Chapters 7 and 8, a significant problem is that they fail to distinguish between "implementation" and "interaction" relationships between modules. The former are useful (and necessary) for understanding how one module is built out of the facilities of others. But the latter are needed to express architectural relationships—such as the nature of the communication between computational components.

1.3   THE STATUS OF SOFTWARE ARCHITECTURE

Good architectural design has always been a major factor in determining the success of a software system. However, while there are many useful architectural paradigms (such as pipelines, layered systems, client-server organizations, etc.), they are typically understood only in an idiomatic way and applied in an ad hoc fashion. Consequently, software system designers have been unable to exploit commonalities in system architectures, make principled choices among design alternatives, specialize general paradigms to specific domains, or teach their craft to others.

Recently, software architecture has begun to emerge as an important field of study for software engineering practitioners and researchers. Architectural issues are being addressed by work in areas such as module interface languages, domain-specific architectures, software reuse, codification of organizational patterns for software, architectural description languages, formal underpinnings for architectural design, and architectural design environments.

While there has been considerable recent activity in this area, much of it has gone on in small groups, and many of these efforts are operating without detailed knowledge of other on-going work. Two recent workshops [GPT95, Gar95a] brought together researchers and practitioners interested in software architecture to discuss the current state of the practice and art. These workshops served to establish a common understanding of the state of the practice, the kinds of research and development efforts that are in progress, and the important challenges for this emerging field. Widespread interest in these workshops (one workshop call elicited 86 responses from over 140 authors) demonstrates the extent of these activities, which can be roughly placed into four categories.

The first category is addressing the problem of architectural characterization by providing new *architectural description languages*. As detailed later, these languages are aimed at giving practitioners better ways of writing down architectures so that they can be communicated to others and in many cases analyzed with tools.

The second category is addressing *codification of architectural expertise*. Work in this area is concerned with cataloging and rationalizing the variety of architectural principles and patterns that engineers have developed through software practice.

The third category is addressing *frameworks for specific domains* [SEI90, Tra94]. This work typically results in an architectural framework for a specific class of software such as avionics control systems, mobile robotics, or user interfaces. When successful, such frameworks can be easily instantiated to produce new products in the domain.

The fourth category addresses *formal underpinnings for architecture*. As new notations are developed, and as the practice of architectural design is better understood, formalisms for reasoning about architectural designs become relevant. Several of these are described in Chapters 6 and 8.

A sound basis for software architecture promises benefits for both development and maintenance. For development it is increasingly clear that effective software engineers require facility in architectural software design. First, it is important to be able to recognize common paradigms, so that high-level relationships among systems can be understood and so that new systems can be built as variations on old systems. Second, getting the right architecture is often crucial to the success of a software system design; the wrong one can lead to disastrous results. Third, detailed understanding of software architectures allows the engineer to make principled choices among design alternatives. Fourth, an architectural system representation is often essential to the analysis and description of the high-level properties of a complex system. Fifth, fluency in the use of notations for describing architectural paradigms allows the software engineer to communicate new system designs to others.

With respect to the software itself, reuse is currently impeded by differences in component packaging. That is, a given functionality may be packaged as a procedure, a communicating process, or a filter; it may interact with other components by calls, message-passing, or shared data. Because these differences in packaging are recognized only informally and not supported by programming languages and tools, and because neither formal nor informal guidance shows when and how to use them, it is often unclear whether components with compatible functionality will actually be able to interact properly. An architectural basis for composition of reusable components should help to address many of these issues.

Beyond the development stage, documenting a system's structure and properties in a rigorous way has obvious advantages for maintenance. Much of the time spent on maintenance goes to understanding the existing code; this effort should be reduced substantially if the original design structure is captured clearly and explicitly. In addition, retaining the designer's intentions about system organization should help maintainers preserve the system's design integrity.

Software architecture found its roots in diagrams and informal prose. Unfortunately, diagrams and descriptions are highly ambiguous. At best they rely on common intuitions and past experience to have any meaning at all. Moreover, system designers generally lack adequate concepts, tools, and decision criteria for selecting and describing system structures that fit the problem at hand. It is virtually impossible to answer with any precision the many questions that arise during system design. What is a "pipeline" architecture, and when should one choose it over, say, a "layered" architecture? What are the consequences of choosing one structural decomposition over another? Which architectures can be composed with others? How are implementation choices related to the overall performance of these architectures? And so on.

Systems often exhibit an overall style that follows a well-recognized, though informal, idiomatic pattern. In Chapter 2 we survey a number of these patterns, and in Chapter 3 we illustrate their use through case studies. We identify pipes and filters, data abstractions or objects, implicit invocation, hierarchical layers, repositories, and interpreters as a useful (though incomplete) set of well-known patterns, or styles, of system organization. These styles differ both in the kinds of components they use and in the way those components interact with each other. As advocates of various of these architectures explain, adherence to the rules of the style enhances both software development and subsequent maintenance. (However, the advocates often neglect to mention that different architectures are appropriate in different situations.)

Choosing the most appropriate architecture for a given problem (or domain) remains an open problem. The rules of the style usually determine how to package components—for example, as procedures, objects, or filters. As a result, components cannot usually be interchanged across styles; code may not be reusable because its interface makes incompatible assumptions. In Unix, for example, the functionality of "sort" is available both in the form of a filter and in the form of a procedure.

A number of component-based languages have been proposed and implemented. These languages describe systems as configurations of modules that interact in specific, predetermined ways (such as remote procedure call, messages, or events [Pur88, Kra90, Pou89, Bea92]) or enforce specialized patterns of organization [D+91, Ros85, L+88]. While such languages provide new ways of describing interactions between components in a large system, they too are typically oriented around a small, fixed set of communication paradigms and programming-level descriptions, or they enforce a very specialized, single-purpose organization. This makes them inappropriate for expressing a broad range of architectural designs.

Some software architectures are carefully documented and often widely disseminated. Examples include the International Standard Organization's Open Systems Interconnection Reference Model (a layered network architecture) [Pau85], the NIST/ECMA Reference Model (a generic software engineering environment framework) [CN92, Nis91], and the X Window System (a distributed, windowed user-interface architecture based on event triggering and callbacks) [SG86].

A growing community of researchers is focusing on software architecture. There has been long-standing interest in particular classes of architectures such as objects (focused by the OOPSLA conference), pipelines (focused by the USENIX conference), and client-server systems (a subject of intense attention in the commercial computing world). Early attention to the variety of idiomatic patterns of system organization and the possibility of organizing this knowledge systematically [Sha88, PW92, BS92, GS93b] have led to enough activity to sustain workshops on architectural design [BW93, Lam96] and interface-definition languages [Win94]. Handbooks of object-oriented patterns are beginning to appear [GHJV95, Pre95]. Software architecture emerged as a key theme at a recent workshop on directions in software engineering [THP92], and has recently spawned its own focused workshops [GPT95, Gar95a]. A major effort to gain design power for specific kinds of problems addresses domain-specific software architectures (DSSAs) in several specific domains [MG92, HRPL+95, Tra94, Ves94]. Formalizations have been proposed [AAG93, AG94c, IN95, MQR95]. New languages for describing architectures are also emerging [SDK+95, LAK+95, DC95].

1.4   The Plan of This Book

Software architecture is evolving rapidly. The bulk of this book describes what we see as its current state, focusing primarily on understanding how people organize systems and their reasons for doing so.

In this book we also consider the need for new higher-level languages specifically oriented to the problem of describing software architecture. First we show how ideas from "classical" language design apply to the task of describing software architectures. We then detail the characteristics such languages should have in the areas of composition, abstraction, reusability, configuration, heterogeneity, and analysis. Finally, we show how existing approaches fail to satisfy these properties, thus motivating the need for new language design. In taking this general point of view, the intention is not to propose a particular language—indeed, we believe that no single language will be sufficient for all aspects of architectural description—but rather to establish the framework within which architectural language design must take place.

Our primary considerations are understanding architectural abstractions, localizing and codifying the ways components interact, and distinguishing among the various ways in which architectural principles can be applied to software system design and analysis. Our focus is largely pragmatic: we are concerned primarily with what good engineers have found useful in practice. Thus, in Chapter 2 we describe a collection of common architectural styles and patterns upon which many systems are currently based. Then in Chapter 3 we present seven case studies to show how these architectural ideas can improve our understanding of software systems. This is followed by a more detailed architectural case study of shared information systems in Chapter 4.

Secondarily, we consider some emerging notations and tools for describing architectures and guiding our use of them. Chapter 5 illustrates how tools can help a designer to select appropriate architectures for a given problem. While such tools are only now beginning to emerge, the two described in that chapter illustrate some of the ways in which we can effectively apply existing technology effectively to the problem.

Chapter 6 takes up the issue providing formal models of architectures and architectural styles. In particular, we illustrate three approaches to formalizing software architecture. The first shows one way to formalize the architecture for a specific system. The second shows how to use formalism to understand a design space for architectural styles and patterns. The third shows one way to provide a formal basis for architectural connection.

In Chapters 7 and 8 we consider languages for describing architectures and tools for processing these descriptions. The first of these chapters considers the essential requirements for architectural description, and then makes the case that connectors deserve first-class treatment in such descriptions. We also illustrate some of the trade-offs that must be made in adding abstractions for new architectural connectors to existing programming languages. The second of these chapters considers three tools for constructing and analyzing architectures. One is an environment for the UniCon Language, which allows a mixture of architectural styles. The second is a toolkit, called Aesop, that supports creation of style-specific architectural design environments. The third is a formal notation and tool, called WRIGHT, for analyzing the consistency of an architectural specification.

CHAPTER

2

ARCHITECTURAL STYLES

ONE OF THE HALLMARKS of architectural design is the use of idiomatic patterns of system organization. Many of these patterns—or architectural styles—have been developed over the years as system designers recognized the value of specific organizational principles and structures for certain classes of software. In this chapter we consider a number of these architectural styles. Our purpose is to illustrate the rich space of architectural choices, and indicate some of the trade-offs involved in choosing one style over another.

2.1 ARCHITECTURAL STYLES

The use of patterns and styles of design is pervasive in many engineering disciplines. Indeed, an established, shared understanding of the common forms of design is one of the hallmarks of a mature engineering field. The shared vocabulary of design idioms and rules for using them is typically codified in engineering handbooks and materials for professional curricula.

Software has organizational styles, too.[1] At the architectural level, these are often associated with phrases such as a *client-server system,* a *pipe-filter design,* or a *layered architecture.* Some of these are commonly associated with specific design methods and notations, such as *object-oriented* and *dataflow* organizations. Other architectural patterns are associated with specific classes of systems such as the traditional organization of a compiler, the International Standard Organization's Open Systems Interconnection Reference Model [Pau85], and common patterns for object-oriented design [GHJV95, Pre95]. While we are still far from a comprehensive taxonomy of architectural idioms, general outlines of

---

[1] In this book we will use the terms *architectural pattern, architectural idiom,* and *architectural style* interchangeably. The problem of understanding precisely what is a style is one of active research and debate. The next section, as well as Chapters 6 and 8 provide one view; others can be found in the literature [Gar95b, PW92, AAG93, MQR95].

such a taxonomy are beginning to emerge. Figure 2.1 shows a partial list of some of the principle categories.

At a more detailed level, in order to make sense of the differences among styles, it helps to have a common framework from which to view them. The framework we will adopt is to treat an architecture of a specific system as a collection of computational components—or simply *components*—together with a description of the interactions among these components—the *connectors*. Examples of components are clients, servers, filters, layers, databases. Examples of connectors are procedure call, event broadcast, database protocols, and pipes.

Dataflow systems   **Virtual machines**
    Batch sequential   Interpreters
    Pipes and filters   Rule-based systems
Call-and-return systems   **Data-centered systems (repositories)**
    Main program and subroutine   Databases
    OO systems   Hypertext systems
    Hierarchical layers   Blackboards
Independent components
    Communicating processes
    Event systems

FIGURE 2.1   A List of Common Architectural Styles

An architectural style, then, defines a family of such systems in terms of a pattern of structural organization. More specifically, an architectural style defines a *vocabulary* of components and connector types, and a set of *constraints* on how they can be combined. For many styles there may also exist one or more *semantic models* that specify how to determine a system's overall properties from the properties of its parts.

Given this framework, we can approach specific architectural styles by answering the following questions:

- What is the design vocabulary—the types of components and connectors?
- What are the allowable structural patterns?
- What is the underlying computational model?
- What are the essential invariants of the style?
- What are some common examples of its use?
- What are the advantages and disadvantages of using that style?
- What are some of the common specializations?

We now consider seven commonly used styles: pipes and filters, objects, implicit invocation, layering, repositories, interpreters, and process control.

2.2   PIPES AND FILTERS

In a pipe-and-filter style each component has a set of inputs and a set of outputs. A component reads streams of data on its inputs and produces streams of data on its outputs. This is usually accomplished by applying a local transformation to the input streams and computing incrementally, so that output begins before input is consumed. Hence components are termed *filters*. The connectors of this style serve as conduits for the streams, transmitting outputs of one filter to inputs of another. Hence the connectors are termed *pipes*.

Among the important invariants of the style is the condition that filters must be independent entities: in particular, they should not share state with other filters. Another important invariant is that filters do not know the identity of their upstream and downstream filters. Their specifications might restrict what appears on the input pipes or make guarantees about what appears on the output pipes, but they may not identify the components at the ends of those pipes. Furthermore, the correctness of the output of a pipe-and-filter network should not depend on the order in which the filters perform their incremental processing—although fair scheduling can be assumed. (See [AG92, AAG93] for in-depth treatment of this style and its formal properties.) Figure 2.2 illustrates this style.

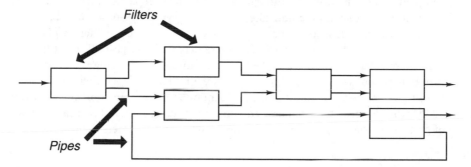

FIGURE 2.2   Pipes and Filters

Common specializations of this style include *pipelines*, which restrict the topologies to linear sequences of filters; bounded pipes, which restrict the amount of data that can reside on a pipe; and typed pipes, which require that the data passed between two filters have a well-defined type.

A degenerate case of a pipeline architecture occurs when each filter processes all of its input data as a single entity.[2] In this case the architecture becomes a *batch sequential* system. In these systems pipes no longer serve the function of providing a stream of data, and therefore are largely vestigial. Hence such systems are best treated as instances of a separate architectural style.

The best-known examples of pipe-and-filter architectures are programs written in the Unix shell [Bac86]. Unix supports this style by providing a notation for connecting components (represented as Unix processes) and by providing run-time mechanisms for implementing pipes. As another well-known example, traditionally compilers have been

---

[2] In general, we find that the boundaries of styles can overlap. This should not deter us from identifying the main features of a style with its central examples of use.

viewed as pipeline systems (though the phases are often not incremental). The stages in the pipeline include lexical analysis, parsing, semantic analysis, and code generation. (We return to this example in the case studies.) Other examples of pipes and filters occur in signal-processing domains [DG90], parallel programming [BAS89], functional programming [Kah74], and distributed systems [BWW88].

Pipe-and-filter systems have a number of nice properties. First, they allow the designer to understand the overall input/output behavior of a system as a simple composition of the behaviors of the individual filters. Second, they support reuse: any two filters can be hooked together, provided they agree on the data that are being transmitted between them. Third, systems are easy to maintain and enhance: new filters can be added to existing systems and old filters can be replaced by improved ones. Fourth, they permit certain kinds of specialized analysis, such as throughput and deadlock analysis. Finally, they naturally support concurrent execution. Each filter can be implemented as a separate task and potentially executed in parallel with other filters.

But these systems also have their disadvantages.[3] First, pipe-and-filter systems often lead to a batch organization of processing. Although filters can process data incrementally, they are inherently independent, so the designer must think of each filter as providing a complete transformation of input data to output data. In particular, because of their transformational character, pipe-and-filter systems are typically not good at handling interactive applications. This problem is most severe when incremental display updates are required, because the output pattern for incremental updates is radically different from the pattern for filter output. Second, they may be hampered by having to maintain correspondences between two separate but related streams. Third, depending on the implementation, they may force a lowest common denominator on data transmission, resulting in added work for each filter to parse and unparse its data. This, in turn, can lead both to loss of performance and to increased complexity in writing the filters themselves.

2.3   DATA ABSTRACTION AND OBJECT-ORIENTED ORGANIZATION

In the style based on data abstraction and object-oriented organization, data representations and their associated primitive operations are encapsulated in an abstract data type or object. The components of this style are the objects—or, if you will, instances of abstract data types. Objects are examples of a type of component we call a *manager* because it is responsible for preserving the integrity of a resource (here the representation). Objects interact through function and procedure invocations. Two important aspects of this style are (1) that an object is responsible for preserving the integrity of its representation (usually by maintaining some invariant over it), and (2) that the representation is hidden from other objects. Figure 2.3 illustrates this style.[4]

---

[3] This is true in spite of the fact that the pipe-and-filter style, like every style, has a set of devout followers—people who believe that all problems worth solving can best be solved using that particular style.

[4] We haven't mentioned inheritance in this description. While inheritance is an important organizing principle for defining the types of objects in a system, it does not have a direct architectural function. In particular, in our view, an inheritance relationship is not a connector, since it does not define the interaction between components in a system. Also, in an architectural setting inheritance of properties is not restricted to object types—but may include connectors and even architectural styles.

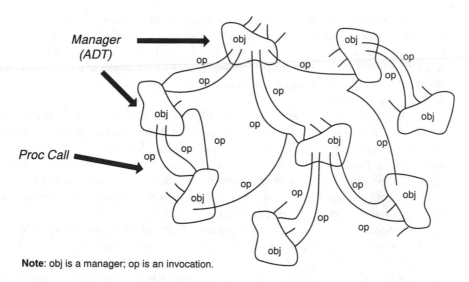

Note: obj is a manager; op is an invocation.

FIGURE 2.3   Abstract Data Types and Objects

The use of abstract data types, and increasingly the use of object-oriented systems, is, of course, widespread. There are many variations. For example, some systems allow "objects" to be concurrent tasks; others allow objects to have multiple interfaces [KG89, Har87b].

Object-oriented systems have many nice properties, most of which are well known. Because an object hides its representation from its clients, it is possible to change the implementation without affecting those clients. Additionally, the bundling of a set of accessing routines with the data they manipulate allows designers to decompose problems into collections of interacting agents.

But object-oriented systems also have some disadvantages. The most significant is that in order for one object to interact with another (via procedure call) it must know the identity of that other object. This is in contrast, for example, to pipe-and-filter systems, where filters do not need to know what other filters are in the system in order to interact with them. In object-oriented systems, then, whenever the identity of an object changes it is necessary to modify all other objects that explicitly invoke it. In a module-oriented language this manifests itself as the need to change the "import" list of every module that uses the changed module. There can also be side-effect problems: if A uses object B and C also uses B, then C's effects on B look like unexpected side effects to A, and vice versa.

2.4 EVENT-BASED, IMPLICIT INVOCATION

In a system in which the component interfaces provide a collection of procedures and functions, such as an object-oriented system, components typically interact with each other by explicitly invoking those routines. Recently, however, there has been considerable interest in an alternative integration technique, variously referred to as *implicit invocation,* *reactive integration,* and *selective broadcast.* This style has historical roots in systems based on actors [Hew69], constraint satisfaction, daemons, and packet-switched networks.

The idea behind implicit invocation is that instead of invoking a procedure directly, a component can announce (or broadcast) one or more events. Other components in the system can register an interest in an event by associating a procedure with it. When the event is announced, the system itself invokes all of the procedures that have been registered for the event. Thus an event announcement "implicitly" causes the invocation of procedures in other modules.

For example, in the Field system [Rei90], tools such as editors and variable monitors register for a debugger's breakpoint events. When a debugger stops at a breakpoint, it announces an event that allows the system to automatically invoke procedures of those registered tools. These procedures might scroll an editor to the appropriate source line or redisplay the value of monitored variables. In this scheme, the debugger simply announces an event, but does not know what other tools or actions (if any) are concerned with that event, or what they will do when that event is announced.

Architecturally speaking, the components in an implicit invocation style are modules whose interfaces provide both a collection of procedures (as with abstract data types) and a set of events. Procedures may be called in the usual way, but a component can also register some of its procedures with events of the system. This will cause these procedures to be invoked when those events are announced at run time.

The main invariant of this style is that announcers of events do not know which components will be affected by those events. Thus components cannot make assumptions about the order of processing, or even about what processing will occur as a result of their events. For this reason, most implicit invocation systems also include explicit invocation (i.e., normal procedure call) as a complementary form of interaction.

Examples of systems with implicit invocation mechanisms abound [GKN92]. They are used in programming environments to integrate tools [Ger89, Rei90], in database management systems to ensure consistency constraints [Hew69, Bal86], in user interfaces to separate presentation of data from applications that manage the data [KP88, SBH+83], and by syntax-directed editors to support incremental semantic checking [HN86, HGN91].

One important benefit of implicit invocation is that it provides strong support for reuse. Any component can be introduced into a system simply by registering it for the events of that system. A second benefit is that implicit invocation eases system evolution [SN92]. Components may be replaced by other components without affecting the interfaces of other components in the system.

The primary disadvantage of implicit invocation is that components relinquish control over the computation performed by the system. When a component announces an event, it cannot assume other components will respond to it. Moreover, even if it does know what other components are interested in the events it announces, it cannot rely on the order in which they are invoked. Another problem concerns exchange of data. Sometimes data can be passed with an event, but in other situations event systems must rely on a shared repository for interaction. In these cases global performance and resource management can become critical issues. Finally, reasoning about correctness can be problematic, since the meaning of a procedure that announces events will depend on the context of bindings in which it is invoked. This is in contrast to traditional reasoning about procedure calls, which need only consider a procedure's pre- and post-conditions when reasoning about the functional behavior of its invocation.

2.5   LAYERED SYSTEMS

A layered system is organized hierarchically, each layer providing service to the layer above it and serving as a client to the layer below. In some layered systems inner layers are hidden from all except the adjacent outer layer, except for certain functions carefully selected for export. Thus in these systems the components implement a virtual machine at some layer in the hierarchy. (In other layered systems the layers may be only partially opaque.) The connectors are defined by the protocols that determine how the layers will interact. Topological constraints include limiting interactions to adjacent layers. Figure 2.4 illustrates this style.

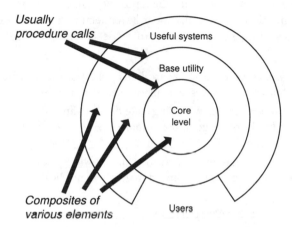

FIGURE 2.4 Layered Systems

The most widely known examples of this kind of architectural style are layered communication protocols [McC91]. In such applications each layer provides a substrate for communication at some level of abstraction. Lower levels define lower levels of interaction, the lowest typically being defined by hardware connections. Other application areas for this style include database systems and operating systems [BO92, FO85, LS79].

Layered systems have several desirable properties. First, they support designs based on increasing levels of abstraction. This allows implementors to partition a complex problem into a sequence of incremental steps. Second, they support enhancement. As with pipelines, because each layer interacts with at most the layers below and above, changes to the function of one layer affect at most two other layers. Third, they support reuse. Like abstract data types, they allow different implementations of the same layer to be used interchangeably, provided they support the same interfaces to their adjacent layers. This leads to the possibility of defining standard layer interfaces upon which different implementors can build. (Good examples are the OSI ISO model and some of the X Window System protocols.)

But layered systems also have disadvantages. Not all systems are easily structured in a layered fashion. (We will see an example of this later in the case studies of Chapter 3.) And even if a system *can* logically be structured in layers, considerations of performance may require closer coupling between logically high-level functions and their lower-level implementations. Additionally, it may be quite difficult to find the right levels of abstraction. This is particularly true for standardized layered models. The communications community, for instance, has had some difficulty mapping existing protocols into the ISO framework because many of those protocols bridge several layers.

2.6 REPOSITORIES

In a repository style there are two quite distinct kinds of components: a central data structure represents the current state, and a collection of independent components operate on the central data store. Interactions between the repository and its external components can vary significantly among systems.

The choice of a control discipline leads to two major subcategories. If the types of transactions in an input stream trigger selection of processes to execute, the repository can be a traditional database. On the other hand, if the current state of the central data structure is the main trigger for selecting processes to execute, the repository can be a blackboard.

Figure 2.5 illustrates a simple view of a blackboard architecture. (We will examine more detailed models in the case studies.) The blackboard model is usually presented with three major parts:

1. **The knowledge sources:** separate, independent parcels of application-dependent knowledge. Interaction among knowledge sources takes place solely through the blackboard.

2. **The blackboard data structure:** problem-solving state data, organized into an application-dependent hierarchy. Knowledge sources make changes to the blackboard that lead incrementally to a solution to the problem.

3. **Control:** driven entirely by the state of the blackboard. Knowledge sources respond opportunistically when changes in the blackboard make them applicable.

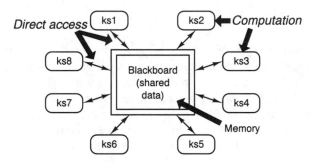

Note: ks is a knowledge source.   **FIGURE 2.5** The Blackboard

The diagram shows no explicit representation of the control component. Invocation of a knowledge source (ks) is triggered by the state of the blackboard. The actual locus of control, and hence its implementation, can be in the knowledge sources, the blackboard, a separate module, or some combination of these.

Blackboard systems have traditionally been used for applications requiring complex interpretations of signal processing, such as speech and pattern recognition. Several of these are surveyed by Nii [Nii86]. They have also appeared in other kinds of systems that involve shared access to data with loosely coupled agents [ACM90].

There are, of course, many other examples of repository systems. Batch-sequential systems with global databases are a special case. Programming environments are often organized as a collection of tools together with a shared repository of programs and program fragments [BSS84]. Even applications that have traditionally been viewed as pipeline architectures may be more accurately interpreted as repository systems. For example, as we will see later, while compiler architecture has traditionally been presented as a pipeline, the "phases" of most modern compilers operate on a base of shared information (symbol tables, abstract syntax tree, etc.).

2.7   INTERPRETERS

In an interpreter organization a virtual machine is produced in software. An interpreter includes the pseudoprogram being interpreted and the interpretation engine itself. The pseudoprogram includes the program itself and the interpreter's analog of its execution state (activation record). The interpretation engine includes both the definition of the interpreter and the current state of *its* execution. Thus an interpreter generally has four components: an interpretation engine to do the work, a memory that contains the pseudo-code to be interpreted, a representation of the control state of the interpretation engine, and a representation of the current state of the program being simulated (see Figure 2.6).

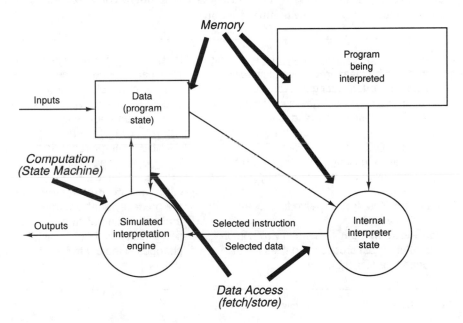

FIGURE 2.6   Interpreter

Interpreters are commonly used to build virtual machines that close the gap between the computing engine expected by the semantics of the program and the computing engine available in hardware. We occasionally speak of a programming language as providing, for example, a "virtual Pascal machine."

2.8   PROCESS CONTROL

Another architectural style is based on process control loops. This system organization is not widely recognized in the software community; nevertheless it seems to quietly appear within designs dominated by other models. Unlike object-oriented or functional designs, which are characterized by the kinds of components that appear, control-loop designs are characterized both by the kinds of components involved and the special relations that must hold among them.

2.8.1   PROCESS-CONTROL PARADIGMS

Continuous processes of many kinds convert input materials to products with specific properties by performing operations on the inputs and on intermediate products. The values of measurable properties of system state (materials, equipment settings, etc.) are called the variables of the process. Process variables that measure the output materials are called the controlled variables of the process. The properties of the input materials, intermediate products, and operations are captured in other process variables. In particular, the manipulated variables are associated with things that can be changed by the control system in order to regulate the process. (Process variables should not be confused with program variables.) Figure 2.7 gives some useful definitions.

Process variables. Properties of the process that can be measured; several specific kinds are often distinguished.

Controlled variable. Process variable whose value the system is intended to control.

Input variable. Process variable that measures an input to the process.

Manipulated variable. Process variable whose value can be changed by the controller.

Set point. The desired value for a controlled variable.

Open-loop system. System in which information about process variables is not used to adjust the system.

Closed-loop system. System in which information about process variables is used to manipulate a process variable to compensate for variations in process variables and operating conditions.

Feedback control system. The controlled variable is measured, and the result is used to manipulate one or more of the process variables.

Feedforward control system. Some of the process variables are measured, and anticipated disturbances are compensated for without waiting for changes in the controlled variable to be visible.

FIGURE 2.7   Process-Control Definitions

The purpose of a control system is to maintain specified properties of the outputs of the process at (sufficiently near) given reference values called the *set points*. If the input materials are pure, if the process is fully defined, and if the operations are completely repeatable, the process can simply run without surveillance. Such a process is called an open-loop system. Figure 2.8 shows such a system, a hot-air furnace that uses a constant burner setting to raise the temperature of the air that passes through. A similar furnace that uses a timer to turn the burner off and on at fixed intervals is also an open-loop system.

The open-loop assumptions are rarely valid for physical processes in the real world. More often, properties such as temperature, pressure, and flow rates are monitored, and their values are used to control the process by changing the settings of apparatus such as valves, heaters, and chillers. Such systems are called *closed-loop systems*. A home thermostat

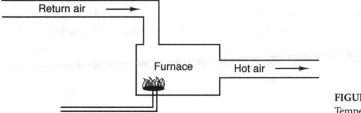

FIGURE 2.8 Open-Loop
Temperature Control

is a common example: the air temperature at the thermostat is measured, and the furnace
is turned on and off as necessary to maintain the desired temperature (the set point). Figure 2.9 shows the addition of a thermostat to convert Figure 2.8 to a closed-loop system.

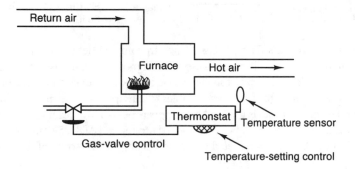

FIGURE 2.9 Closed-Loop
Temperature Control

There are two general forms of closed-loop control. Feedback control, illustrated in
Figure 2.10, adjusts the process according to measurements of the controlled variable. The
important components of a feedback controller are the process definition, the process variables (including designated input and controlled variables), a sensor to obtain the controlled variable from the physical output, the set point (target value for the controlled
variable), and a control algorithm. Figure 2.9 corresponds to Figure 2.10 as follows: the
furnace with burner is the process; the thermostat is the controller; the return air temperature is the input variable; the hot air temperature is the controlled variable; the thermostat
setting is the set point; and the temperature sensor is the sensor.

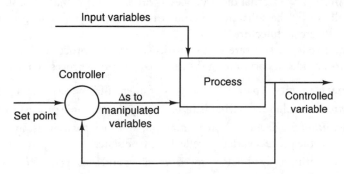

FIGURE 2.10 Feedback
Control

Feedforward control, shown in Figure 2.11, anticipates future effects on the controlled variable by measuring other process variables whose values may be more timely; it adjusts the process based on these variables. The important components of a feedforward controller are essentially the same as for a feedback controller except that the sensor(s) obtains values of input or intermediate variables. It is valuable when lags in the process delay the effect of control changes.

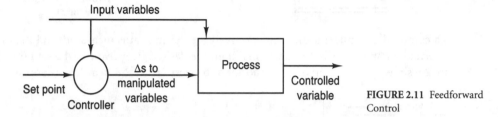

FIGURE 2.11 Feedforward Control

These are simplified models. They do not deal with complexities such as properties of sensors, transmission delays, and calibration issues. They ignore the response characteristics of the system, such as gain, lag, and hysteresis. They don't show how to combine feedforward and feedback or how to choose which process variables to manipulate. Chemical engineering provides excellent quantitative models for predicting how processes will react to various control algorithms; indeed there are a number of standard strategies [P+84, Section 22]. These are mentioned in Section 3.4.3, but a detailed discussion is beyond the scope of this book.

2.8.2   A SOFTWARE PARADIGM FOR PROCESS CONTROL

We usually think of software as algorithmic: we compute outputs (or execute continuous systems) solely on the basis of the inputs. This normal model does not allow for external perturbations; if noninput values of a computation change spontaneously, this is regarded as a hardware error. The normal software model corresponds to an open-loop system, and in most cases it is entirely appropriate. However, when the operating conditions of a software system are not completely predictable—especially when the software is operating a physical system—the purely algorithmic model breaks down. When the execution of a software system is affected by external disturbances—forces or events that are not directly visible to or controllable by the software—then a control paradigm should probably be considered for the software architecture.

An architectural style for software that controls continuous processes can be based on the process-control model, incorporating the essential parts of a process-control loop:

1. **Computational elements:** separate the process of interest from the control policy.
   - *Process definition,* including mechanisms for manipulating some process variables.
   - *Control algorithm* for deciding how to manipulate process variables, including a model for how the process variables reflect the true state.
2. **Data elements:** continuously updated process variables and sensors that collect them.
   - *Process variables,* including designated input, controlled, and manipulated variables, and knowledge of which can be sensed.

- *Set point*, or reference value for controlled variable.
- *Sensors* to obtain values of process variables pertinent to control.

3. **The control loop paradigm:** establishes the relation that the control algorithm exercises. It collects information about the actual and intended states of the process, and tunes the process variables to drive the actual state toward the intended state.

The two computational elements separate issues about desired functionality from issues about responses to external disturbances. For a software system, we can bundle the process and the process variables; that is, we can regard the process definition together with the process variables and sensors as a single subsystem whose input and controlled variables are visible in the subsystem interface. We can then bundle the control algorithm and the set point as a second subsystem; this controller has continuous access to current values of the set point and the monitored variables. For a feedback system, this will be the controlled variable. There are two interactions between these major systems: the controller receives values of process variables from the process, and the controller supplies continuous guidance to the process about changes to the manipulated variables.

The result is a particular kind of dataflow architecture. The primary characteristic of dataflow architectures is that the components interact by providing data to each other, each component executing when data is available. Most dataflow architectures involve independent (often concurrent) processes and pacing that depend on the rates at which the processes provide data for each other. The control-loop paradigm assumes further that data related to process variables is updated continuously. Moreover, unlike many dataflow architectures, which are linear, the control-loop architecture requires a cyclic topology. Finally, the control loop establishes an intrinsic asymmetry between the control element and the process element.

2.9   OTHER FAMILIAR ARCHITECTURES

There are numerous other architectural styles and patterns. Some are widespread, and others are specific to particular domains. While a detailed treatment is beyond the scope of this chapter, we briefly note a few of the important categories.

- **Distributed processes:** Distributed systems have developed a number of common organizations for multiprocess systems [And91]. Some can be characterized primarily by their topological features, such as ring and star organizations. Others are better characterized in terms of the kinds of interprocess protocols that are used for communication (e.g., heartbeat algorithms).

  One common form of distributed system architecture is a *client-server* organization [Ber92]. In these systems a server represents a process that provides services to other processes (the clients). Usually the server does not know in advance the identities or number of clients that will access it at run time. On the other hand, clients know the identity of a server (or can find it out through some other server) and access it by remote procedure call.

- **Main program/subroutine organizations**: The primary organization of many systems mirrors the programming language in which the system is written. For languages without support for modularization, this often results in a system organized around a main program and a set of subroutines. The main program acts as the driver for the subroutines, typically providing a control loop for sequencing through the subroutines in some order.

- **Domain-specific software architectures**: Recently there has been considerable interest in developing "reference" architectures for specific domains [MG92, Tra94]. These architectures provide an organizational structure tailored to a family of applications, such as avionics, command and control, or vehicle-management systems. By specializing the architecture to the domain, it is possible to increase the descriptive power of structures. Indeed, in many cases the architecture is sufficiently constrained that an executable system can be generated automatically or semi-automatically from the architectural description itself.

- **State transition systems**: A common organization for many reactive systems is the state transition system [Har87a]. These systems are defined in terms of a set of states and a set of named transitions that move a system from one state to another.

2.10 HETEROGENEOUS ARCHITECTURES

Thus far we have been speaking primarily of "pure" architectural styles. While it is important to understand the individual nature of each of these styles, most systems typically involve some combination of several styles.

Architectural styles can be combined in several ways. One way is through hierarchy. A component of a system organized in one architectural style may have an internal structure that is developed in a completely different style. For example, in a Unix pipeline the individual components may be represented internally using virtually any style—including, of course, another pipe-and-filter system.[5]

What is perhaps more surprising is that connectors, too, can often be hierarchically decomposed. For example, a pipe connector may be implemented internally as a FIFO queue accessed by insert and remove operations.

A second way to combine styles is to permit a single component to use a mixture of architectural connectors. For example, a component might access a repository through part of its interface, but interact through pipes with other components in a system, and accept control information through another part of its interface. (In fact, Unix pipe-and-filter systems do this; the file system plays the role of the repository, and initialization switches play the role of control.)

Another example is an "active database." This is a repository which activates external components through implicit invocation. In this organization external components register interest in portions of the database. The database automatically invokes the appropriate tools on the basis of this association.

A third way to combine styles is to completely elaborate one level of architectural description in a completely different architectural style. We will see examples of this in the case studies of the next chapter.

---

[5] More likely, a component is defined with spaghetti code—i.e., no style.

CHAPTER 3

CASE STUDIES

WE NOW PRESENT seven examples and case studies to illustrate how we can use architectural principles to increase our understanding of software systems. The first case study shows how different architectural solutions to the same problem provide different benefits. The second case study summarizes experience in developing a domain-specific architectural style for a family of industrial products. The third case study contrasts several styles for implementing mobile robotics systems. The fourth case study illustrates how to apply a process-control style to system design. The remaining three case studies present examples of heterogeneous architectures.

3.1 KEY WORD IN CONTEXT

In his paper of 1972, Parnas proposed the following problem [Par72]:

> The KWIC [Key Word in Context] index system accepts an ordered set of lines; each line is an ordered set of words, and each word is an ordered set of characters. Any line may be "circularly shifted" by repeatedly removing the first word and appending it at the end of the line. The KWIC index system outputs a listing of all circular shifts of all lines in alphabetical order.

Parnas used the problem to contrast different criteria for decomposing a system into modules. He describes two solutions, one based on functional decomposition with shared access to data representations, and a second based on a decomposition that hides design decisions. Since its introduction, the problem has become well-known and is widely used as a teaching device in software engineering.

While KWIC can be implemented as a relatively small system, it is not simply of pedagogical interest. Practical instances of it are widely used by computer scientists. For example, the "permuted" [*sic*] index for the Unix Man pages is essentially such a system.

From the point of view of software architecture, the problem is appealing because we can use it to illustrate the effect of changes on software design. Parnas shows that different problem decompositions vary greatly in their ability to withstand design changes. Among the changes he considers are the following:

1. **Changes in the processing algorithm:** For example, line shifting can be performed on each line as it is read from the input device, on all the lines after they are read, or on demand when the alphabetization requires a new set of shifted lines.

2. **Changes in data representation:** For example, lines, words, and characters can be stored in various ways. Similarly, circular shifts can be stored explicitly or implicitly (as pairs of index and offset).

Garlan, Kaiser, and Notkin also use the KWIC problem to illustrate modularization schemes based on implicit invocation [GKN92]. To do this, they extend Parnas's analysis by also considering the following:

3. **Enhancement to system function:** For example, modify the system to eliminate circular shifts that start with certain noise words (such as *a, an, and,* etc.). Change the system to be interactive, and allow the user to delete lines from the original lists (or from the circularly shifted lists).

4. **Performance:** Both space and time.

5. **Reuse:** To what extent can the components serve as reusable entities?

We now outline four architectural designs for the KWIC system. All four are grounded in published solutions (including implementations). The first two are those considered in Parnas's original article. The third solution uses an implicit invocation style and represents a variant on the solution examined by Garlan, Kaiser, and Notkin. The fourth is a pipeline solution inspired by the Unix index utility.

After presenting each solution and briefly summarizing its strengths and weakness, we contrast the different architectural decompositions in a table organized along the five design dimensions itemized above.

3.1.1   SOLUTION 1: MAIN PROGRAM/SUBROUTINE WITH SHARED DATA

The first solution decomposes the problem according to the four basic functions performed: input, shift, alphabetize, and output. These computational components are coordinated as subroutines by a main program that sequences through them in turn. Data is communicated between the components through shared storage ("core storage"). Communication between the computational components and the shared data is an unconstrained read-write protocol. This is possible because the coordinating program guarantees sequential access to the data (see Figure 3.1).

This solution allows data to be represented efficiently, since computations can share the same storage. The solution also has a certain intuitive appeal, since distinct computational aspects are isolated in different modules.

However, as Parnas argues, it has a number of serious drawbacks in terms of its ability to handle changes. In particular, a change in the data storage format will affect almost all of the modules. Similarly, changes in the overall processing algorithm and enhance-

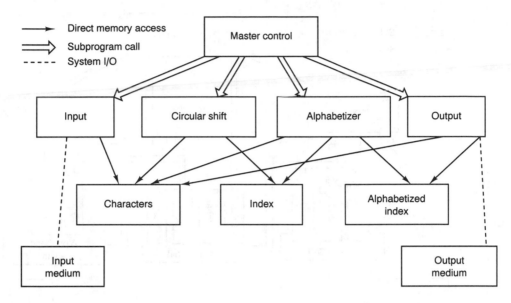

FIGURE 3.1   KWIC: Shared Data Solution

ments to system function are not easily accommodated. Finally, this decomposition is not particularly supportive of reuse.

3.1.2   Solution 2: Abstract Data Types

The second solution decomposes the system into a similar set of five modules. However, in this case data is no longer directly shared by the computational components. Instead, each module provides an interface that permits other components to access data only by invoking procedures in that interface. (See Figure 3.2, which illustrates how each component now has a set of procedures that determine the form of access to it by other components in the system.)

This solution provides the same logical decomposition into processing modules as the first. However, it has a number of advantages over the first solution when design changes are considered. In particular, both algorithms and data representations can be changed in individual modules without affecting others. Moreover, reuse is better supported than in the first solution because modules make fewer assumptions about the others with which they interact.

On the other hand, as discussed by Garlan, Kaiser, and Notkin, the solution is not particularly well suited to certain kinds of functional enhancements. The main problem is that to add new functions to the system, the implementor must either modify the existing modules—compromising their simplicity and integrity—or add new modules that lead to performance penalties. (See [GKN92] for a detailed discussion.)

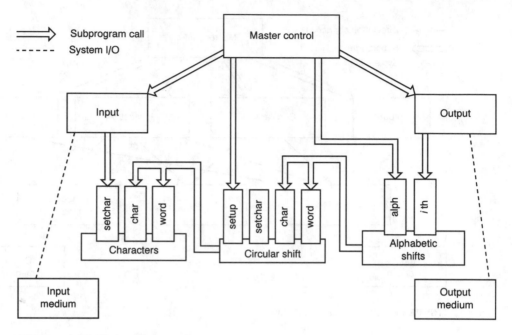

FIGURE 3.2   KWIC: Abstract Data Type Solution

3.1.3   SOLUTION 3: IMPLICIT INVOCATION

The third solution uses a form of component integration based on shared data, similar to the first solution (see Figure 3.3). However, there are two important differences. First, the interface to the data is more abstract. Rather than exposing the storage formats to the computing modules, this solution accesses data abstractly (for example, as a list or a set). Second, computations are invoked implicitly as data is modified. Thus interaction is based on an "active data" model. For example, the act of adding a new line to the line storage causes an event to be sent to the shift module. This allows it to produce circular shifts (in a separate, abstract shared-data store), which in turn causes the alphabetizer to be implicitly invoked, so that it can alphabetize the lines.

This solution easily supports functional enhancements to the system: additional modules can be attached to the system by registering them to be invoked on data-changing events. Because data is accessed abstractly, the solution also insulates computations from changes in data representation. It also supports reuse, since the implicitly invoked modules only rely on the existence of certain externally triggered events.

However, the solution suffers from the fact that it can be difficult to control the processing order of the implicitly invoked modules. Further, because invocations are data-driven, the most natural implementations of this kind of decomposition tend to use more space than the previously considered decompositions.

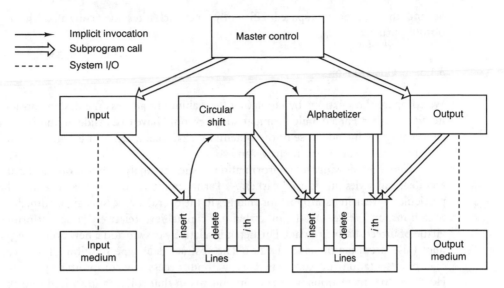

FIGURE 3.3   KWIC: Implicit Invocation Solution

3.1.4   SOLUTION 4: PIPES AND FILTERS

The fourth solution uses a pipeline approach. In this case there are four filters: input, shift, alphabetize, and output. Each filter processes the data and sends it to the next filter. Control is distributed: each filter can run whenever it has data on which to compute. Data sharing between filters is strictly limited to that transmitted on pipes (see Figure 3.4).

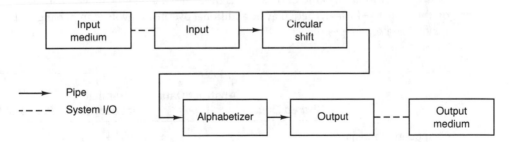

FIGURE 3.4   KWIC: Pipe-and-Filter Solution

This solution has several nice properties. First, it maintains the intuitive flow of processing. Second, it supports reuse, since each filter can function in isolation (provided upstream filters produce data in the form it expects). New functions are easily added to the system by inserting filters at the appropriate points in the processing sequence. Third, it is amenable to modification, since filters are logically independent of other filters.

On the other hand the solution has a number of drawbacks. First, it is virtually impossible to modify the design to support an interactive system. For example, deleting a line would require some persistent shared storage, violating a basic tenet of this approach.

Second, the solution uses space inefficiently, since each filter must copy all of the data to its output ports.

3.1.5 COMPARISONS

We compare the solutions by tabulating their ability to address the design considerations itemized earlier. For a detailed comparison, we would have to consider a number of factors concerning the intended use of the system: for example, whether it is batch or interactive, update-intensive or query-intensive, and so on.

Figure 3.5 provides an approximation to such an analysis, based on the discussion of architectural styles introduced earlier. As Parnas pointed out, the shared-data solution is particularly weak in its support for changes in the overall processing algorithm, data representations, and reuse. On the other hand it can achieve relatively good performance, by virtue of direct sharing of data. Further, it is relatively easy to add a new processing component (also accessing the shared data). The abstract data type solution allows changes to data representation and supports reuse, without necessarily compromising performance. However, the interactions between components in that solution are wired into the modules themselves, so changing the overall processing algorithm or adding new functions may involve a large number of changes to the existing system.

The implicit invocation solution is particularly good for adding new functionality. However, it suffers from some of the problems of the shared-data approach: poor support for change in data representation and reuse. Moreover, it may introduce extra execution overhead. The pipe-and-filter solution allows new filters to be placed in the stream of text processing. Therefore it supports changes in processing algorithm, changes in function, and reuse. On the other hand, decisions about data representation will be wired into the assumptions about the kind of data that is transmitted along the pipes. Further, depending on the exchange format, there may be additional overhead involved in parsing and unparsing the data onto pipes.

	Shared Data	Abstract Data Type	Implicit Invocation	Pipe and Filter
Change in Algorithm	–	–	+	+
Change in Data Rep	–	+	–	–
Change in Function	+	–	+	+
Performance	+	+	–	–
Reuse	–	+	–	+

FIGURE 3.5   KWIC: Comparison of Solutions

3.2   INSTRUMENTATION SOFTWARE

Our second case study describes the industrial development of a software architecture at Tektronix, Inc. This work was carried out as a collaborative effort between several Tektronix product divisions and the Computer Research Laboratory over a three-year period [DG90, GD90].

The purpose of the project was to develop a reusable system architecture for oscilloscopes. An oscilloscope is an instrumentation system that samples electrical signals and displays pictures (called *traces*) of them on a screen. Oscilloscopes also perform measurements on the signals, and display them on the screen. Although they were once simple analogue devices involving little software, modern oscilloscopes rely primarily on digital technology and have quite complex software. It is not uncommon for a modern oscilloscope to perform dozens of measurements, supply megabytes of internal storage, support an interface to a network of workstations and other instruments, and provide a sophisticated user interface, including a touch-panel screen with menus, built-in help facilities, and color displays.

Like many companies that have had to rely increasingly on software to support their products, Tektronix was faced with a number of problems. First, there was little reuse across different oscilloscope products. Instead, different oscilloscopes were built by different product divisions, each with its own development conventions, software organization, programming language, and development tools. Moreover, even within a single product division, each new oscilloscope typically had to be completely redesigned to accommodate changes in hardware capability and new requirements on the user interface. This problem was compounded by the fact that both hardware and interface requirements were changing increasingly rapidly. Furthermore, there was a perceived need to address "specialized markets," which meant that it would have to be possible to tailor a general-purpose instrument to a specific set of uses, such as patient monitoring or automotive diagnostics.

Second, performance problems were increasing because the software was not rapidly configurable within the instrument. These problems arose because an oscilloscope may be configured in many different modes, depending on the user's task. In old oscilloscopes reconfiguration was handled simply by loading different software to handle the new mode. But the total size of software was increasing, which led to delays between a user's request for a new mode and a reconfigured instrument.

The goal of the project was to develop an architectural framework for oscilloscopes that would address these problems. The result of that work was a domain-specific software architecture that formed the basis of the next generation of Tektronix oscilloscopes. Since then the framework has been extended and adapted to accommodate a broader class of systems, while at the same time being better adapted to the specific needs of instrumentation software. In the remainder of this section, we outline the stages in this architectural development.

3.2.1   AN OBJECT-ORIENTED MODEL

The first attempt at developing a reusable architecture focused on producing an object-oriented model of the software domain, which clarified the data types used in oscilloscopes:

waveforms, signals, measurements, trigger modes, and so on (see Figure 3.6). While this was a useful exercise, it fell far short of producing the hoped-for results. Although many types of data were identified, there was no overall model that explained how the types fit together. This led to confusion about the partitioning of functionality. For example, should measurements be associated with the types of data being measured, or represented externally? Which objects should the user interface interact with?

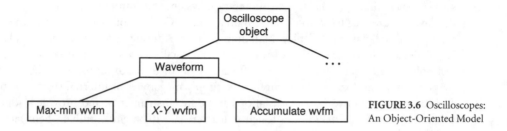

FIGURE 3.6 Oscilloscopes:
An Object-Oriented Model

3.2.2   A LAYERED MODEL

The second phase attempted to correct these problems by providing a layered model of an oscilloscope (see Figure 3.7), in which the core layer represented the signal-manipulation functions that filter signals as they enter the oscilloscope. These functions are typically implemented in hardware. The next layer represented waveform acquisition. Within this layer signals are digitized and stored internally for later processing. The third layer consisted of waveform manipulation, including measurement, waveform addition, Fourier transformation, and so on. The fourth layer consisted of display functions, which were responsible for mapping digitized waveforms and measurements to visual representations. The outermost layer was the user interface. This layer was responsible for interacting with the user and for deciding which data should be shown on the screen (see Figure 3.7).

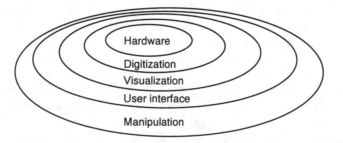

FIGURE 3.7 Oscilloscopes:
A Layered Model

The layered model was intuitively appealing since it partitioned the functions of an oscilloscope into well-defined groups. Unfortunately it was the wrong model for the application domain. The main problem was that the boundaries of abstraction enforced by the layers conflicted with the needs for interaction among the various functions. For example, the model suggests that all user interactions with an oscilloscope should be in terms of the visual representations. In practice, however, real oscilloscope users need to directly affect the functions in all layers, such as setting attenuation in the signal-manipulation layer, choosing acquisition mode and parameters in the acquisition layer, or creating derived waveforms in the waveform-manipulation layer.

3.2.3   A PIPE-AND-FILTER MODEL

The third attempt yielded a model in which oscilloscope functions were viewed as incremental transformers of data. Signal transformers are used to condition external signals. Acquisition transformers derive digitized waveforms from these signals. Display transformers convert these waveforms into visual data (see Figure 3.8).

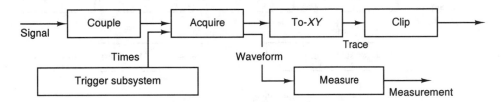

FIGURE 3.8   Oscilloscopes: A Pipe-and-Filter Model

This architectural model was a significant improvement over the layered model because it did not isolate the functions in separate partitions. For example, nothing in this model would prevent signal data from feeding directly into display filters. Further, the model corresponded well with the engineers' view of signal processing as a dataflow problem, and allowed the clean intermingling and substitution of hardware and software components within a system design.

The main problem with the model was that it was not clear how the user should interact with it. If the user were simply at the visual end of the system, this would represent an even worse decomposition than the layered system.

3.2.4   A MODIFIED PIPE-AND-FILTER MODEL

The fourth solution accounted for user inputs by associating with each filter a control interface that allowed an external entity to set parameters of operation for the filter. For example, the acquisition filter could have parameters that determined sample rate and waveform duration. These inputs serve as configuration parameters for the oscilloscope. One can think of such filters as having a "control panel" interface that determines what function will be performed across the conventional input/output dataflow interface. Formally, the filters can be modeled as "higher-order" functions, for which the configuration parameters determine what data transformation the filter will perform. (In Section 6.2 we sketch this formal model.) Figure 3.9 illustrates this architecture.

The introduction of a control interface solves a large part of the user interface problem. First, it provides a collection of settings that determine what aspects of the oscilloscope can be modified dynamically by the user. It also explains how the user can change oscilloscope functions by incremental adjustments to the software. Second, it decouples the signal-processing functions of the oscilloscope from the actual user interface: the signal-processing software makes no assumptions about how the user actually communicates changes to its control parameters. Conversely, the actual user interface can treat the signal-processing functions solely in terms of the control parameters. Designers can therefore change the implementation of the signal-processing software and hardware without affecting the implementation of the user interface (provided the control interface remained unchanged).

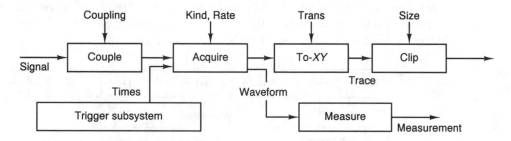

FIGURE 3.9   Oscilloscopes: A Modified Pipe-and-Filter Model

3.2.5   FURTHER SPECIALIZATION

The adapted pipe-and-filter model was a great improvement, but it, too, had some problems. The most significant problem was that the pipe-and-filter computational model led to poor performance. In particular, because waveforms can occupy a large amount of internal storage, it is simply not practical for each filter to copy waveforms every time they process them. Further, different filters may run at radically different speeds: it is unacceptable to slow one filter down because another filter is still processing its data.

To handle these problems the model was further specialized. Instead of using a single kind of pipe, we introduced several "colors" of pipes. Some of these allowed data to be processed without copying. Others permitted slow filters to ignore incoming data if they were in the middle of processing other data. These additional pipes increased the stylistic vocabulary and allowed the pipe/filter computations to be tailored more specifically to the performance needs of the product.

3.2.6   SUMMARY

This case study illustrates some of the issues involved in developing an architectural style for a real application domain. It underscores the fact that different architectural styles have different effects on the solution to a set of problems. Moreover, it illustrates that architectural designs for industrial software must typically be adapted from pure forms to specialized styles that meet the needs of the specific domain. In this case, the final result depended greatly on the properties of pipe-and-filter architectures, but adapted that generic style so that it could also satisfy the performance needs of the product family.

3.3   MOBILE ROBOTICS

By Marco Schumacher

A mobile robotics system is one that controls a manned or partially manned vehicle, such as a car, a submarine, or a space vehicle. Such systems are finding many new uses in areas such as space exploration, hazardous waste disposal, and underwater exploration.

Building the software to control mobile robots is a challenging problem. These systems must deal with external sensors and actuators, and they must respond in real time at rates commensurate with the activities of the system in its environment. In particular, the software functions of a mobile robot typically include acquiring input provided by its sensors, controlling the motion of its wheels and other moveable parts, and planning its future path. Several factors complicate the tasks: obstacles may block the robot's path; the sensor input may be imperfect; the robot may run out of power; mechanical limitations may restrict the accuracy with which it moves; the robot may manipulate hazardous materials; and unpredictable events may demand a rapid response.

Over the years, many architectural designs have been proposed for robotic systems. The richness of the field permits interesting comparisons of the emphases chosen by different researchers. In this section we consider four representative architectural designs.

3.3.1   DESIGN CONSIDERATIONS

To help create a framework for comparison of the architectural approaches, we enumerate below some of the basic requirements (Req1 through Req4) for a mobile robot's architecture.

- **Req1:** The architecture must accommodate *deliberative and reactive behavior*. The robot must coordinate the actions it undertakes to achieve its designated objective (e.g., collect a rock sample) with the reactions forced on it by the environment (e.g., avoid an obstacle).
- **Req2:** The architecture must allow for *uncertainty*. The circumstances of a robot's operation are never fully predictable. The architecture must provide a framework in which the robot can act even when faced with incomplete or unreliable information (e.g., contradictory sensor readings).
- **Req3:** The architecture must *account for dangers* inherent in the robot's operation and its environment. By considering fault tolerance, safety, and performance, the architecture must help maintain the integrity of the robot, its operators, and its environment. Problems like reduced power supply, dangerous vapors, or unexpectedly opening doors should not lead to disaster.
- **Req4:** The architecture must give the designer *flexibility*. Application development for mobile robots frequently requires experimentation and reconfiguration. Moreover, changes in tasks may require regular modification.

The degree to which these requirements apply in a given situation depends both on the complexity of the work the robot is programmed to perform and the predictability of its environment. For instance, fault tolerance is paramount when the robot is operating on another planet as part of a space mission; it is still important, but less crucial, when the robot can be brought to a nearby maintenance facility.

We now examine four architectural designs for mobile robots: Lozano's control loops [LP90], Elfes's layered organization [Elf87], Simmons's task-control architecture [Sim92], and Shafer's application of blackboards [SST86]. We will use the four requirements listed above to guide the evaluation of these alternatives.

3.3.2   SOLUTION 1: CONTROL LOOP

Unlike mobile robots, most industrial robots only need to support minimal handling of unpredictable events: the tasks are fully predefined (e.g., welding certain automobile parts together), and the robot has no responsibility with respect to its environment. (Rather, the environment is responsible for not interfering with the robot.) The open-loop paradigm applies naturally to this situation: the robot initiates an action or series of actions without bothering to check on their consequences [LP90].

Upgrading this paradigm to mobile robots involves adding feedback, thus producing a closed-loop architecture. The controller initiates robot actions and monitors their consequences, adjusting the future plans according to the monitored information. Figure 3.10 illustrates the control-loop paradigm. Let us consider how this model handles the four requirements listed above.

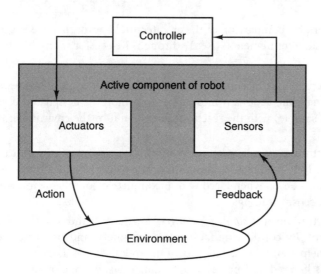

FIGURE 3.10 A Control-Loop Solution for Mobile Robots

- **Req1:** An advantage of the closed-loop paradigm is its simplicity: it captures the basic interaction between the robot and the outside. However, its simplicity is also a drawback in the more unpredictable environments. One expert [LP90] notes that the feedback loop assumes that changes in the environment are continuous and require continuous reactions (e.g., the control of pressure through the gradual opening and closing of a valve). Robots, though, are mostly confronted with disparate, discrete events that require them to switch between very different behavior modes (e.g., between controlling manipulator motions and adjusting the base position, to avert loss of equilibrium). The model does not suggest how such mode changes should be handled.

For complex tasks, the control loop gives no leverage for decomposing the software into cooperating components. If the steps of sensing, planning, and acting must be refined, other paradigms must provide the details that the control-loop model lacks.

- **Req2:** For the resolution of uncertainty, the control-loop paradigm is biased towards one method: reducing the unknowns through iteration. A trial-and-error process with action and reaction eliminates possibilities at each turn. If more subtle steps are needed, the architecture offers no framework for integrating these with the basic loop or for delegating them to separate entities.
- **Req3:** Fault tolerance and safety are supported by the closed-loop paradigm in the sense that its simplicity makes duplication easy and reduces the chance of errors creeping into the system.
- **Req4:** The major components of a robot architecture (supervisor, sensors, motors) are separated from each other and can be replaced independently. More refined tuning must take place inside the modules, at a level of detail that the architecture does not show.

In summary, the closed-loop paradigm seems most appropriate for simple robotic systems that must handle only a small number of external events and whose tasks do not require complex decomposition.

3.3.3   Solution 2: Layered Architecture

Figure 3.11 shows Alberto Elfes's definition of the idealized layered architecture [Elf87], which influenced the design of the Dolphin sonar and navigation system, implemented on the Terregator and Neptune mobile robots [CBCD93, PDB84].

- At level 1, the lowest level, reside the robot control routines (motors, joints, etc.).
- Levels 2 and 3 deal with input from the real world. They perform sensor interpretation (the analysis of the data from one sensor) and sensor integration (the combined analysis of different sensor inputs).
- Level 4 is concerned with maintaining the robot's model of the world.
- Level 5 manages the navigation of the robot.
- Levels 6 and 7 schedule and plan the robot's actions. Dealing with problems and replanning is also part of the level-7 responsibilities.
- The top level provides the user interface and overall supervisory functions.
- **Req1:** Elfes's model sidesteps some of the problems encountered with the control loop by defining more components to which the required tasks can be delegated. Being specialized to autonomous robots, it indicates the concerns that must be addressed (e.g., sensor integration). Furthermore, it defines abstraction levels (e.g., robot control vs. navigation) to guide the design.

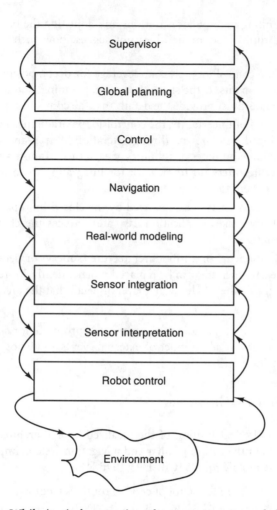

FIGURE 3.11 A Layered Solution for Mobile Robots

While it nicely organizes the components needed to coordinate the robot's operation, the layered architecture does not fit the actual data and control-flow patterns. The layers suggest that services and requests are passed between adjacent components. In reality, as Elfes readily acknowledges, information exchange is less straightforward. For instance, data requiring fast reaction may have to be sent directly from the sensors to the problem-handling agent at level 7, and the corresponding commands may have to skip levels to reach the motors in time.

Another problem in the model is that it does not separate two abstraction hierarchies that actually exist in the architecture:

- The data hierarchy, with raw sensor input (level 1), interpreted and integrated results (2 and 3), and finally the world model (4).
- The control hierarchy, with motor control (level 1), navigation (5), scheduling (6), planning (7), and user-level control (8).

(Some other layered architectures, such as NASREM, do a better job in this respect. We will mention some of these later.)

- **Req2:** The existence of abstraction layers addresses the need for managing uncertainty: what is uncertain at the lowest level may become clear with the added knowledge available in the higher layers. For instance, the context embodied in the world model can provide the clues to disambiguate conflicting sensor data.

- **Req3:** Fault tolerance and passive safety (when you strive not to do something) are also served by the abstraction mechanism. Data and commands are analyzed from different perspectives. It is possible to incorporate many checks and balances into the system. As already mentioned, performance and active safety (when you have to do something rather than avoid doing something) may require that the communication pattern be short-circuited.

- **Req4:** The interlayer dependencies are an obstacle to easy replacement and addition of components. Further, complex relationships between the layers can become more difficult to decipher with each change.

In summary, the abstraction levels defined by the layered architecture provide a framework for organizing the components that succeeds because it is precise about the roles of the different layers. The major drawback of the model is that it breaks down when it is taken to the greater level of detail demanded by an actual implementation. The communication patterns in a robot are not likely to follow the orderly scheme implied by the architecture.

3.3.4   SOLUTION 3: IMPLICIT INVOCATION

The third solution is based on a form of implicit invocation, as embodied in the Task-Control Architecture (TCA) [Sim92]. Figure 3.12 sketches the architecture. It has been used to control numerous mobile robots, such as the Ambler robot [Sim90].

The TCA architecture is based on hierarchies of tasks, or *task trees*. Figure 3.13 shows a sample task tree, in which parent tasks initiate child tasks. The software designer can define temporal dependencies between pairs of tasks; for example, a common temporal constraint is that A must complete before B starts. These features permit the specification of selective concurrency. The implementation of TCA includes many operations for dynamic reconfiguration of task trees at run time in response to changing robot state and environmental conditions.

TCA uses implicit invocation to coordinate interactions between tasks. Specifically, tasks communicate by multicasting messages via a message server, which redirects those messages to tasks that are registered to handle them.

In addition to the communication of messages, TCA's implicit invocation mechanisms support three functions:

1. **Exceptions:** Certain conditions cause the execution of an associated exception handler. Exceptions override the currently executing task in the subtree that causes the exception. They quickly change the processing mode of the robot and are thus better suited for managing spontaneous events (such as a dangerous change in terrain) than the feedback loop or the long communication paths of the pure layered archi-

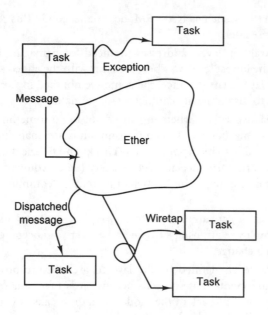

FIGURE 3.12 An Implicit Invocation Architecture for Mobile Robots

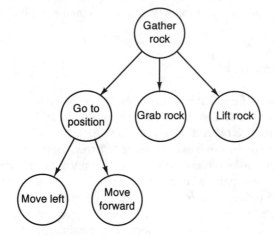

FIGURE 3.13 A Task Tree for Mobile Robots

tecture. Exception handlers have at their disposal all the operations for manipulating the task trees: for example, they can abort or retry tasks.

2. **Wiretapping:** Messages can be intercepted by tasks superimposed on an existing task tree. For instance, a safety-check component can use this feature to validate outgoing motion commands.

3. **Monitors:** Monitors read information and execute some action if the data fulfills a certain criterion. An example from the TCA manual is the battery check: if the battery level falls below a given level, the actions necessary for recharging it are invoked. This feature offers a convenient way of dealing with fault-tolerance issues by setting aside agents to supervise the system.

We turn now to the requirements.

- **Req1:** Task trees on the one hand, and exceptions, wiretapping, and monitors on the other, permit a clear-cut separation of action (the behavior embodied in the task trees) and reaction (the behavior dictated by extraneous events and circumstances).

  TCA also distinguishes itself from the previous paradigms by explicitly incorporating concurrent agents in its model. In TCA it is evident that multiple actions can proceed at the same time, more or less independently. The other two models do not explicitly address concurrency.

  In practice, the amount of concurrency of a TCA system is limited by the capabilities of the central server. In general, its reliance on a central control point may be a weak point of TCA.

- **Req2:** How TCA addresses uncertainty is less clear. If imponderables exist, a tentative task tree can be built, to be modified by the exception handlers if its fundamental assumptions turn out to be erroneous.

- **Req3:** As illustrated by the examples above, the TCA exception, wiretapping, and monitoring features take into account the needs for performance, safety, and fault tolerance.

  Fault tolerance by redundancy is achieved when multiple handlers register for the same signal; if one of them becomes unavailable, TCA can still provide the service by routing the request to another. Performance also benefits, since multiple occurrences of the same request can be handled concurrently by multiple handlers.

- **Req4:** The use of implicit invocation makes incremental development and replacement of components straightforward. It is often sufficient to register new handlers, exceptions, wiretaps, or monitors with the central server; no existing components are affected.

In summary, TCA offers a comprehensive set of features for coordinating the tasks of a robot while respecting the requirements for quality and ease of development. The richness of the scheme makes it most appropriate for more complex robot projects.

3.3.5   SOLUTION 4: BLACKBOARD ARCHITECTURE

Figure 3.14 describes a blackboard architecture for mobile robots. This paradigm was used in the NAVLAB project, as part of the CODGER system [SST86]. The *whiteboard* architecture, as it is termed in [SST86], works with abstractions reminiscent of those encountered in the layered architecture. The components of CODGER are the following:

- The "captain": the overall supervisor.
- The "map navigator": the high-level path planner.
- The "lookout": a module that monitors the environment for landmarks.
- The "pilot": the low-level path planner and motor controller.
- The perception subsystem: the modules that accept the raw input from multiple sensors and integrate it into a coherent interpretation.

Let us consider the requirements.

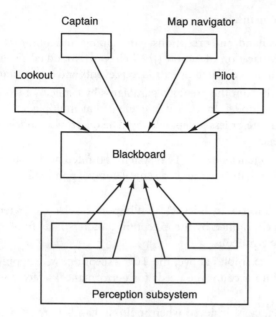

FIGURE 3.14 A Blackboard Solution for Mobile Robots

- **Req1:** The components (including the modules inside the perception subsystem) communicate via the shared repository of the blackboard system. Modules indicate their interest in certain types of information. The database returns them such data either immediately or when some other module inserts it into the database. For instance, the lookout may watch for certain geographic features; the database informs it when the perception subsystem stores images matching the description.

  One difficulty with the CODGER architecture is that control flow has to be coerced to fit the database mechanism, even under circumstances where direct interaction between components would be more natural.

- **Req2:** The blackboard is also the means for resolving conflicts or uncertainties in the robot's world view. For instance, the lookout's landmark detections provide a reality check for the distance estimation by dead-reckoning; both sets of data are stored in the database. The modules responsible for resolving the uncertainty register with the database to obtain the necessary data. (A good example of this activity is sensor fusion, performed by the perception subsystem to reconcile the input from its diverse sensors.)

- **Req3:** Communication via the database is similar to the communication via TCA's central message server. The exception mechanism, wiretapping, and monitoring—guarantors of reaction speed, safety, and reliability—can be implemented in COD-GER by defining separate modules that watch the database for the signs of unexpected occurrences or the beginnings of troublesome situations.

- **Req4:** As with TCA, the blackboard architecture supports concurrency and decouples senders from receivers, thus facilitating maintenance.

In summary, the blackboard architecture is capable of modeling the cooperation of tasks, both for coordination and resolving uncertainty in a flexible manner, thanks to an implicit invocation mechanism based on the contents of the database. These features are only slightly less powerful than TCA's equivalent capabilities.

3.3.6   COMPARISONS

In this section we have examined four architectures for mobile robotics to illustrate how architectural designs can be used to evaluate the satisfaction of a set of requirements. The four architectures differ substantially in their control regimes, their communications, and their specificity of components, which affects the degree to which they satisfy the requirements, as shown in Figure 3.15.

	Control Loop	Layers	Implicit invocation	Blackboard
Task Coordination	+ –	–	+ +	+
Dealing with uncertainty	–	+ –	+ –	+
Fault intolerance	+ –	+ –	+ +	+
Safety	+ –	+ –	+ +	+
Performance	+ –	+ –	+ +	+
Flexibility	+ –	–	+	+

FIGURE 3.15   Table of Comparisons

Naturally, these architectures are not the only possibilities; dozens of other architectures exist. Many of these are hybrids. For example, the The NASA/NBS Standard Reference Model for Telerobots (NASREM) [LFW90] is an architecture that combines control loops with layers, while Hayes-Roth's architecture combines layers with data flow [HRPL+95].

3.4   CRUISE CONTROL

In this section we illustrate how to apply the control-loop paradigm to a simple problem that has traditionally been cast in object-oriented terms. As we will show, the use of control-loop architectures can contribute significantly to clarifying the important architectural dimensions of the problem.

Booch and others have used the cruise-control problem to explore the differences between object-oriented and functional (traditional procedural) programming [AG93, Boo86,War84]. As described by Booch, this problem is:

A cruise-control system that exists to maintain the speed of a car, even over varying terrain. Figure 3.16 shows the block diagram of the hardware for such a system.

There are several inputs:

System on/off	If on, denotes that the cruise-control system should maintain the car speed.
Engine on/off	If on, denotes that the car engine is turned on; the cruise-control system is only active if the engine is on.
Pulses from wheel	A pulse is sent for every revolution of the wheel.
Accelerator	Indication of how far the accelerator has been pressed.
Brake	On when the brake is pressed; the cruise-control system temporarily reverts to manual control if the brake is pressed.
Increase/Decrease Speed	Increase or decrease the maintained speed; only applicable if the cruise-control system is on.
Resume Speed	Resume the last maintained speed; only applicable if the cruise-control system is on.
Clock	Timing pulse every millisecond.

There is one output from the system:

Throttle	Digital value for the engine throttle setting.

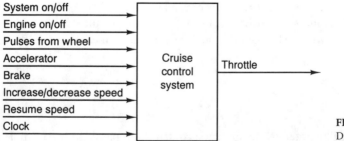

FIGURE 3.16 Booch Block Diagram for Cruise Control

The problem does not clearly state the rules for deriving the output from the set of inputs. Booch elaborates the description in the form of a dataflow diagram, but some questions remain unanswered. In the design below, missing details are supplied to match the apparent behavior of the cruise control on the authors' cars. Moreover, the inputs provide two kinds of information: whether the cruise control is active, and if so, what speed it should maintain.

The problem statement says the output is a value for the engine throttle setting. In classical process control, the corresponding signal would be a change in the throttle setting; this avoids calibration and wear problems with the sensors and engine. A more conventional cruise-control requirement would thus specify control of the current speed of the vehicle. However, current speed is not explicit in the problem statement, though it does appear implicitly as "maintained speed" in the descriptions of some of the inputs. If the requirement addresses current speed, throttle setting remains an appropriate output from the control algorithm. To avoid unnecessary changes in the problem we assume accurately calibrated digital control and achieve the effect of incremental signals by retaining the previous throttle value in the controller.

The problem statement also specifies a millisecond clock. In Booch's object-oriented solution, the clock is used only in combination with the wheel pulses to determine the current speed. Presumably the process that computes the speed will count the number of clock pulses between wheel pulses. The problem is overspecified in this respect: a slower clock or one that delivered current time on demand with sufficient precision would also work and would require less computing. Further, a single system clock is not required by the problem, though it might be convenient for other reasons.

These considerations lead to a restatement of the problem: *Whenever the system is active, determine the desired speed, and control the engine throttle setting to maintain that speed.*

3.4.1   Object View of Cruise Control

Booch organizes an object-oriented decomposition of the system around objects that exist in the task description. The elements of the decomposition correspond to important quantities and physical entities in the system, as shown in Figure 3.17, where the blobs represent objects, and the directed lines represent dependencies among objects. Although the target speed did not appear explicitly in the problem statement, it does appear in Figure 3.17 as "Desired Speed."

3.4.2   Process-Control View of Cruise Control

Section 2.8.1 suggests that a control-loop architecture is appropriate when the software is embedded in a physical system that involves continuing behavior, especially when the system is subject to external perturbations. These conditions hold in the case of cruise control: the system is supposed to maintain constant speed in an automobile despite variations in terrain, vehicle load, air resistance, fuel quality, and so on. To develop a control-loop architecture for this system, we begin by identifying the essential system elements as described in Section 2.8.1.

Computational elements

- **Process definition:** Since the cruise-control software is driving a mechanical device (the engine), the details are not relevant. For our purposes, the process receives a

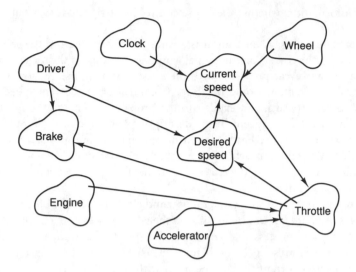

FIGURE 3.17   Booch's Object-Oriented Design for Cruise Control

throttle setting and turns the car's wheels. There may in fact be more computers involved, for example, in controlling the fuel-injection system. From the standpoint of the cruise-control subsystem, however, the process takes a throttle setting as input and controls the speed of the vehicle.

• **Control algorithm:** This algorithm models the current speed from the wheel pulses, compares it to the desired speed, and changes the throttle setting. The clock input is needed to determine current speed from the intervals between wheel pulses. Since the problem requires an exact throttle setting rather than a change, the current throttle setting must be maintained by the control algorithm. The policy decision about how much to change the throttle setting for a given discrepancy between current speed and desired speed is localized in the control algorithm.

Data elements

• **Controlled variable:** For the cruise control, this is the current speed of the vehicle.

• **Manipulated variable:** For the cruise control, this is the throttle setting.

• **Set point:** The desired speed is set and modified by the accelerator input and the increase/decrease speed input, respectively. Several other inputs determine whether the cruise control is currently controlling the car: system on/off, engine on/off, brake, and resume. These inputs interact: resume restores automatic control, but only if the entire system is on. These inputs are provided by the human driver (the operator, in process terms).

• **Sensor for controlled variable:** For cruise control, the current state is the current speed, which is modeled on data from a sensor that delivers wheel pulses, using the clock. (See the discussion below about the accuracy of this model.)

In the restated control task, note that only the current speed output, the wheel pulses input, and the throttle manipulated variable are used outside the set point and active/

inactive determination. This leads immediately to two subproblems: the interface with the driver, concerned with "Whenever the system is active determine the desired speed," and the control loop, concerned with "Control the engine throttle setting to maintain that speed."

The latter is the actual control problem; we'll examine it first. Figure 3.18 shows a suitable architecture for the control system. The first task is to model the current speed from the wheel pulses. The designer should validate this model carefully. The model could fail if the wheels spin, which could affect control in two ways. If the wheel pulses are being taken from a drive wheel and the wheel is spinning, the cruise control would keep the wheel spinning (at constant speed) even if the vehicle stops moving. Even worse, if the wheel pulses are being taken from a nondrive wheel and the drive wheels are spinning, the controller will act as if the current speed is too slow and continually increase the throttle setting. The designer should also consider whether the controller has full control authority over the process. In the case of cruise control, the only manipulated variable is the throttle; the brake is not available. As a result, if the automobile is coasting faster than the desired speed, the controller is powerless to slow it down.

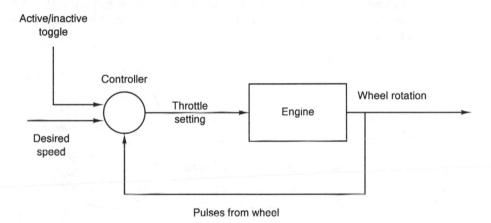

FIGURE 3.18   Control Architecture for Cruise Control

The controller also receives two inputs from the set-point computation: the active/inactive toggle, which indicates whether the controller is in charge of the throttle, and the desired speed, which only needs to be valid when the vehicle is under automatic control. All this information should be either state or continuously updated data, so all lines in the diagram represent dataflow. The controller is implemented as a continuously evaluating function that matches the dataflow character of the inputs and outputs. Several implementations are possible, including variations on simple on/off control, proportional control, and more sophisticated disciplines. Each of these has a parameter that controls how quickly and tightly the control tracks the set point; analysis of these characteristics is discussed in Section 3.4.3. As noted above, the engine is of little interest here; it might very well be implemented as an object or as a collection of objects.

The set-point calculation divides naturally into two parts: (1) determining whether or not the automatic system is active—in control of the throttle—and (2) determining the desired speed for use by the controller in automatic mode.

Some of the inputs in the original problem definition capture state (system on/off, engine on/off, accelerator, brake), and others capture events (wheel pulses, increase/ decrease speed, resume, clock). We will treat accelerator as state, specifically as a continuously updated value. However, determining whether the automatic cruise control is actively controlling the car is cleaner if everything it depends on is of the same kind. We will therefore use transitions between states for system on/off, engine on/off, and brake. For simplicity we assume brake application is atomic, so that other events are blocked when the brake is on. A more detailed analysis of the system states would relax this assumption [AG93].

The active/inactive toggle is triggered by a variety of events, so a state transition design, shown in Figure 3.19, is natural. The system is completely off whenever the engine is off. Otherwise there are three inactive states and one active state. In the first inactive state no set point has been established. In the other two, the previous set point must be remembered. When the driver accelerates to a speed greater than the set point, the manual accelerator controls the throttle through a direct linkage (note that this is the only use of the accelerator position in this design, and it relies on relative effect rather than absolute position); when the driver uses the brake, the control system is inactivated until the resume signal is sent. The active/inactive toggle input of the control system is set to active precisely when this state machine is in state Active.

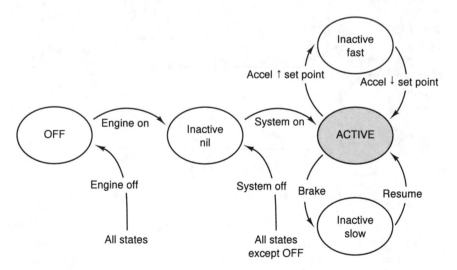

FIGURE 3.19   State Machine for Activation

Determining the desired speed is simpler, since it does not require state other than the current value of desired speed (the set point). Whenever the system is off, the set point is undefined. Whenever the system on signal is given (including when the system is already on), the set point is set to the current speed as modeled by wheel pulses. The driver also has a control that increases or decreases the set point by a set amount. This, too, can be invoked at any time (assume that arithmetic on undefined values yields undefined values). Figure 3.20 summarizes the events involved in determining the set point. Note that this process requires access to the clock in order to estimate the current speed from the pulses from the wheel.

Event	Effect on desired speed
Engine off, system off	Set to "undefined."
System on	Set to current speed as estimated from wheel pulses.
Increase speed	Increment desired speed by constant.
Decrease speed	Decrement desired speed by constant.

FIGURE 3.20   Event Table for Determining Set Point

We can now (Figure 3.21) combine the control architecture, the state machine for activation, and the event table for determining the set point into an entire system. Although the control unit and set point determination do not need to use the same clock, we have them do so to minimize changes to the original problem statement. Then, since current speed is used in two components, it would be reasonable for the next elaboration of the design to encapsulate that model in a reusable object; this would encapsulate the clock.

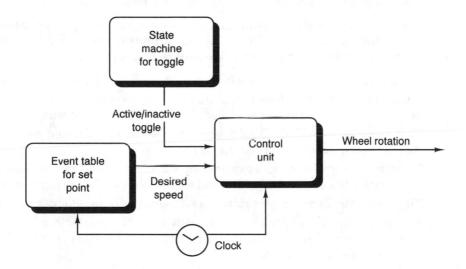

FIGURE 3.21   Complete Cruise Control System

All of the objects in Booch's design (Figure 3.17) have clear roles in the resulting system. It is entirely reasonable to anticipate a design strategy that uses the control-loop architecture for the system as a whole, and uses a number of other architectures, including objects and state machines, to elaborate the elements of the control-loop architecture. The shift from an object-oriented view to a control view of the cruise-control architecture raised a number of design questions that had previously been slighted. The separation of process from control concerns led to explicit choice of the control discipline. The limitations of the control model also became clear, including possible inaccuracies in the current speed model and incomplete control at high speed. The dataflow character of the model showed irregularities in the way the input was specified, for example, mixture of state and event inputs and the inappropriateness of absolute position of the accelerator.

We now compare the two approaches in more detail.

3.4.3 ANALYSIS AND DISCUSSION

CORRESPONDENCE BETWEEN ARCHITECTURE AND PROBLEM

The selection of an architecture commits the designer to a particular view of a problem. Like any abstraction, this view emphasizes some aspects of the problem and suppresses others. Booch [Boo86] characterizes the views inherent in object-oriented and functional architectures as follows:

> Simply stated, object-oriented development is an approach to software design in which the decomposition of a system is based upon the concept of an object. An object is an entity whose behavior is characterized by the actions that it suffers and that it requires of other objects. Object-oriented development is fundamentally different from traditional functional methods, for which the primary criteria for decomposition is that each module in the system represents a major step in the overall process.

The issue, of course, is deciding which abstractions are most useful for any particular problem. We have argued that the control view is particularly appropriate for a certain class of problems. In this case, the control view clarifies the design in several ways:

- The control view leads us to respecify the output as the actual speed of the vehicle.
- The separation of control from process makes the model of actual speed explicit and hence more likely to be validated; similarly it raises the question of control authority.
- The explicit element for the control algorithm also sets up a design decision about the kind of control to be exercised (see Section 3.4.3).
- By establishing special relations among components, the control paradigm discriminates among different kinds of inputs, and makes the feedback loop more obvious.
- The control paradigm clearly separates manual operation from automatic operation.
- Determination of the set point is easier to verify when it's separated from control; for example, Booch's design does not appear to reset the desired speed to undefined when the engine is turned off.

METHODOLOGICAL IMPLICATIONS

Object-oriented architectures are supported by associated methodologies. What can we say about methodologies for control-loop organizations and when they are useful? First, a methodology should help the designer decide when the architecture is appropriate. Second, a methodology should help the designer identify the elements of the design and their interactions. This corresponds to instructions for "finding the objects" in object-oriented methodologies. Third, a methodology should help the designer identify critical design decisions. In the case of control, these include potential safety problems.

Åström and Wittenmark give a collection of examples of common solutions for process control problems [AW90]. Each identifies a typical control situation and gives advice for suitable strategies. They provide a top-down methodology that also serves as the control paradigm for software:

- Choose the control principle.
- Choose the control variables.
- Choose the measured variables.
- Create subsystems.

A methodology should also provide for system modifications. Booch proposes two for the object-oriented design; both would be simple changes in the control-loop design:

- Add a digital speedometer: The wheel pulses are directly available as a control signal that can be picked up by any other component and used independently of the control paradigm. In addition, Section 3.4.1 suggested the creation of an object for current speed.
- Use separate microcomputers for current/desired speed and throttle: The most likely assignment of function to multiple processors would put the control on one and engine-related operations on another. This corresponds directly to the design.

PERFORMANCE: SYSTEM RESPONSE TO CONTROL

Process control provides powerful tools for selecting and analyzing the response characteristics of systems. For example, the cruise controller can set the throttle in several ways [P+84]:

- **On/Off Control:** The simplest and most common mode of control simply turns the process off and on. This is more appropriate for thermostats than throttles, but it could be considered. In order to prevent the power from fluttering rapidly on and off, on/off control usually provides some form of hysteresis (actual speed must deviate from the set point by some amount before control is exercised, or power setting can't be switched more often than a preset limit).
- **Proportional Control:** The output of a proportional controller is a fixed multiple of the measured error. The gain of a cruise controller is the amount by which the speed deviation is multiplied to determine the change in throttle setting. This is a parameter of control. Depending on the properties of the engine, this can lead to a steady-state value not quite equal to the set point or to oscillation of the speed about the set point.
- **Proportional plus Reset Control:** The controller has two parts; the first is proportional to the error, and the second causes the controller output to change as long as an error is present. This has the effect of forcing the error to zero. Adding a further correction based on the derivative of the error speeds up the response but is probably overkill for the cruise-control application.

For each of these alternatives, mathematical models of the system responses are well understood.

CORRECTNESS

When software controls a physical system, correctness and safety are critically important. We have seen how the control paradigm's methodology leads the designer to consider the accuracy of design assumptions that have significant safety implications. For cruise control, the possibility of runaway feedback is a significant safety concern.

3.4.4   SUMMARY

Much of the power of a design methodology arises from how well it focuses attention on significant decisions at appropriate times. Methodologies generally do this by decomposing the problem in such a way that development of the software structure proceeds hand in hand with the analysis for significant decisions. This localizes decisions and limits the ripples caused by changes. Our exploration of cruise control has shown that the significant high-level decisions are better elicited by a methodology based on process control than on the more common object-oriented methodology. In particular, the control paradigm separates the operation of the main process from compensation for external disturbances. This separation of concerns yields appropriate abstractions and reveals design issues that might otherwise be neglected.

Cruise control exemplifies a class of design problems in which a real-time process is controlled by embedded software. Conceptually, such processes update the control status continuously. Thinking about these designs explicitly as process-control problems leads the designer to a software organization that separates process concerns from control concerns and requires explicit attention to the appropriateness and correctness of the control strategy. This leads to early consideration of performance and correctness questions that might not otherwise arise.

3.5   THREE VIGNETTES IN MIXED STYLE

3.5.1   A LAYERED DESIGN WITH DIFFERENT STYLES FOR THE LAYERS

The PROVOX™ system by Fisher Controls offers distributed process control for chemical production processes [Fis89]. The process-control capabilities of the system range from simple control loops that control pressure, flow, or levels to complex strategies involving interrelated control loops. Provisions are made for integration with plant management and information systems in support of computer-integrated manufacturing. The system architecture integrates process control with plant management and information systems in a five-level layered hierarchy, shown in Figure 3.22. The right side of the figure shows the software view, and the left side shows the hardware view. Each level corresponds to a different process-management function with its own decision-support requirements.

- **Level 1:** Process measurement and control—direct adjustment of final control elements.
- **Level 2:** Process supervision—operations console for monitoring and controlling Level 1.

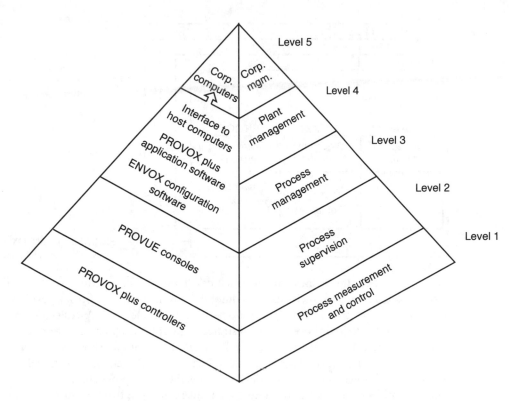

FIGURE 3.22   PROVOX—Hierarchical Top Level

- **Level 3:** Process management—computer-based plant automation, including management reports, optimization strategies, and guidance to the operations console.
- **Levels 4 and 5:** Plant and corporate management—higher-level functions such as cost accounting, inventory control, and order processing/scheduling.

Different computation and response times are required at different levels of this hierarchy. (This is similar to the concerns addressed by the layered architecture for mobile robotics discussed in Section 3.3.3.) Accordingly, different computational models are used. Levels 1 to 3 are object-oriented; Levels 4 and 5 are largely based on conventional data-processing repository models. In this section we examine only the object-oriented model of Level 2 and the repositories of Levels 4 and 5.

For the control and monitoring functions of Level 2, PROVOX uses a set of *points*, or loci of process control. Figure 3.23 shows the canonical form of a point definition; seven specialized forms support the most common kinds of control. Points are, in essence, object-oriented design elements that encapsulate information about control points of the process. The points are individually configured to achieve the desired control strategy. Data associated with a point includes the following: operating parameters, including current process value, setpoint (target value), valve output, and mode (automatic or manual); tuning parameters, such as gain, reset, derivative, and alarm trip-points; and configuration parameters, including tag (name) and I/O channels.

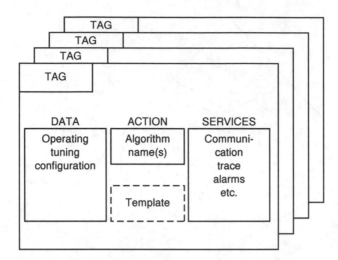

FIGURE 3.23 PROVOX—
Object-Oriented Elaboration

In addition, the point's data can include a template for a control strategy. Like any good object, a point also includes procedural definitions such as control algorithms, communication connections, reporting services, and trace facilities. A collection of points implements the desired process-control strategy through the communication services and through the actual dynamics of the process (e.g., if one point increases flow into a tank, the current value of a point that senses tank level will reflect this change). Although the communication through process state deviates from the usual procedural or message-based control of objects, points are conceptually very like objects in their encapsulation of essential state and action information.

Reports from points appear as input transactions to data-collection and analysis processes at higher design levels. The organization of the points into control processes can be defined by the designer to match the process-control strategy. These processes can be further aggregated into Plant Process Areas (points related to a set of equipment, such as a cooling tower) and thence into Plant Management Areas (segments of a plant that would be controlled by single operators).

PROVOX makes provisions for integration with plant management and business systems at Levels 4 and 5. Selection of those systems is often independent of process control design; PROVOX does not itself provide MIS systems directly but does provide for integrating a conventional host computer with conventional database management. The data-collection facilities of Level 3, the reporting facilities of Level 2, and the network that supports distributed implementation suffice to provide process information as transactions to these databases. Such databases are commonly designed as repositories, with transaction-processing functions supporting a central data store—quite a different style from the object-oriented design of Level 2.

The use of hierarchical layers at the top design level of a system is fairly common. This permits strong separation of different classes of functions and clean interfaces between the layers. However, within each layer the interactions among components are often too intricate to permit strict layering.

3.5.2   AN INTERPRETER USING DIFFERENT IDIOMS FOR THE COMPONENTS

Rule-based systems provide a means of codifying the problem-solving skills of human experts. These experts tend to capture problem-solving techniques as sets of situation-action rules whose execution or activation is sequenced in response to the conditions of the computation rather than by a predetermined scheme. Because these rules are not directly executable by available computers, systems for interpreting such rules must be provided. Hayes-Roth has surveyed the architecture and operation of rule-based systems [HR85].

The basic features of a rule-based system, shown in Hayes-Roth's rendering as Figure 3.24, are essentially the features of a table-driven interpreter, as outlined earlier.

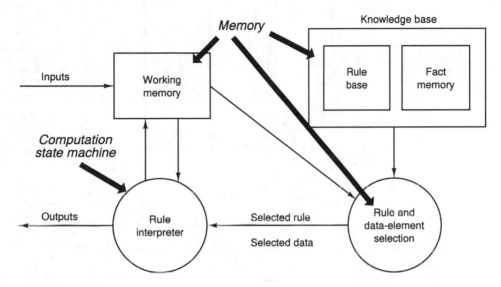

FIGURE 3.24   Basic Rule-Based System

- The *pseudocode* to be executed, in this case the knowledge base
- The *interpretation engine*, in this case the rule interpreter, the heart of the inference engine
- The *control state of the interpretation engine*, in this case the rule and data-element selector
- The *current state of the program* running on the virtual machine, in this case the working memory

Rule-based systems make heavy use of pattern matching and context (currently relevant rules). Adding special mechanisms for these facilities to the design yields the more complicated view shown in Figure 3.25. With this added complexity, the original simple interpreter vanishes in a sea of new interactions and dataflows. Although the interfaces among the original modules remain, they are not distinguished from the newly added interfaces.

However, we can rediscover the interpreter model by identifying the components of Figure 3.25 with their design antecedents in Figure 3.24, as in Figure 3.26. Viewed in this

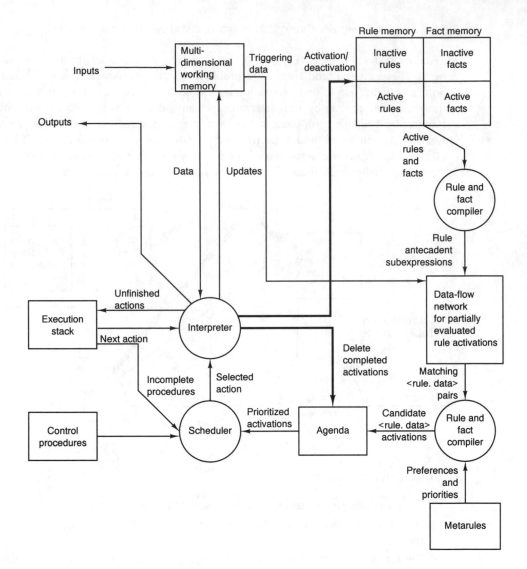

FIGURE 3.25   Sophisticated Rule-Based System

way, the elaboration of the design becomes much easier to explain and understand. For example, we can see the following:

- The knowledge base remains a relatively simple memory structure, merely gaining substructure to distinguish active from inactive contents.
- The rule interpreter is expanded with the interpreter idiom (that is, the interpretation engine of the rule-based system is itself implemented as a table-driven interpreter), with control procedures playing the role of the pseudocode to be executed and the execution stack the role of the current program state.

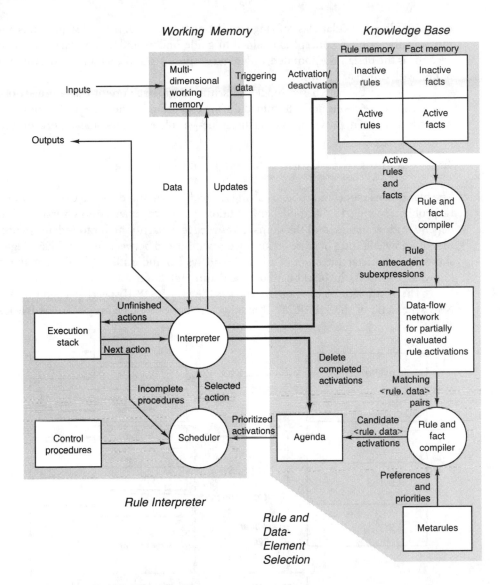

FIGURE 3.26   Simplified Rule-Based System

- "Rule and data-element selection" is implemented primarily as a pipeline that progressively transforms active rules and facts to prioritized activations; in this pipeline the third filter ("nominators") also uses a fixed database of metarules.
- Working memory is not further elaborated.

The interfaces among the rediscovered components are unchanged from the simple model except for the two bold lines over which the interpreter controls activations.

This example illustrates two points. First, in a sophisticated rule-based system the elements of the simple rule-based system are elaborated in response to execution characteristics of the particular class of languages being interpreted. If the design is presented in this way, the original concept is retained to guide understanding and later maintenance. Second, as the design is elaborated, different components of the simple model can be elaborated with different idioms.

Note that the rule-based model is itself a design structure: it calls for a set of rules whose control relations are determined during execution by the state of the computation. A rule-based system provides a virtual machine—a rule executor—to support this model.

3.5.3   A BLACKBOARD GLOBALLY RECAST AS AN INTERPRETER

The blackboard model of problem solving is a highly structured special case of opportunistic problem solving. In this model, the solution space is organized into several application-dependent hierarchies, and the domain knowledge is partitioned into independent modules of knowledge that operate on knowledge within and between levels [Nii86]. Figure 2.5 showed the basic architecture of a blackboard system and outlined its three major parts: knowledge sources, the blackboard data structure, and control.

The first major blackboard system was the HEARSAY-II speech-recognition system. Nii's schematic of the HEARSAY-II architecture appears in Figure 3.27. The blackboard

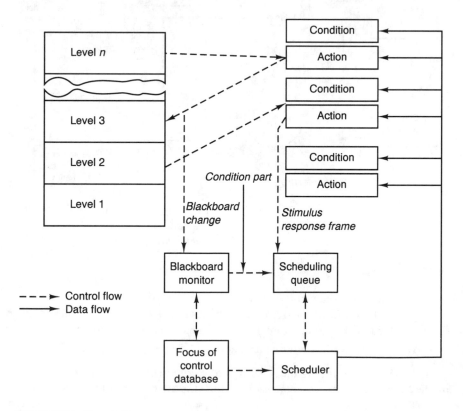

FIGURE 3.27   Hearsay-II

structure is a six- to eight-level hierarchy in which each level abstracts information on its adjacent lower level, and blackboard elements represent hypotheses about the interpretation of an utterance. Knowledge sources correspond to such tasks as segmenting the raw signal, identifying phonemes, generating word candidates, hypothesizing syntactic segments, and proposing semantic interpretations. Each knowledge source is organized as a condition part that specifies when it is applicable and an action part that processes relevant blackboard elements and generates new ones. The control component is realized as a blackboard monitor and a scheduler; the scheduler monitors the blackboard and calculates priorities for applying the knowledge sources to various elements on the blackboard.

HEARSAY-II was implemented between 1971 and 1976 on DEC PDP-10s. These machines were not directly capable of condition-triggered control, so it should not be surprising to find that an implementation provides the mechanisms of a virtual machine that realizes the implicit invocation semantics required by the blackboard model.

Figure 3.27 elaborates the individual components of Figure 2.5 and also adds components for the previously implicit control component. In the process, the figure becomes rather complex, because it is now illustrating two concepts: the blackboard model and realization of that model by a virtual machine. The blackboard model can be recovered as in Figure 3.28 by suppressing the control mechanism and regrouping the conditions and

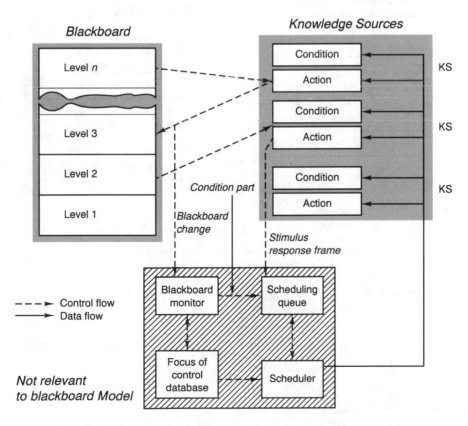

FIGURE 3.28   Blackboard View of Hearsay-II

actions into knowledge sources. The virtual machine can be seen to be realized by an interpreter by using the assignment of function in Figure 3.29. Here the blackboard corresponds cleanly to the current state of the recognition task. The collection of knowledge sources roughly supplies the pseudocode of the interpreter; however, the actions also contribute to the interpretation engine. The interpretation engine includes several components that appear explicitly in Figure 3.27: the blackboard monitor, the focus-of-control database, and the scheduler, as well as the actions of the knowledge sources. The scheduling queue corresponds roughly to the control state. To the extent that execution of conditions determines priorities, the conditions contribute to rule selection as well as forming pseudocode.

Here we see a system initially designed with one model (blackboard, a special form of repository), and then realized through a different model (interpreter). The realization does not involve a component-by-component expansion as in the previous two examples; the view as an interpreter involves a different aggregation of components than the view as blackboard.

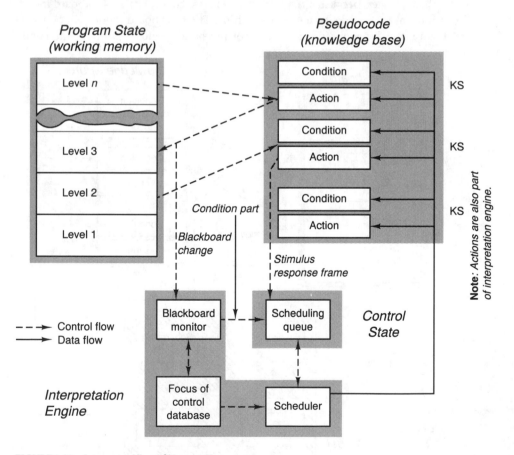

FIGURE 3.29   Interpreter View of Hearsay-II

4

SHARED INFORMATION SYSTEMS

As THE REQUIREMENTS for a class of systems evolve, so do the architectures that are needed to satisfy those requirements. In this chapter we examine the interplay between evolution and architecture in the context of shared information systems. By considering how the architectures of three kinds of shared information systems have evolved in response to changing technology and user expectations, we discover a common pattern of architectural evolution over the broader domain.

4.1 SHARED INFORMATION SYSTEMS

One particularly significant class of system is responsible for collecting, manipulating, and preserving large bodies of complex information. These are *shared information systems*. Systems of this kind appear in many different domains; this chapter examines three.

- *Data processing*, driven primarily by the need to build business decision systems from conventional databases.
- *Software development environments*, driven primarily by the need to represent and manipulate programs and their designs.
- *Building design*, driven primarily by the need to couple independent design tools to allow for the interactions of their results in structural design.

The earliest shared information systems consisted of separate programs for separate subtasks. Later, multiple independent processing steps were composed into larger tasks by passing data in a known, fixed format from one step to another. This organization is not flexible in responding to variations or discrepancies in data. Nor is it tolerant of structural modification, especially the addition of components developed under different assumptions. It is also not responsive to the needs of interactive processing, which must handle individual requests as they arrive.

Still later, often as requirements for interaction appeared, new organizations allowed independent processing subsystems to interact through a shared data store. While this organization is an improvement, it still encounters integration problems—especially when multiple data stores with different representations must be shared, when the system is distributed, when many user tasks must be served, and when the suite of processing and data subsystems changes regularly. Several newer approaches now compensate for these differences in representation and operating assumptions, but the problem is not completely solved. A common pattern, the *shared information system evolution pattern*, is evident in the application areas examined here.

4.2   DATABASE INTEGRATION

Business data processing has traditionally been dominated by database management, in particular by database updates. Originally, separate databases served separate purposes, and implementation issues revolved around efficient ways to do massive, coordinated, periodic updates. As time passed, interactive demands required individual transactions to complete in real time. Still later, as databases proliferated and organizations merged, information proved to have value far beyond its original needs. Diversity in representations and interfaces arose, information began to appear redundantly in multiple databases, and geographic distribution added communication complexity. As this happened, the challenges shifted from individual transaction processing to integration.

Individual database systems must support transactions of predetermined types and also periodic summary reports. Bad requests require a great deal of special handling. Originally the updates and summary reports were collected into batches, with database updates and reports produced during periodic batch runs. However, when interactive queries became technologically possible, the demand for interaction generated demand for on-line processing of both individual requests and exceptions. Reports remained on roughly the same cycles as before, so reporting became decoupled from transaction processing.

As databases became more common, information about a business became distributed among multiple databases, which made it even easier for the data to become inconsistent and incomplete. In addition, the representations, or schemas, for different databases were usually different; even the portion of the data shared by two databases was likely to have different representations in each database. The total volume of data to handle was correspondingly larger, and it was often distributed across multiple machines. Two general strategies emerged for dealing with data diversity: unified schemas and multidatabases.

4.2.1   BATCH SEQUENTIAL

Some of the earliest large computer applications were databases. In these applications individual database operations—transactions—were collected into large batches. The application consisted of a small number of large stand-alone programs that performed sequential updates on flat (unstructured) files. A typical organization included the following:

- A massive *edit program*, which accepted transaction inputs and performed whatever validation was possible without access to the database
- A massive *transaction sort*, which got the transactions into the same order as the records on the sequential master file
- A sequence of *update programs*, one for each master file; these huge programs actually executed the transactions by moving sequentially through the master file, matching each type of transaction to its corresponding account and updating the account records
- A *print program* that produced periodic reports

The steps were independent of each other; they had to run in a fixed sequence, and each ran to completion, producing an output file in a new format, before the next step began. This is a *batch sequential* architecture. The organization of a typical batch sequential update system appears in Figure 4.1 [Bes90, p. 29]. This figure also shows the possibility of on-line queries (but not modifications). In this structure the files to support the queries are reloaded periodically, so recent transactions (e.g., within the past few days) are not reflected in the query responses.

Figure 4.1 is a Yourdon dataflow diagram. Processes are depicted as circles, or "bubbles"; dataflow (here, large files) is depicted with arrows, and data stores such as computer files are depicted with parallel lines. This notation is conventional in this application area for showing the relations among processes and dataflow. Within a bubble, however, the approach changes. Figure 4.2 [Bes90, p. 150] shows the internal structure of an update process. There is one of these for each of the master data files, and each is responsible for handling all possible updates to that data file.

In Figure 4.2, the boxes represent subprograms, and the lines represent procedure calls. A single driver program processes all batch transactions. Each transaction has a standard set of subprograms that check the transaction request, access the required data, validate the transaction, and post the result. Thus all the program logic for each transaction is localized in a single set of subprograms. The figure indicates that the transaction-processing template is replicated, so that each transaction has its own set. Note the difference even in graphical notation as the design focus shifts from the architecture to the code level.

The essential—batch sequential—parts of Figure 4.1 are redrawn in Figure 4.3 in a form that allows comparison to other architectures. The redrawn figure emphasizes the sequence of operations to be performed and the completion of each step before the start of its successor. It suppresses the on-line query support and updates to multiple master files, or databases.

4.2.2   SIMPLE REPOSITORY

Two trends forced a movement away from batch sequential processing. First, interactive technology provided the opportunity and demand for continuous processing of on-line updates as well as on-line queries. On-line queries of stale data are not very satisfactory; interaction requires incremental updates of the database, at least for on-line transactions (there is less urgency about transactions that arrive by slow means such as mail, since they

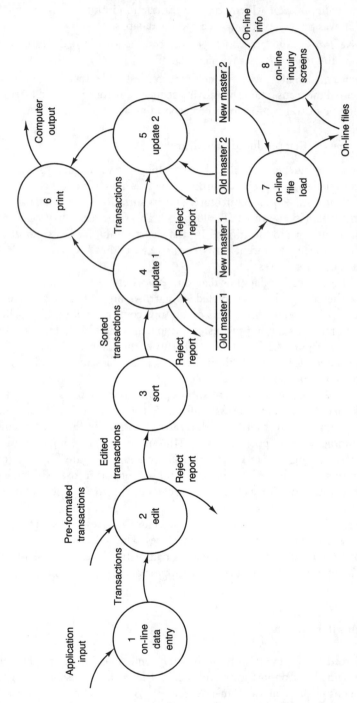

FIGURE 4.1 Dataflow Diagram for Batch Databases (Reprinted by permission of John Wiley and Sons from Laurence J. Best's *Application Architecture* ©1990 John Wiley and Sons.)

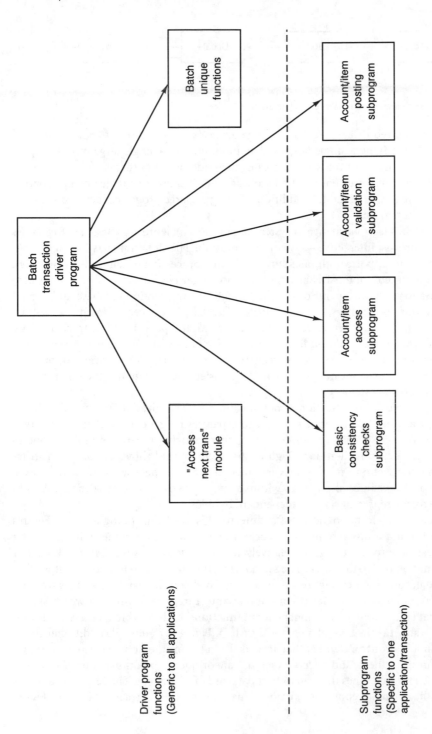

Note: The driver calls a different set of subprograms for each transaction type.

FIGURE 4.2   Internal Structure of Batch Update Process (Reprinted by permission of John Wiley and Sons from Laurence J. Best's *Application Architecture* ©1990 John Wiley and Sons.)

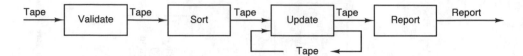

FIGURE 4.3   Batch Sequential Database Architecture

have already incurred delays). Second, as organizations grew, the set of transactions and queries grew. Modifying a single large update program and a single large reporting program for each change to a transaction creates methodological bottlenecks. New types of processing were added often enough to discourage modification of a large update program for each new processing request. In addition, starting up large programs incurred substantial overheads at that time.

These trends led to a change in system organization. Figure 4.4 [Bes90, p. 81] shows a "modern"—that is, interactive—system organization. The notation is as for Figure 4.1. This organization supports both interactive and batch processing for all transaction types; updates can occur continuously. Since these are no longer periodic operations, the system also provides for periodic operations. Here, though, the transaction database and extract database are transient buffers; the account/item database is the central permanent store. The transaction database serves to synchronize multiple updates. The extract database solves a problem created by the addition of interactive processing—namely the loss of synchronization between the updating and reporting cycles. This figure obscures not only the difference between a significant database and a transient buffer but also the separation of transactions into separate processes.

It is possible for transaction processing in this organization to resemble batch sequential processing. However, it is useful to separate the general overhead operations from the transaction-specific operations. It may also be useful to perform multiple operations on a single account all at once. Figure 4.5 [Bes90, p. 158] shows the program structure for the transactions in this new architecture. Since the transactions now exist individually rather than as alternatives within a single program, several of the bubbles in Figure 4.4 actually represent sets of independent bubbles.

There is not a clean separation of architectural issues from coding issues in Figures 4.4 and 4.5. It is not unusual to find this, because explicit attention to the architecture as a separate level of software design is relatively recent. Indeed, Figures 4.4 and 4.5 suffer from information overload as well. The system structure is easier to understand if we first isolate the database updates. Figure 4.6 focuses narrowly on the database and its transactions. This is an instance of a fairly common architecture, a repository, in which shared persistent data is manipulated by independent functions, each of which has essentially no permanent state. It is the core of a database system. Figure 4.7 adds two additional structures. The first is a control element that accepts the batch or interactive stream of transactions, synchronizes them, and selects which update or query operations to invoke, and in which order. This subsumes the transaction database of Figure 4.4. The second is a buffer that serves the periodic reporting function. This subsumes the extract database of Figure 4.4.

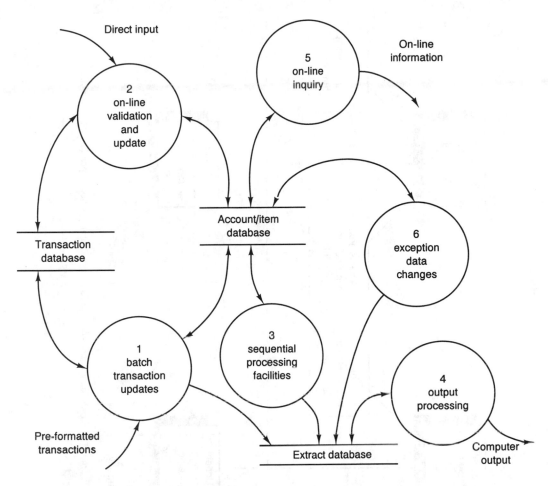

FIGURE 4.4   Dataflow Diagram for Interactive Database (Reprinted by permission of John Wiley and Sons from Laurence J. Best's *Application Architecture* ©1990 John Wiley and Sons.)

4.2.3   VIRTUAL REPOSITORY

As organizations grew, databases came to serve multiple functions. Since this was usually a result of incremental growth, individual, independent programs continued to be the locus of processing. In response, simple repositories gave way to databases that supported multiple views through schemas. Corporate reorganizations, mergers, and other consolidations of data forced the joint use of multiple databases. As a result, information could no longer be localized in a single database. Figure 4.8 [KS91, p. 13] hints at the extent of the problem through schemas that describe books in four libraries. Note, for example, that the call number is represented in different ways in all four schemas; in this case they're all Library of Congress numbers, so the more difficult case of a mixture of Library of Congress and Dewey numbering doesn't arise. Note also the variety of ways in which the publisher's name, address, and (perhaps) telephone number are represented.

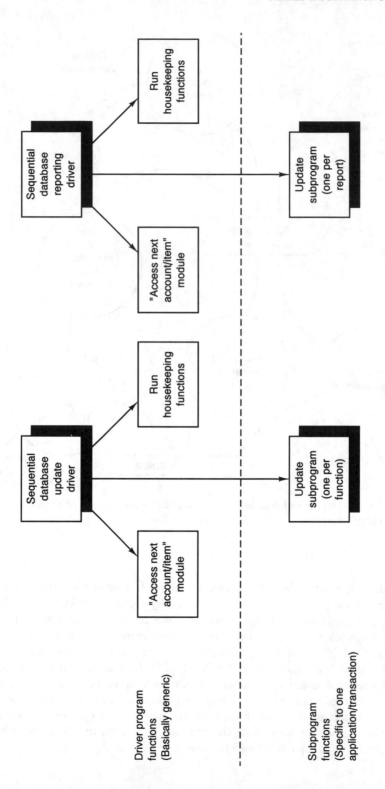

Note: One driver program for each file processed sequentially.

FIGURE 4.5 Internal Structure of Interactive Update Process (Reprinted by permission of John Wiley and Sons from Laurence J. Best's *Application Architecture* © 1990 John Wiley and Sons.)

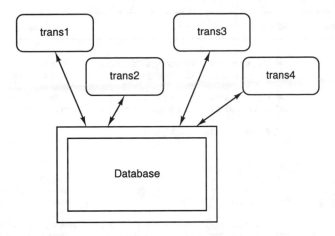

FIGURE 4.6   Simple Repository Database Architecture

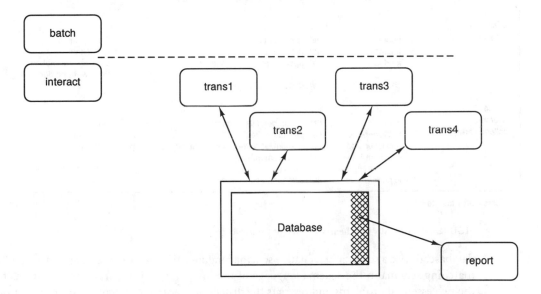

FIGURE 4.7   Repository Architecture for Database, Showing Control and Reporting

Developing applications that rely on multiple, diverse databases like these requires the solution of two problems. First, the system must reconcile representation differences. Second, it must communicate results across distributed systems that may have not only different data representations but also different database schema representations. One approach to the unification of multiple schemas is called the *federated approach*. Figure 4.9 [A+91, p. 21] shows one version of this, relying on the well-understood technology for handling multiple views on databases. The top of this figure shows how the usual database mechanisms integrate multiple schemas into a single schema. The bottom of the figure suggests an approach to importing data from autonomous external databases: For each

Library	Table name	Attributes	General description
CDB1: Main (Main library)	item	(i#*, title, author-name, subject, type, language)	Library items
	lc-num	(i#*, c-letter, f-digit, s-digit, cuttering)	Library of Congress number
			Publishers
	publisher	(i#*, name, tel, street, city, zip, state, country)	Lending information
	lend-info	(i#*, lend-period, library-use-only. checked-out)	Borrower and due date
	checkout-info	(i#*, dl-num, hour, day, month, year)	
CDB1: Engineering (Engineering library)	items	(i#*, title, a-name, type, c-letter, f-digit, s-digit, cuttering)	Library items
	item-subject	(i#*, subject)	Subject of each item
	item language	(i#*, language)	Language used in each item
			Publishers
	publisher	(i#*, p-name, str-num, str-name, city, zip, state)	Lending information
	lend info	(i#*, lend-period, library-use-only, checked out)	Borrower and due date
	checkout-info	(i#*, dl-num, hour, day, month, year)	
CDB3: City (City public library)	books	(i#*, lc-num, name, title, subject)	Library items
	publisher	(i#*, p-name, p-address)	Publishers
	lend-info	(i#*, l-period, reference, checked out)	Lending information
			Borrower and due date
	checkout-info	(i#*, dl-num, day, month, year)	
CDB4: Comm (Community college library)	item	(i#*, lc-number, title, a-name)	Library items
	publisher-info	(i#*, p#*, name, tel)	Publishers
	publisher-add	(p#*, st-num, st-name, room-num, city, state, zip)	Publisher address
	checkout-info	(i#*, id, day, month, year)	Borrower and due date
			Library card number
	lc-num	(i#*, category, user-name)	

*Indicates key attribute

FIGURE 4.8   Diversity of Schemas for a Single Construct

database, devise a schema in its native schema language that exports the desired data, and a matching schema in the schema language of the importer. This separates the solutions to the two essential problems and restricts the distributed system problem to communication between matching schemas.

Figure 4.9 combines solutions to two problems. Here again, the design is clearer if the discussion and diagram separate the two sets of concerns. Figure 4.10 shows the integration of multiple databases by unified schemas. It shows a simple composition of projections. The details about whether the data paths are local or distributed and whether the local schema and import schema are distinct are suppressed at this level of abstraction; these communication questions should be addressed in an expansion of the abstract filter design (and they may not need to be the same for all of the constituents).

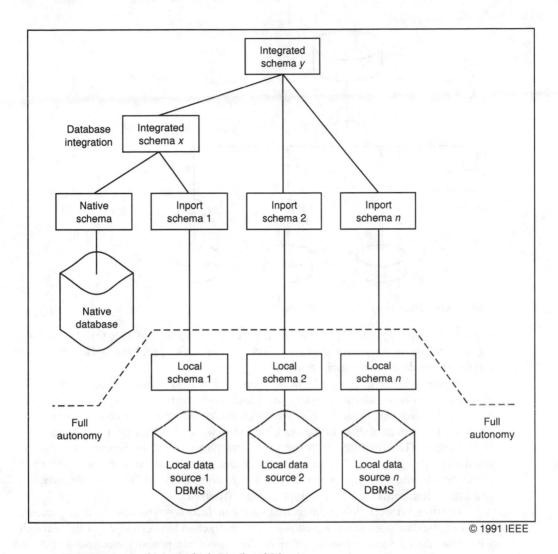

FIGURE 4.9   Combining Multiple Distributed Schemas

4.2.4   HIERARCHICAL LAYERS

Unified schemas allow for the merger of information, but their mappings are fixed, passive, and static. The designers of the views must anticipate all future needs; the mappings simply transform the underlying data, and there are essentially no provisions for recognizing and adapting to changes in the set of available databases. In the real world, each database serves multiple users, and indeed the set of users changes regularly. The set of available databases also changes, both because the population of databases itself changes and because network connectivity changes the set that is accessible. This exacerbates the usual problems of inconsistency across a set of databases. The commercial database community has begun to respond to this problem of dynamic reconfiguration. Distributed database

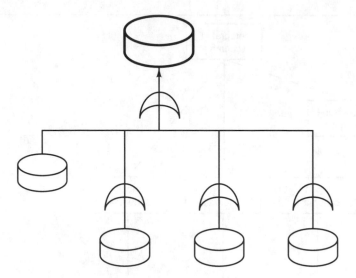

FIGURE 4.10   Integration of Multiple Databases

products organized on a client-server model are beginning to challenge traditional main-frame database management systems [Hov92]. This set of problems is also of current interest in the database research community.

Figure 4.11 [Wie92, p. 45] depicts one research scenario for active mediation between a constantly changing set of users and a constantly changing set of databases. Wiederhold proposes introducing active programs, called *experts*, to accept queries from users, recast them as queries to the available databases, and deliver appropriate responses to the users. These experts, or active mediators ("mediators" in Figure 4.11), localize knowledge about how to discover what databases are available and interact with them, about how to recast user queries in useful forms, and about how to reconcile, integrate, and interpret information from multiple, diverse databases.

In effect, Wiederhold's architecture uses *hierarchical layers* to separate the business of the users, the databases, and the mediators. The interaction between layers of the hierarchy will most likely be a *client-server* relation. This is not a repository, because there is no enforced coherence of central shared data; it is not a batch sequential system (or any other form of pipeline), because the interaction with the data is incremental. Figure 4.12 recasts this in a form similar to the other examples.

4.2.5   EVOLUTION OF SHARED INFORMATION SYSTEMS IN BUSINESS DATA PROCESSING

These business data processing applications exhibit the following pattern of development driven by changing technology and changing needs.

- *Batch processing:* Stand-alone programs; results are passed from one to another on magtape. *Batch sequential model.*

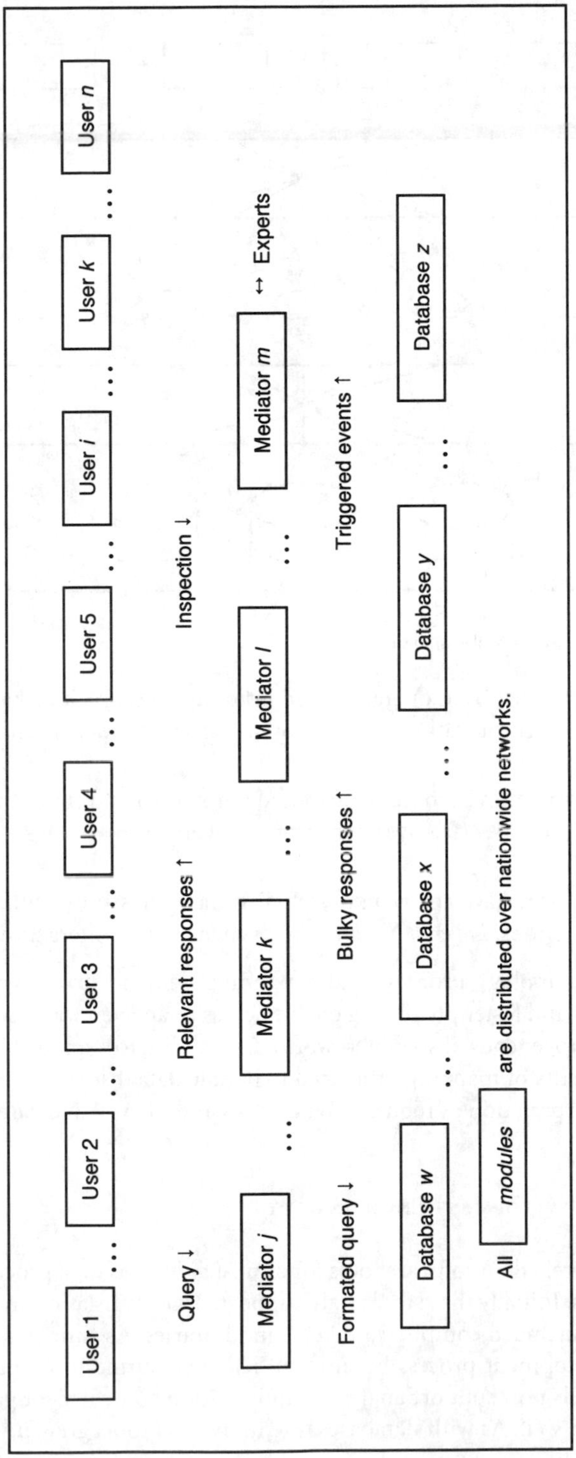

© 1992 IEEE

FIGURE 4.11 Multidatabase with Mediators

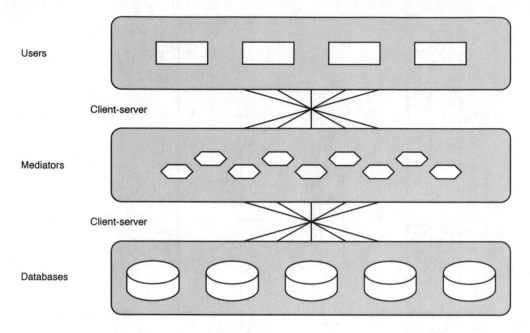

FIGURE 4.12   Layered Architecture for Multidatabase

- *Interactive processing:* Concurrent operation and faster updates preclude batching, so updates are out of synchronization with reports. *Repository model* with external control.
- *Unified schemas:* Information becomes distributed among many different databases. One *virtual repository* defines (passive) consistent conversion mappings to multiple databases.
- *Multidatabase:* Databases have many users; passive mappings don't suffice; active agents mediate interactions. *Layered hierarchy* with client-server interaction.

In this evolution, technology progress and expanding demand drive evolutionary progress. Larger memories and faster processing enable access to an ever-wider assortment of data resources in a heterogeneous, distributed world. Our ability to exploit this remains limited by volume, complexity of mappings, the need to handle data discrepancies, and the need for sophisticated interpretation of requests for services and of available data.

4.3   INTEGRATION IN SOFTWARE DEVELOPMENT ENVIRONMENTS

Software development has relied on software tools for almost as long as data processing has relied on on-line databases. Initially these tools only supported the translation from source code to object code; they included compilers, linkers, and libraries. As time passed, many steps in the software development process became sufficiently routine to be partially or wholly automated, and tools now support analysis, configuration control, debugging, testing, and documentation as well. As with databases, the individual tools grew up independently. Although the integration problem has been recognized for nearly two decades [Tor74], individual tools still work well together only in isolated cases.

4.3.1 BATCH SEQUENTIAL

The earliest software development tools were stand-alone programs. Often their output appeared only on paper—perhaps in the form of object code on cards or paper tape. Eventually most of the tools produced results that were at least in some magnetic (universally readable) form, but the output of each tool was likely to be in the wrong format, the wrong units, or the wrong conceptual model for other tools to use. Even today, execution profiles are customarily provided in human-readable form but not propagated back to the compiler for optimization. Effective sharing of information was thus limited by lack of knowledge about how information was encoded in representations. As a result, manual translation of one tool's output to another tool's input format was common.

As time passed, new tools incorporated prior knowledge of related tools, and the usefulness of shared information became more evident. Scripts were developed to invoke tools in fixed orders. These scripts essentially defined batch sequential architectures, which still represent the most common style of integration for most environments. For example, in Unix both shell scripts and *make* follow this paradigm. ASCII text is the universal exchange representation, but the conventions for encoding internal structure in ASCII remain idiosyncratic.

4.3.2 TRANSITION FROM BATCH SEQUENTIAL TO REPOSITORY

Our view of the architecture of a system can change in response to improvements in technology. The way we think about compilers illustrates this. In the 1970s, compilation was regarded as a sequential process, and the organization of a compiler was typically drawn as shown in Figure 4.13. Text enters at the left end and is transformed in a variety of ways—to lexical token stream, parse tree, intermediate code—before emerging as machine code on the right. We often refer to this compilation model as a pipeline, even though it was (at least originally) closer to a batch sequential architecture in which each transformation (pass) ran to completion before the next one started.

FIGURE 4.13 Traditional Compiler Model

In fact, even the batch sequential version of this model was not completely accurate. Most compilers created a separate symbol table during lexical analysis and used or updated it during subsequent passes. It was not part of the data that flowed from one pass to another; it existed outside all the passes, so the system structure was more properly drawn as in Figure 4.14.

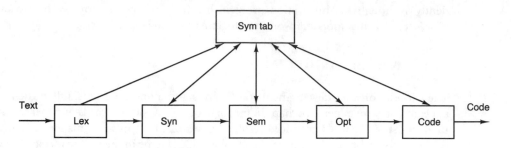

FIGURE 4.14   Traditional Compiler Model with Symbol Table

As time passed, compiler technology grew more sophisticated. The algorithms and representations of compilation grew more complex, and increasing attention turned to the intermediate representation of the program during compilation. Improved theoretical understanding, such as attribute grammars, accelerated this trend. The consequence was that by the mid-1980s the intermediate representation (for example, an attributed parse tree), was the center of attention. It was created early during compilation, manipulated during the remainder, and discarded at the end. The data structure might change in detail, but it remained substantially one growing structure throughout. However, we continued (sometimes to the present) to model the compiler with sequential dataflow, as in Figure 4.15.

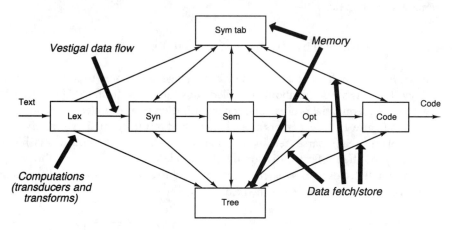

FIGURE 4.15   Modern Canonical Compiler

In fact, a more appropriate view of this structure would redirect attention from the sequence of passes to the central shared representation. When you declare that the tree is the locus of compilation information, and the passes define operations on the tree, it becomes natural to redraw the architecture as in Figure 4.16. Now the connections between passes denote control flow, which is a more accurate depiction; the rather stronger connections between the passes and the tree/symbol table structure denote data access and manipulation. In this fashion, the architecture has become a repository, and this is indeed a more appropriate way to think about a compiler of this class.

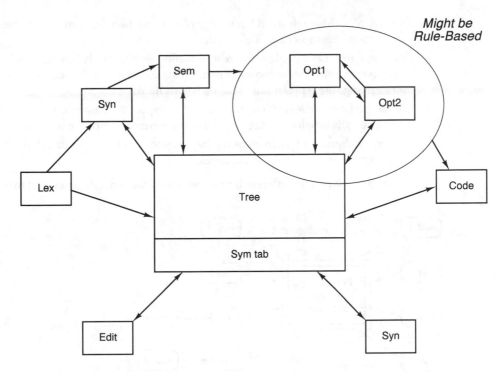

FIGURE 4.16   Repository View of Modern Compiler

Happily, this new view also accommodates various tools that operate on the internal representation rather than the textual form of a program; these include syntax-directed editors and various analysis tools.

Note that this repository resembles the database repository in some respects and differs in others. Like the database, the information of the compilation is localized in a central data component and operated on by a number of independent computations that interact only through the shared data. However, whereas the execution order of the operations in the database was determined by the types of the incoming transactions, the execution order of the compiler is predetermined, except possibly for opportunistic optimization.

4.3.3   REPOSITORY

Batch sequential tools and compilers—even when organized as repositories—do not retain information from one use to another. As a result, a body of knowledge about the program is not accumulated. The need for auxiliary information about a program to supplement the various source, intermediate, and object versions became apparent, and tools started retaining information about the prior history of a program.

The repository of the compiler provided a focus for this data collection. Efficiency considerations led to incremental compilers that updated the previous version of the augmented parse tree, and some tools came to use this shared representation as well. Figure 4.17 shows some of the ways that tools could interact with a shared repository.

- *Tight coupling:* Share detailed knowledge of the common, but proprietary, representation among the tools of a single vendor

- *Open representation:* Publish the representation so that tools can be developed by many sources. Often these tools can manipulate the data, but they are in a poor position to change the representation for their own needs.

- *Conversion boxes:* Provide filters that import or export the data in foreign representations. The tools usually lose the benefits of incremental use of the repository.

- *No contact:* Prevent a tool from using the repository, either explicitly, through excess complexity, or through frequent changes.

These alternatives have different implications for function, efficiency, and marketing.

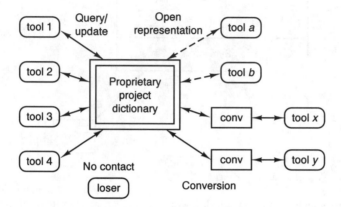

FIGURE 4.17   Software Tools with Shared Representation

4.3.4   HIERARCHICAL LAYERS

Current work on integration emphasizes the interoperability of tools, especially in distributed systems. Figure 4.18 [CN92, p. 19] shows one approach, the NIST/ECMA reference model. Although its designers do not regard it as a layered architecture, it resembles in some ways the layered architecture with mediators for databases, but it is more elaborate because it attempts to integrate communications and user interfaces as well as representation. It also embeds knowledge of software development processes, such as the order in which tools must be used and what situations call for certain responses.

Note, however, that whereas this model provides for the integration of data, it provides communication and user interface services directly. That is, this model allows for integration of multiple representations but fixes the models for user interfaces and communication.

In one variation on the integrated-environment theme, the integration system defines a set of "events" (e.g., "module foo.c recompiled") and provides support for tools to announce or to receive notice of the occurrence of events. This provides a means of communicating the need for action, but it does not solve the central problem of sharing information.

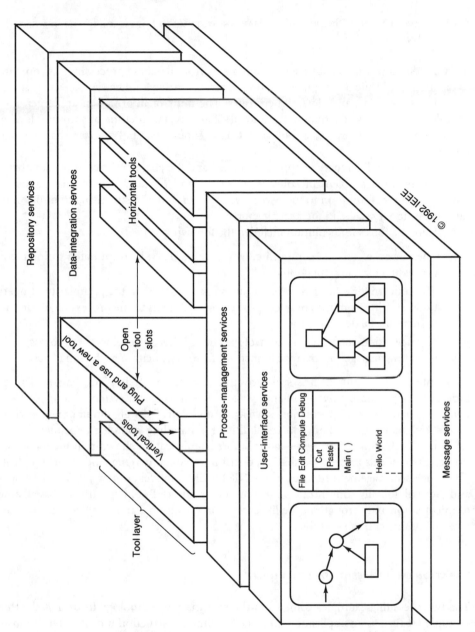

FIGURE 4.18 NIST/ECMA Reference Model for Environment Integration

© 1992 IEEE

4.3.5   EVOLUTION OF SHARED INFORMATION SYSTEMS IN SOFTWARE DEVELOPMENT ENVIRONMENTS

Software development has different requirements from database processing. As compared to databases, software development involves a greater variety of data types, fewer instances of each distinct type, and slower query rates. The units of information are larger, more complex, and less discrete than in traditional databases. The lifetime of software development information, however, is not (or at least should not be) shorter than database lifetimes.

Despite the differences in application areas and the characteristics of the supporting data, the essential problem of collecting, storing, and retrieving shared data about an ongoing process is common to the two areas. It is therefore not surprising to find comparable evolutionary stages in their architectures.

Here the forces for evolution included the following:

- The advent of on-line computing, which drove the shift from batch to interactive processing for many functions
- The concern for efficiency, which is driving a reduction in the granularity of operations, shifting from the complete processing of systems to the processing of modules to incremental development
- The need for management to control the entire software development process, which is leading managerial coverage to increase from compilation to the full life cycle

Integration in this area is still incomplete. Data conversions are passive, and the ordering of operations remains relatively rigid. The integration systems can exploit only relatively coarse system information, such as file and date. Software development environments are under pressure to add capabilities for handling complex dependencies and selecting which tools to use. Steps toward more sophistication show up in the incorporation of metamodels to describe sharing, distribution, data merging, and security policies. The process-management services of the NIST/ECMA model are not yet well developed, and they will initially concentrate on project-level support. But integration across all kinds of information and throughout the life cycle is on the agenda, and intelligent assistance is often mentioned on the wish-list.

4.4   INTEGRATION IN THE DESIGN OF BUILDINGS

The two preceding examples come from the information technology fields. For the third example we turn to an application area, the building construction industry. This industry requires a diverse variety of expertise. Distinct responsibilities correspond to matching sets of specialized functions. Indeed, distinct subindustries support these specialties. A project generally involves a number of independent, geographically dispersed companies. The diversity of expertise and dispersion of the industry inhibit communication and limit the scope of responsibilities. Each new project creates a new coalition, so there is little accumulated shared experience and no special advantage for pairwise compatibility between companies. However, the subtasks interact in complex, sometimes nonobvious ways, and coordination among specialties (global process expertise) is itself a specialty [Ter92].

The construction community employs divide-and-conquer problem solving, with interactions among the subproblems. This is naturally a distributed approach; teams of independent subcontractors map naturally to distributed problem-solving systems with coarse-grained cooperation among specialized agents. However, the separation into subproblems is forced by the need for specialization and the nature of the industry; the problems are not inherently decomposable, and the subproblems are often interdependent.

In this setting it was natural for computing to evolve bottom-up. Building designers have exploited computing for many years for tasks ranging from accounting to computer-aided design. We are concerned here with the software that performs analysis for various stages of the design activity. The 1960s and 1970s gave rise to a number of algorithmic systems directed at aiding in the performance of individual phases of the facility development. However, a large number of tasks in facility development depend on judgment, experience, and rules of thumb accumulated by experts in the domain. Such tasks cannot be performed efficiently in an algorithmic manner [Ter92].

The early stages of development, involving stand-alone programs and batch sequential compositions, are sufficiently similar to the two previous examples that it is not illuminating to review them. The first steps toward integration focused on support-supervisory systems, which provided basic services such as data management and information flow control to individual independent applications, much as software development environments did. The story picks up from the point of these early integration efforts.

Integrated environments for building design are frameworks for controlling a collection of stand-alone applications that solve part of the building-design problem [Ter92]. They must be

- Efficient in managing problem solving and information exchange
- Flexible in dealing with changes to tools
- Graceful in reacting to changes in information and problem-solving strategies

These requirements derive from the lack of standardized problem-solving procedures; they reflect the separation into specialties and the geographical distribution of the facility-development process.

4.4.1   REPOSITORY

The selection of tools and the composition of individual results require judgment, experience, and rules of thumb. Because of coupling between subproblems, this process is not algorithmic, so integrated systems require a planning function. The goal of an integrated environment is integration of data, design decisions, and knowledge. Two approaches emerged: the closely-coupled Master Builder, or monolithic system, and the design environment with cooperating tools. These early efforts at integration added elementary data management and information flow control to a tool-set.

The common responsibilities of a system for distributed problem-solving follow:

- Problem partitioning (divide into tasks for individual agents)

- Task distribution (assign tasks to agents for best performance)
- Agent control (strategy that assures tasks are performed in organized fashion)
- Agent communication (exchange of information essential when subtasks interact or conflict)

Terk [Ter92] surveyed and classified many of the integrated building-design environments that were developed in the 1980s. Here's what he found:

- *Data:* Mostly repositories: shared common representation with conversions to private representations of the tools
- *Communication:* Mostly shared data, some messaging
- *Tools:* Split between closed (tools specifically built for this system) and open (external tools can be integrated)
- *Control:* Mostly single-level hierarchy; tools at bottom; coordination at top
- *Planning:* Mostly fixed partitioning of kind and processing order; scripts sometimes permit limited flexibility

So the typical system was a repository with a sophisticated control and planning component. A fairly typical such system, IBDE [F+90] appears in Figure 4.19. Although the depiction is not typical, the distinguished position of the global data shows clearly the repository character. A list of the tools that populate this IBDE follows.

- ARCHPLAN develops architectural plan from site, budget, geometric constraints .
- CORE lays out building service core (elevators, stairs, etc.).
- STRYPES configures the structural system (e.g., suspension, rigid frame, etc.).
- STANLAY performs preliminary structural design and approximate analysis of the structural system.
- SPEX performs preliminary design of structural components.
- FOOTER designs the foundation.
- CONSTRUCTION PLANEX generates construction schedule and estimates cost.

4.4.2　INTELLIGENT CONTROL

As integration and automation proceed, the complexity of planning and control grows to be a significant problem. Indeed, as this component grows more complex, its structure starts to dominate the repository structure of the data. The difficulty of reducing the planning to pure algorithmic form makes this application a candidate for intelligent control.

The Engineering Design Research Center at CMU is exploring the development of intelligent agents that can learn to control external software systems, or systems intended for use with interactive human intervention. Integrated building design is one of the areas they have explored. Figure 4.21 [NS91] shows their design for an intelligent extension of the original IBDE system, Soar/IBDE. That figure is easier to understand when presented in two stages, so Figure 4.20 shows the relation of the intelligent agent to the external software systems before Figure 4.21 adds the internal structure of the intelligent agent. Figure 4.20 is clearly derived from Figure 4.19, with the global data moved to the status of just

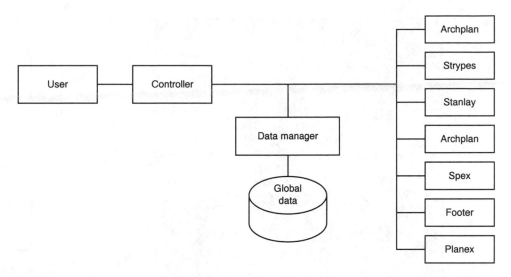

FIGURE 4.19   Integrated Building-Design Environment

another external software system. The emphasis in Soar/IBDE was control of the interaction with the individual agents of IBDE.

From the standpoint of the designers' general position on intelligent control, this organization seems reasonable, as the agent is portrayed as interacting with whatever software is provided. However, the global data plays a special role in this system. Each of the seven other components must interact with the global data (or else it makes no sense to retain the global data). Also, the intelligent agent may also find that the character of interaction with the global data is special, since it was designed to serve as a repository, not to interact with humans. Future enhancements of this system will probably need to address the interactions among components as well as the components themselves.

Figure 4.21 adds the fine structure of the intelligent agent. The agent has six major components. It must be able to identify and formulate subtasks for the set of external software systems and express them in the input formats of those systems. It must receive the output and interpret it in terms of a global overview of the problem. It must be able to understand the actions of the components as they work toward solution of the problem, both in terms of general knowledge of the task and specific knowledge of the capabilities of the set of external software systems.

The most significant aspect of this design is that the seven external software systems are interactive. This means that their input and output are incremental, so a component that needs to understand their operation must retain and update a history of the interaction. The task becomes vastly more complex when pointer input and graphical output are included, though this is not the case here.

4.4.3   EVOLUTION OF SHARED INFORMATION SYSTEMS IN BUILDING DESIGN

Integration in the area of building design is less mature than in databases and software development environments. Nevertheless, the early stages of integrated building or facility

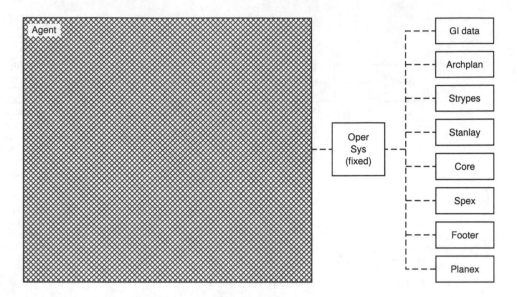

FIGURE 4.20   High-Level Architecture for Intelligent IBDE

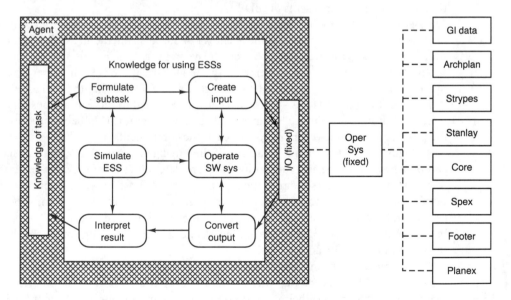

FIGURE 4.21   Detailed Architecture for Soar/IBDE

environments resemble the early stages of the first two examples. The evolutionary shift to layered hierarchies seems to come when many users must select from a diverse set of tools, and they need extra system structure to coordinate the effort of selecting and managing a useful subset. These systems have not reached this stage of development yet, so we have no information on how that will emerge.

In this case, however, the complexity of the task makes it a prime candidate for intelligent control. This opens the question of whether intelligent control could be of assistance in the other two examples, and if so what form it would take. The single-agent model developed for Soar/IBDE is one possibility, but the enrichment of database mediators to make them capable of independent intelligent action (like knowbots) is clearly another.

4.5   ARCHITECTURAL STRUCTURES FOR SHARED INFORMATION SYSTEMS

While examining examples of software integration, we have seen a variety of general architectural patterns, or idioms for software systems. In this section we reexamine the dataflow and repository idioms to see the variety that can occur within a single idiom.

Current software tools do not distinguish among different kinds of components at this level. These tools treat all modules equally, and they mostly assume that modules interact only via procedure calls and perhaps shared variables. By providing only a single model of component, they tend to blind designers to useful distinctions among modules. Moreover, by supporting only a fixed pair of low-level mechanisms for module interaction, they distract designers from the rich classes of high-level interactions among components. These tools provide little support for documenting design intentions in such a way that they become visible in the resulting software artifacts.

By making the richness of these structures explicit, we focus the attention of designers on the need for coherence and consistency in systems design. Incorporating this information explicitly in a system design would provide a record that simplifies subsequent changes and helps to ensure that later modifications will not compromise the integrity of the design. The architectural descriptions focus on design issues such as the gross structure of the system, the kinds of parts from which it is composed, and the kinds of interactions that take place.

The use of well-known patterns leads to reuse of design templates. These templates capture intuitions that are a common part of our folklore: it is now common practice to draw box-and-line diagrams that depict the architecture of a system, but no uniform meaning is yet associated with these diagrams. Many anecdotes suggest that simply providing some vocabulary to describe parts and patterns is a good first step.

By way of recapitulation, we now examine variations on two of the architectural forms that appear above: dataflow and repositories.

4.5.1   VARIANTS ON DATAFLOW SYSTEMS

The dataflow architecture that repeatedly occurs in the evolution of shared information systems is the batch sequential pattern. However, the most familiar example of this genre is probably the Unix pipe-and-filter system. The similarity of these architectures is apparent in the diagrams used for systems of the respective classes, as indicated in Figure 4.22. Both decompose a task into a (fixed) sequence of computations. They interact only through the data passed from one to another and share no other information. They assume that the components read and write the data as a whole—that is, the input or output contains one complete instance of the result in some standard order. There are differences, though. Batch sequential systems have the following characteristics:

- Very coarse-grained
- Unable to provide feedback in real time
- Unable to exploit concurrency
- Unlikely to proceed at an interactive pace

On the other hand, pipe-and-filter systems are characterized as follows:

- Fine-grained, beginning to compute as soon as they consume a few input tokens
- Able to start producing output right away (processing is localized in the input stream)
- Able to provide feedback (though most shells can't express it)
- Often interactive

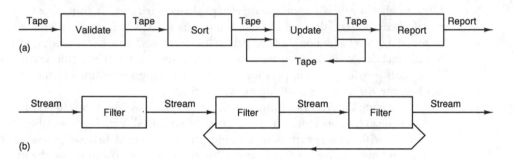

FIGURE 4.22   Comparison of (a) Batch Sequential and (b) Pipe/Filter Architectures

4.5.2   VARIANTS ON REPOSITORIES

The other architectural pattern that figured prominently in our examples was the repository. Repositories in general are characterized by a central shared data store coupled tightly to a number of independent computations, each with its own expertise. The independent computations interact only through the shared data, and they do not retain any significant amount of private state. The variations differ chiefly in the apparatus that controls the order in which the computations are invoked, in the access mechanisms that allow the computations access to the data, and in the granularity of the operations.

Figures 4.6 and 4.7 show a database system. Here the control is driven by the types of transactions in the input stream, the access mechanism is usually supported by a specialized programming language, and the granularity is that of a database transaction. Figure 4.16 shows a programming language compiler. Here control is fixed (compilation proceeds in the same order each time), the access mechanism may be full conversion of the shared data structure into an in-memory representation, or direct access (when components are compiled into the same address space), and the granularity is that of a single pass of a compiler.

Figure 4.17 shows a repository that supports independent tools. Control may be determined by the direct requests of users, or it may in some cases be handled by an event mechanism also shared by the tools. A variety of access methods are available, and the granularity is that of the tool-set.

One prominent repository has not appeared here; it is mentioned now for completeness—to extend the comparison of repositories. This is the blackboard architecture, most frequently used for signal-processing applications in artificial intelligence [Nii86] and depicted in Figure 4.23. Here the independent computations are various knowledge sources that can contribute to solving the problem—for example, syntactic-semantic connection, phoneme recognition, word-candidate generation, and signal segmentation for speech understanding. The blackboard is a highly structured representation especially designed for the representations pertinent to the application. Control is completely opportunistic, driven by the current state of the data on the blackboard. The abstract model for access is direct visibility, as with many human experts watching each other solve a problem at a real blackboard (understandably, implementations support this abstraction with more feasible mechanisms). The granularity is quite fine, at the level of interpreting a signal segment as a phoneme.

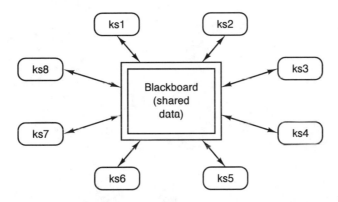

FIGURE 4.23   Blackboard Architecture

4.6   Some Conclusions

Three tasks arising in different communities deal with collecting, manipulating, and preserving shared information. In each case changing technologies and requirements drove changes in the architectural form commonly used for the systems. We can identify that sequence as a common evolutionary pattern for shared information systems:

- Isolated applications without interaction
- Batch sequential processing
- Repositories for integration via shared data
- Layered hierarchies for dynamic integration across distributed systems

Since problems remain and new technology continues to emerge, this pattern may grow in the future, for example, to include active control by intelligent agents.

These examples show one case in which a common problem structure appears in several quite different application areas. This suggests that attempts to exploit "domain knowledge" in software design should characterize domains by their computational requirements (e.g., shared information systems) as well as by industry (e.g., data processing, software development, or facility design). In addition, the examples show that within a single domain, differences among requirements or operational settings may change the preferred architecture. Taken together, these insights suggest that the notion of a single domain-specific architecture serving a segment of an industry may not fully exploit our growing architectural capabilities.

CHAPTER 5

ARCHITECTURAL DESIGN GUIDANCE

How DOES ONE GO ABOUT choosing an appropriate architecture to satisfy a given set of requirements? Currently architectural expertise lives in the minds of good system designers who often have years of experience in building systems for specific domains. As the field of architecture matures, however, we can hope that some of this expertise will find its way into tools that can help software architects to make principled choices within an architectural design space. In this chapter we consider two prototype tools that do just that. The first tool was constructed as part of Thomas Lane's Ph.D. thesis research: it provides an expert system that helps design user-interface architectures. The second tool was constructed as a project by a group of graduate students in software engineering: it builds on Lane's notion of design spaces and provides a spreadsheet-based tool for evaluating the strengths and weaknesses of a set of architectural styles for a given set of requirements.

5.1 GUIDANCE FOR USER-INTERFACE ARCHITECTURES

by Thomas G. Lane

5.1.1 DESIGN SPACES AND RULES

We can describe and classify the architectural alternatives available to a system designer by constructing a *design space*. Within a design space, we can formulate design rules that indicate good and bad combinations of choices, and use them to select an appropriate system design based on functional requirements. The design space is useful in its own right as a shared vocabulary for describing and understanding systems.

This work should be viewed as a means of codifying software design knowledge for use in day-to-day practice and in the training of new software engineers. For this purpose, a set of design rules need not produce a "perfect" or "best possible" design. The rules will make a valuable contribution if they can help a journeyman designer to make choices comparable to those that a master designer would make—or even just help the journey-man to choose a reasonable design with no major errors. With sufficient experience, designers may create a set of such rules that is complete and reliable enough to serve as the basis for automated system design, but the rules can be applied in practice long before that stage is reached.

The work described in this chapter tested these ideas by constructing a design space and rules for the architecture of user-interface software systems. These rules were experimentally tested by comparing their recommendations to actual system designs. The results showed that a rather simple set of rules could achieve a promising degree of agreement with the choices of expert designers. These exploratory results suggest that the approach sketched here is a viable way to create an organized body of knowledge for software engineering.

THE UTILITY OF CODIFIED KNOWLEDGE

The underlying goal of this work is to organize and express software design knowledge in a useful form. One way of doing this is to develop a vocabulary of well-understood, reusable design concepts and patterns. If widely adopted, a design vocabulary has three major benefits. First, it aids in creating a system design by providing mental building blocks. Second, it helps in understanding or predicting the properties of a design by offering a context for the creation and application of knowledge. Third, it reduces the effort needed to understand another person's design by reducing the number of new concepts to be learned.

An example of such a vocabulary is the codification of control structures that took place about two decades ago. Programmers learned to perceive control flow in terms of a few standard concepts (conditionals, iteration, selection, subroutine calls, etc.) rather than as a complex pattern of low-level tests and branches. By reducing apparent complexity and providing a shared understanding of control-flow patterns, these conceptual building blocks made programs both easier to write and easier to read. Researchers discovered key properties of these structures, for example, the invariant and termination conditions of loops. Using the standard structures helped practitioners to focus on these properties, and produce better-understood, more reliable programs. Finally, codification made it possible to build tools (programming languages) that supported the structural concepts directly, providing further productivity gains.

As software engineering matures and research attention shifts to ever-larger problems, we can expect to see similar codification occurring for larger software entities. The time now seems ripe to begin codifying structural patterns in medium-size software systems, that is, in the characteristics of modules and the interconnections between them. (We can already anticipate that even higher levels of design abstraction will be needed to design very large systems, but we are far from having enough experience to be able to discern patterns at that scale.)

A different analogy for this work is the compilation of engineering design handbooks, such as Perry's [P+84]. The established fields of engineering have long distinguished between innovative and routine design. Innovative design relies upon raw invention or derivation from abstract principles, while routine design uses standardized methods to solve problems similar to those that have been solved before. These methods are often collected and presented in handbooks. When they will work, routine design methods are cheaper and more likely to yield an acceptable (though not necessarily optimum) design than are innovative methods. The primary purpose of handbooks, then, is to support routine design.

A good handbook arms its user with a number of standard design approaches and with knowledge of their strengths and limitations. Software engineering handbooks could therefore combat two opposite evils now widely seen in practice: both the tendency to invent every new system from scratch and the tendency to reuse a single design for every problem regardless of its suitability. Handbook-style texts are now widely available for the selection of algorithms and data structures (e.g., [Knu73, Sed88]), but they do not yet exist for higher levels of software design.

The work reported here offers an organizational scheme (namely, design spaces and rules) for handbooks of software system structure, as well as the beginnings of specific knowledge for one such handbook covering user-interface systems.

THE NOTION OF A DESIGN SPACE

The central concept here is that of a multidimensional design space that classifies system architectures. Each dimension of a design space describes variation in one system characteristic or design choice. Values along a dimension correspond to alternative requirements or design choices. For example, required response time could be a dimension, as could the means of interprocess synchronization (e.g., messages or semaphores). A specific system design corresponds to a point in the design space, identified by the dimensional values that correspond to its characteristics and structure. Figure 5.1 illustrates a tiny design space.

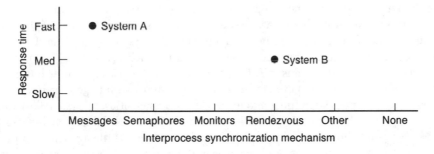

FIGURE 5.1   A Simple Design Space

The different dimensions are not necessarily independent; in fact, it is important to discover correlations between dimensions, in order to create design rules describing appropriate and inappropriate combinations of choices. One empirical way of discovering such correlations is to see whether successful system designs cluster in some parts of the space and are absent from others.

A key part of the design space approach is to choose some dimensions that reflect requirements or evaluation criteria (function and/or performance), while other dimensions reflect structure (or other available design choices). Correlations found among such dimensions can provide direct design guidance: they show which design choices are most likely to meet the functional requirements for a new system. For example, the hypothetical data in Figure 5.1 suggests that a message mechanism is more likely to provide fast response time than a rendezvous mechanism. (Of course, one would want more than just two data points before drawing this conclusion.)

The dimensions that describe functional and performance requirements make up the *functional design space*, while those that describe structural choices make up the *structural design space*. We can regard these groupings either as independent spaces or as subspaces of a single large design space. In the context of a stepwise ("waterfall") model of the software design process, the functional design space represents the results of the requirements analysis and gross functional design steps, while the structural design space represents the results of initial system decomposition.

The dimensions of a design space are usually not continuous and need not possess any useful metric (distance measure). A dimension that represents a structural choice is likely to have a discrete set of possible values, which may or may not have any meaningful ordering. For example, methods for specifying user-interface behavior include state transition diagrams, context-free grammars, menu trees, and many others. Each of these techniques has many small variations, so one of the key problems in constructing a design space is finding the most useful granularity of classification. Even when a dimension is in principle continuous (e.g., a performance number), one may choose to aggregate it into a few discrete values (e.g., "low," "medium," "high"). This is appropriate when such gross estimates provide as much information as one needs or can get, as is often true in the early stages of design.

5.1.2   A DESIGN SPACE FOR USER-INTERFACE ARCHITECTURES

The design space reported here, together with its associated rules, describes architectural alternatives for user-interface software: systems whose main focus is on providing an interactive user interface for some software function(s). The system studied need not provide the whole user interface. Thus the scope of the study included not only complete user-interface management systems (UIMSs), but also graphics packages, user-interface toolkits, window managers, and even stand-alone applications with large user-interface components. This scope is large enough to include a wide range of useful system structures, yet not so large as to be intractable. Another domain might have been chosen, but user interfaces are a good choice because the field is in ferment, with little agreement on the best possible structures. Hence the results may be useful immediately, as well as serving to illustrate the larger argument made above.

The design space is too large to cover completely in this chapter; we will only describe some representative dimensions and rules. (For a more complete presentation of the space, see [Lan90a].) The complete design space contains 25 functional dimensions, 6 of which are described here. In each dimension 3–5 alternatives are recognized. There are 19 structural dimensions, 5 of which are described here, each offering 2–7 alternatives. Figure 5.3 presents the dimensions covered here.

A BASIC STRUCTURAL MODEL

To describe structural alternatives, we need some terminology that identifies the components of a system. The terminology must be quite general, or it will not apply to some structures. A useful scheme for user-interface systems divides any complete system into three components, or groups of modules:

1. An **application-specific** component. This consists of code that is specific to one particular application program and is not intended to be reused in other applications. In particular, this component includes the functional core of the application. It may also include application-specific user-interface code. (The term *code* should be read as including tables, grammars, and other nonprocedural specifications, as well as conventional programming methods.)

2. A **shared user interface** component. This consists of code that is intended to support the user interface of multiple application programs. If the software system can accommodate different types of I/O devices, only code that applies to all device types is included here.

3. A **device-dependent** component. This consists of code that is specific to a particular I/O device class (and is not application-specific).

In a simple system the second or third component might be empty: there might be no shared code other than device drivers, or the system might not provide support for multiple device types (and hence show no clear demarcation of device-specific code).

The intermodule divisions that the design space considers are the division between application-specific code and shared user-interface code on the one hand, and between device-specific code and shared user-interface code on the other. These divisions are called the *application interface* and *device interface* respectively. Figure 5.2 illustrates the structural model.

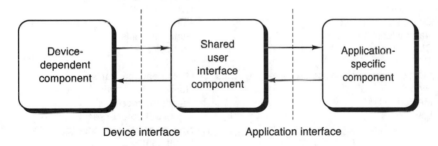

FIGURE 5.2   A Basic Structural Model for User Interface Software

There is some flexibility in dividing a real system into these three components. This apparent ambiguity is very useful, for we can analyze different levels of the system by adopting different labelings. For example, in the X Window System [SG86] one may analyze the window server's design by regarding everything outside the server as application-specific, and then dividing the server into shared user-interface and device-dependent levels. To analyze an X toolkit package, it is more useful to label the toolkit as the shared code, regarding the server as a device-specific black box.

SAMPLE FUNCTIONAL DIMENSIONS

The functional dimensions identify the requirements for a user-interface system that most affect its structure (see Figure 5.3). These dimensions fall into three groups:

Functional Dimensions	Structural Dimensions
External event handling	**Application interface abstraction level**
• No external events	• Monolithic program
• Process events while waiting for input	• Abstract device
• External events preempt user commands	• Toolkit
	• Interaction manager with fixed data types
User customizability	• Interaction manager with extensible data types
• High	• Extensible interaction manager
• Medium	
• Low	**Abstract device variability**
	• Ideal device
User interface adaptability across devices	• Parameterized device
• None	• Device with variable operations
• Local behavior changes	• Ad-hoc device
• Global behavior change	
• Application semantics changes	**Notation for user interface definition**
	• Implicit in shared user interface code
Computer system organization	• Implicit in application code
• Uniprocessing	• External declarative notation
• Multiprocessing	• External procedural notation
• Distributed processing	• Internal declarative notation
	• Internal procedural notation
Basic interface class	
• Menu selection	**Basis of communication**
• Form filling	• Events
• Command language	• Pure state
• Natural language	• State with hints
• Direct manipulation	• State plus events
Application portability across user interface styles	**Control thread mechanism**
• High	• None
• Medium	• Standard processes
• Low	• Lightweight processes
	• Non-preemptive processes
	• Event handlers
	• Interrupt service routines

FIGURE 5.3   The Sample Design-Space Dimensions

- **External requirements.** This group includes the requirements of the particular applications, users, and I/O devices to be supported, as well as constraints imposed by the surrounding computer system.

- **Basic interactive behavior.** This group includes the key decisions about user-interface behavior that fundamentally influence internal structure.

- **Practical considerations.** This group covers development cost considerations; primarily, the required degree of adaptability of the system.

These dimensions are not intended to correspond to the earliest requirements that one might write for a system, but to identify the specifications that immediately precede the gross structural design phase. Thus, some design decisions have already been made in arriving at these choices.

External Requirements.

External event handling is an example of a dimension that reflects an application-imposed external requirement. This dimension indicates whether the application program needs to respond to external events (defined as events not originating in the user interface), and if so, on what time scale. The design space recognizes three alternatives:

- *No external events:* The application is not influenced by external events, or checks for them only in the course of executing specific user commands. For example, a mail program might check for new mail, but only when an explicit command to do so is given. In this case no support for external events is needed in the user interface.

- *Process events while waiting for input:* The application must handle external events, but response-time requirements are not so stringent that it must interrupt processing of user commands. It is sufficient for the user interface to allow response to external events while waiting for input. Automatic reporting of mail arrival might be handled this way.

- *External events preempt user commands:* External-event servicing has sufficiently high priority that execution of user commands must be interrupted when an external event occurs. This requirement is common in real-time control systems.

User customizability is an example of a user-imposed external requirement. The design space recognizes three levels of end-user customizability of a user interface:

- *High:* User can add new commands and redefine commands (e.g., via a macro language), as well as modify user-interface details.

- *Medium:* User can modify details of the user interface that do not affect semantics, for instance, change menu-entry wording, window sizes, colors, and so on.

- *Low:* Little or no user customizability is required.

User-interface adaptability across devices depends on the expected range of I/O devices that the user-interface system must support. This dimension indicates the extent of change in user-interface behavior that may be required when changing to a different set of I/O devices.

- *None:* All aspects of behavior are the same across all supported devices.

- *Local behavior changes:* Only changes in small details of behavior occur across devices, for example, in the appearance of menus.

- *Global behavior changes:* There are major changes in surface user-interface behavior across devices, for example, a change in basic interface class (see below).

- *Application semantics changes:* There are changes in the underlying semantics of commands (e.g., continuous display of state versus display on command).

Computer system organization is an example of a dimension describing the surrounding computer system. This dimension classifies the basic nature of the environment as follows:

- *Uniprocessing:* Only one application executes at a time.

- *Multiprocessing:* Multiple applications execute concurrently.
- *Distributed processing:* Environment is a computer network, with multiple CPUs and non-negligible communication costs.

Basic Interactive Behavior.
Basic interface class identifies the basic kind of interaction supported by the user-interface system. (A general-purpose system might support more than one of these classes.) The design space uses a classification proposed by Shneiderman [Shn86]:

- *Menu selection:* Based on repeated selection from groups of alternatives; at each step the alternatives are (or can be) displayed.
- *Form filling:* Based on entry (usually text entry) of values for a given set of variables.
- *Command language:* Based on an artificial, symbolic language; often allows extension through procedure definitions that resemble a programming language.
- *Natural language:* Based on (a subset of) a human language such as English. Resolution of ambiguous input is a key problem.
- *Direct manipulation:* Based on direct graphical representation and incremental manipulation of the program's data.

It turns out that menu selection and form filling can be supported by similar system structures, but each of the other classes has unique requirements.

Practical Considerations.
Application portability across user interface styles is an example of a dimension defining the required degree of adaptability of a user-interface system. This dimension specifies the degree to which application-specific code is insulated from user-interface style changes.

- *High:* Applications should be portable across significantly different styles (e.g., command language versus menu-driven).
- *Medium:* Applications should be independent of minor stylistic variations (e.g., menu appearance).
- *Low:* User interface variability is not a concern, or application changes are acceptable when modifying the user interface.

SAMPLE STRUCTURAL DIMENSIONS

The structural dimensions represent the decisions determining the overall structure of a user-interface system. These dimensions also fall into three major groups:

- **Division of functions and knowledge among modules.** This group considers how system functions are divided into modules, the interfaces between modules, and the information contained within each module.
- **Representation issues.** This group considers the data representations used within the system. We must consider both actual data, in the sense of values passing through the user interface, and *metadata* that specifies the appearance and behavior of the user interface. Metadata may exist explicitly in the system (for example, as a data structure describing the layout of a dialogue window), or only implicitly.

- **Control flow, communication, and synchronization issues.** This group considers the dynamic behavior of the user-interface code.

Division of Functions and Knowledge Among Modules.
Application interface abstraction level is in many ways the key structural dimension. The design space identifies six general classes of application interface, which are most easily distinguished by their level of abstraction in communication:[1]

- *Monolithic program:* There is no separation between application-specific and shared code, hence no such interface (and no device interface, either). This can be an appropriate solution in small, specialized systems where the application needs considerable control over user-interface details and/or little processing power is available. (Video games are a typical example.)
- *Abstract device:* The shared code is simply a device driver, presenting an abstract device for manipulation by the application. The operations provided have specific physical interpretations (e.g., "draw line," but not "present menu"). Most aspects of interactive behavior are under the control of the application, although some local interactions may be handled by the shared code (e.g., character echoing and backspace handling in a keyboard/display driver). In this category the application interface and device interface are the same.
- *Toolkit:* The shared code provides a library of interaction techniques (e.g., menu or scroll bar handlers). The application is responsible for selecting appropriate toolkit elements and composing them into a complete interface. Hence the shared code can control only local aspects of user-interface style; global behavior remains under application control. The interaction between application and shared code is in terms of specific interactive techniques (e.g., "obtain menu selection"). The application can bypass the toolkit, reaching down to an underlying abstract device level, if it requires an interaction technique not provided by the toolkit. In particular, the application performs conversions between specialized application data types and their device-oriented representations by accessing the underlying abstract device directly.
- *Interaction manager with fixed data types:* The shared code controls both local and global interaction sequences and stylistic decisions. Its interaction with the application is expressed in terms of abstract information transfers, such as "get command" or "present result" (notice that no particular external representation is implied). These abstract transfers use a fixed set of standard data types (e.g., integers, strings); the application must express its input and output in terms of the standard data types. Hence some aspects of the conversion between application internal data formats and user-visible representations remain in the application code.
- *Interaction manager with extensible data types:* Similar to the previous category, except that the application can extend the set of data types used for abstract communication. It does so by specifying (in some notation) the input and output conversions required for the new data types. If properly used, this approach allows

---

[1] Recognition of abstraction level as a key property in user interfaces goes back at least to Hayes [HSL85]. The classification used here is a practical one, but is based on the theoretical distinctions made by Hayes.

knowledge of the external representation to be separated from the main body of the application.

- *Extensible interaction manager:* Again, communication between the application and shared code is in terms of abstract information transfers. The interaction manager provides extensive opportunities for application-specific customization. This is accomplished by supplying code that augments or overrides selected internal operations of the interaction manager. (Most existing systems of this class are coded in an object-oriented language, and the language's inheritance mechanism is used to control customization.) Usually there is a significant body of application-specific code that customizes the interaction manager; this code is much more tightly coupled to the internal details of the interaction manager than is the case for clients of nonextensible interaction managers.

This classification turns out to be sufficient to predict most aspects of the application interface, including the division of user-interface functions, the type and extent of application knowledge made available to the shared user-interface code, and the kinds of data types used in communication. For instance, we have already suggested the division of local versus global control of interactive behavior that is typically found in each category.

Abstract device variability is the key dimension describing the device interface. We view the device interface as defining an *abstract device* for the device-independent code to manipulate. The design space classifies abstract devices according to the degree of variability perceived by the device-independent code.

- *Ideal device:* The provided operations and their results are well specified in terms of an "ideal" device; the real device is expected to approximate the ideal behavior fairly closely. An example is the PostScript imaging model, which ignores the limited resolution of real printers and displays [Ado85]. In this approach, all questions of device variability are hidden from software above the device-driver level, so application portability is high. This approach is most useful where the real devices deviate only slightly from the ideal model, or at least do not deviate in ways that require rethinking of user-interface behavior.

- *Parameterized device:* A class of devices is covered, differing in specified parameters such as screen size, number of colors, number of mouse buttons, and so on. The device-independent code can inquire about the parameter values for the particular device at hand and adapt its behavior as necessary. Operations and their results are well specified, but depend on parameter values. An example is the X Windows graphics model, which exposes display resolution and color handling [SG86]. The advantage of this approach is that higher-level code has both more knowledge of acceptable trade-offs and more flexibility in changing its behavior than is possible for a device driver. The drawback is that device-independent code may have to perform complex case analysis in order to handle the full range of supported devices. If this must be done in each application, the cost is high, and there is a great risk that programmers will omit support for some devices. To reduce this temptation, it is best to design a parameterized model to have just a few well-defined levels of capability, so as to reduce the number of cases to be considered.

- *Device with variable operations:* A well-defined set of device operations exists, but the device-dependent code has considerable leeway in choosing how to implement the operations; device-independent code is discouraged from being closely concerned with the exact external behavior. Results of operations are thus not well specified. Examples are GKS logical input devices [RMP+82] and the Scribe formatting model [RW80]. This approach works best when the device operations are chosen at a level of abstraction high enough to give the device driver considerable freedom of choice. Hence the device-independent code must be willing to give up much control of user-interface details. This restriction means that direct manipulation (with its heavy dependence on semantically controlled feedback) is not well supported.

- *Ad-hoc device:* In many real systems, the abstract device definition has developed in an ad-hoc fashion, and so it is not tightly specified; behavior varies from device to device. Applications therefore must confine themselves to a rather small set of device semantics if they wish to achieve portability, even though any particular implementation of the abstract device may provide many additional features. Alphanumeric terminals are an excellent example. While aesthetically displeasing, this approach has one redeeming benefit: applications that do not care about portability are not hindered from exploiting the full capabilities of a particular real device.

These categories lend themselves to different situations. For example, an abstract device with variable operations is useful when much of the system's "intelligence" is to be put into the device-specific layer, but it is only appropriate for handling local changes in user-interface behavior across devices.

Representation Issues.
Notation for user-interface definition is a representation dimension. It classifies the techniques used for defining the appearance and behavior of the user interface.

- *Implicit in shared user-interface code:* Information "wired into" shared code. For example, the visual appearance of a menu might be implicit in the menu routines supplied by a toolkit. In systems where strong user-interface conventions exist, this is a perfectly acceptable approach.

- *Implicit in application code:* Information buried in the application and not readily available to shared user-interface code. This is most appropriate where the application is already tightly involved in the user interface, for example, in handling semantic feedback in direct-manipulation systems.

- *External declarative notation:* A nonprocedural specification separate from the body of the application program, for example, a grammar or tabular specification. External declarative notations are particularly well suited for supporting user customization and for use by nonprogramming user-interface experts. *Graphical specification* methods are an important special case.

- *External procedural notation:* A procedural specification separate from the body of the application program; often cast in a specialized programming language. Procedural notations are more flexible than declarative ones but are harder to use. User-accessible procedural mechanisms, such as macro definition capability or the programming language of EMACS-like editors [BG88], provide very powerful customization possibilities for sophisticated users. By definition, however, an external notation has limited access to the state of the application program, which may restrict its capability.

- *Internal declarative notation:* A nonprocedural specification within the application program. Unlike an implicit representation, this is available for use by the shared user-interface code. Parameters supplied to shared user-interface routines often amount to an internal declarative notation. An example is a list of menu entries provided to a toolkit menu routine.

- *Internal procedural notation:* A procedural specification within the application program. Unlike an implicit representation, this is available for use by the shared user-interface code. A typical example is a status-inquiry or data-transformation function that is provided for the user-interface code to call. This is the most commonly used notation for customization of extensible interaction managers. It provides an efficient and flexible notation, but because it is not accessible to the end user, it is useless for user customization. It is particularly useful for handling application-specific feedback in direct-manipulation interfaces, since it has both adequate flexibility and efficient access to application semantics.

Each of these categories offers different trade-offs among power, runtime cost, ease of use, and ease of modification. For example, declarative notation is the easiest to use (especially for nonprogramming designers) but it has the least power, since it can only represent a predetermined range of possibilities. Typically, a system uses several notational techniques, with different aspects of the user interface being controlled by different techniques. For example, the position and size of a screen button might be specified graphically, while its highlighting behavior is specified implicitly by the code of a toolkit routine.

Control Flow, Communication, and Synchronization Issues.
Basis of communication is a communication dimension. This dimension classifies systems according to whether communication between modules depends upon shared state, events, or both. An *event* is a transfer of information occurring at a discrete time, for example via a procedure call or message. Communication through shared state variables is significantly different, because the recipient always has access to the current values and need not use information in the same order in which it is sent. The classification follows:

- *Events:* There is no shared state; all communication relies on events.
- *Pure state:* Communication is strictly via shared state; the recipient must repeatedly inspect the state variables to detect changes.
- *State with hints:* Communication is via shared state, but the recipient is actively informed of changes via an event mechanism; hence polling of the state is not required. However, the recipient could ignore the events and reconstruct all necessary information from the shared state, so the events are efficiency hints rather than essential information.
- *State plus events:* Both shared state and events are used; the events are crucial because they provide information not available from state monitoring.

State-based mechanisms are popular for dealing with incrementally updated displays. The hybrid state/event categories allow for performance optimization in return for their extra complexity. State-based communication requires access to shared storage, which may be impossible or unreasonably expensive in some system architectures.

Different bases of communication may be used at the application and device interfaces, but this is rare. It is fairly common to have different bases of communication for input and output; hence the design space provides separate dimensions for input and output communication basis.

Control-thread mechanism describes the method, if any, used to support multiple logical threads of control. Multiple threads are extremely useful in user-interface systems, for example, in handling multiple input devices or for decoupling application processing from user-interface logic. Often, full-fledged processes are too difficult to implement, or impose too much overhead, so many partial implementations are used. This dimension classifies the possibilities as follows:

- *None:* Only a single control thread is used.
- *Standard processes:* Independently scheduled entities with interprocess protection (typically, separate address spaces). These provide security against other processes, but interprocess communication is relatively expensive. For a user-interface system, security may or may not be a concern, while communication costs are almost always a major concern. In network environments, standard processes are usually the only kind that can be executed on different machines.
- *Lightweight processes:* Independently scheduled entities within a shared address space. These are only suitable for mutually trusting processes due to lack of security, but that is not often an issue for user interface systems. The benefit is substantially reduced communication cost, especially for use of shared variables. Few operating systems provide lightweight processes, and building one's own lightweight process mechanism can be difficult.
- *Nonpreemptive processes:* Processes without preemptive scheduling (must explicitly yield control), usually in a shared address space. These are relatively simple to implement. Guaranteeing short response time is difficult and affects the entire system: long computations must be broken up explicitly.
- *Event handlers:* Pseudoprocesses that are invoked via a series of subroutine calls; each such call must return before another event-handler process can be executed. Hence control flow is restricted; for example, waiting for another process cannot occur inside a subroutine called by an event handler. Again, response-time constraints require system-wide attention. The main advantage of this method is that it requires virtually no support mechanism.
- *Interrupt-service routines:* Hardware-level event handling. A series of interrupt-service routine executions form a control thread, but one with restricted control flow and communication abilities. The control-flow restrictions are comparable to event handlers; but unlike event handlers, they allow for preemptive scheduling.

Event handlers are easily implemented within a user-interface system; nonpreemptive processes are harder but can still be implemented without operating system support.

The other mechanisms usually must be provided by the operating system. Some form of preemptive scheduling is often desirable to reduce timing dependencies between threads.

5.1.3 DESIGN RULES FOR USER-INTERFACE ARCHITECTURE

There are very few hard-and-fast rules at this level of design. Most connections between design dimensions are better described by saying that a given choice along one dimension favors or disfavors particular choices along another dimension; the strength of this correlation varies from case to case. The designer's task is to consider all such correlations and to select the alternative favored by the preponderance of the evidence.

Therefore, a natural notation for a design rule is a positive or negative weight associated with particular combinations of alternatives from two (or more) dimensions. A given design can be evaluated by summing the weights of all applicable rules. The "best" design is then the one with the highest score. The author prepared a set of design rules of this form that could be mechanically evaluated and an evaluation program that would rank the structural alternatives when given a set of values for the functional dimensions. (Section 5.1.5 describes an experimental test of this rule set.) The rules can also be viewed less formally as guidelines for human designers.

It is useful to distinguish two categories of rules: those linking functional to structural dimensions, and those interconnecting structural dimensions. The first group allows system requirements to drive a structural design, while the second group ensures the internal consistency of the design.[2] This second group complicates the task of finding the design with the highest score, since choices in different dimensions affect each other. The author resorted to combinatorial searching to locate the best designs; better algorithms may be found in the future. A possible source of better methods is "neural network" techniques, which seem to have some similarity to this problem.

The mechanical rule set contains 622 design rules. They are written in a very primitive notation and can be reduced to about 170 rules at a more reasonable level of abstraction. The very abbreviated descriptions below account for about 10 percent of the formal rules.

SAMPLE RULES

The earlier descriptions of structural alternatives have already mentioned some of the conditions under which one alternative may be preferred to another. This section presents more formally some of the specific design rules that connect the sample dimensions. Each of the sample rules is given in prose form, together with a brief justification.

- If external event handling requires preemption of user commands, then a preemptive control-thread mechanism (standard processes, lightweight processes, or interrupt-service routines) is strongly favored. Without such a mechanism, very severe constraints must be placed on all user-interface and application processing in order to guarantee adequate response time.

---

[2] Rules interconnecting functional dimensions could be useful for evaluating proposed sets of requirements, for example, to estimate the cost of meeting the requirements. The present work has not investigated this possibility.

- High user customizability requirements favor external notations for user-interface behavior. Implicit and internal notations are usually more difficult to access and more closely coupled to application logic than external notations.

- Stronger requirements for user-interface adaptability across devices favor higher levels of application-interface abstraction, so as to decouple the application from user-interface details that may change across devices. If the requirement is for global behavior or application semantics changes, then parameterized abstract devices are also favored. Such changes generally must be implemented in shared user-interface code or application code, rather than in the device driver; thus, information about the device at hand cannot be hidden from the higher levels, as the other classes of abstract devices try to do.

- A distributed system organization favors event-based communication. State-based communication requires shared memory or some equivalent, which is often expensive to access in such an environment.

- The basic user-interface class affects the best choice of application-interface abstraction level. For example, menu-selection and form-filling user interfaces are well served by toolkits and nonextensible interaction managers. But experience has shown that nonextensible interaction managers are not adequate for direct manipulation, because they don't handle semantic feedback well. Extensible interaction managers and toolkits are the favored alternatives for direct manipulation.

- A high requirement for application portability across user-interface styles favors the higher levels of application-interface abstraction. Less obviously, it favors event-based or pure state-based communication over the hybrid forms (state with hints or state plus events). A hybrid communication protocol is normally tuned to particular communication patterns, which may change when the user-interface style changes.

The preceding rules all relate functional to structural dimensions. Following are some examples of the rules that interconnect structural dimensions.

- The choice of application-interface abstraction level influences the choice of notation for user-interface behavior.

- In monolithic programs and abstract-device application interfaces, implicit representation is usually sufficient.

- Toolkit systems include implicit and internal declarative notations (parameters to toolkit routines being of the latter class).

- Interaction managers of all types use external and/or internal declarative notations.

- Extensible interaction managers rely heavily on procedural notations, particularly internal procedural notation, since customization is often done by supplying procedures.

5.1.4   APPLYING THE DESIGN SPACE: AN EXAMPLE

To illustrate these ideas, this section presents a concrete example. The sample system is the cT programming language and environment [SS88]. The cT language is designed for the creation of high-quality, interactive educational applications, for example, physics simula-tions or instruction in musical notation. It must accommodate authors who are experts in their particular subject matter but have only limited programming experience. Implementations exist on a variety of personal computers and workstations, and portability of application programs across these platforms is an important goal.

We can describe cT's functional requirements in the terms of the design space. For the sample dimensions previously cited, we have the following:

- There is no requirement for external event handling; it's not needed in the target class of applications.
- Little or no end-user customizability is needed.
- User-interface adaptability across devices may require local behavior changes, for instance to fill areas with different patterns when color is not available. The range of supported platforms is not so wide that global behavior changes might be necessary.
- Computer system organization may be uniprocessing or multiprocessing; cT does not make special provisions for distributed systems.
- Basic interface class is usually direct manipulation, but menu selection is also used. Each application determines its basic interactive behavior.
- Medium portability of applications across user-interface styles is required. In such things as menu appearance, cT follows the conventions of the host platform, and the application should be independent of such details.

To describe cT structurally, we classify the cT programming system itself as the shared user-interface code, instructional programs written in cT as application-specific code, and the underlying platform (including graphics packages, etc.) as device-specific code. (Notice that this division is already implicit in the functional classification above.)

The architecture of cT can then be classified in the sample structural dimensions as follows:

- The application-interface abstraction level falls in the toolkit class. Toolkit elements are provided for common constructs such as menus or scrolling text boxes; cT's toolbox is particularly strong in the analysis of text input (recognition of misspelled words, equivalent forms of algebraic expressions, etc). For other interactive behavior the application resorts to manipulation of the underlying abstract device.
- The device interface uses a parameterized abstract device. Decisions such as how to scale displays to fit the available hardware are handled largely by the shared user-interface code (but the application can set policy, such as whether to preserve aspect ratio).
- User-interface notation is mostly implicit; some aspects are implicit in the shared code, while others are implicit in the application. Limited use is made of internal procedural notation, and there are some toolbox parameters that qualify as internal declarative notation.
- Communication is based on events; no shared state variables are used.
- cT uses basically a single thread of execution. An exception occurs in the development environment: while editing a cT program, incremental recompilation is done while waiting for user input. The "background" control thread used for this purpose is implemented with an event-handler mechanism.

The mechanical rule set is largely able to replicate these design decisions. For example, the rules recommend implicit and internal-procedural user-interface notations, because the requirements for user customizability and application portability are not high enough to justify the extra cost of external or declarative notations. The rules recommend strict single-thread control flow, so they disagree on the last of the sample dimensions. This is unsurprising since the decision to provide background recompilation is outside the scope of the present design space.

5.1.5   A Validation Experiment

To test the validity of the design space and rules, the rules' recommendations were compared to the actual designs of some user-interface systems. This experiment used six systems that had not been studied in the course of preparing the design space and rules. The test was carried out as follows:

- A designer of each system was asked to describe his system in the terms of the design space; that is, to choose the most descriptive category in each functional and structural dimension.
- Each system's functional description was fed into a program that searched for the structural alternatives that were most highly rated by the rule set.
- The resulting structural recommendations were compared to the actual system descriptions.

The six systems covered a fairly wide range of user-interface requirements. Among them were two radically different UIMSs, an integrated programming environment for teaching novice programmers, the cT system described above, a system for automatic creation of graphical database displays, and a flight-simulator control program. Most of the systems have seen extensive use, so the designers' functional descriptions generally reflect actual experience rather than goals or guesses.

The test showed a moderate to substantial degree of agreement between the rules' predictions and the actual system designs, according to the standard interpretation of the kappa statistic [LK77]. Most of the discrepancies could be classified either as legitimate differences of design opinion, or as small errors or oversights in the rules that had not come to light in prior test cases. (An example of such an error is that the rules treat all varieties of state-based communication as about equally expensive in processing power, whereas actually the forms providing hints are more efficient than pure-state communication. To maintain experimental rigor, the rules were not modified to correct such errors after the formal experiment began.)

The only area in which the rules showed little correlation to the actual designs was that of representational choices: the notation for the user-interface definition dimension described previously, and one other dimension that provides a similar classification for representation of application-specific semantic information. It may be that corrections and additions to the rules would improve this result. However, both of these design choices are heavily influenced by considerations of design-time methods and procedure. Since the present design space deals mainly with issues of run-time structure, it may well be that the space provides insufficient information to make correct choices in these two dimensions.

In that case, the space would need to be extended to cover questions of design procedure before these dimensions could be handled reliably.

These are remarkably good results when one considers the limited amount of information in the rules (Section 5.1.3 contains about 10 percent of the full set). This suggests that the design space provides considerable leverage for the rules; that is, the classifications made by the design space make it easier to select the right type of design.

Furthermore, these rules were developed and tuned to follow the author's own judgments and those of the designers whose systems he studied while preparing the design space. This experiment compared the rules to the judgments of a completely separate group of designers. The extent of correlation is therefore especially striking: it depends not only on the rules successfully representing the knowledge on which they were based, but on agreement between two unrelated groups of designers. Therefore, this experiment shows that

- There is a significant body of agreement among expert user-interface system designers about structural choices.
- The design space and rules capture (at least part of) that agreement.

Though the particular set of rules tested in this experiment has many flaws, these results strongly suggest that the overall approach is valid and powerful.

This experiment is described in more detail in [Lan90b].

5.1.6   How the Design Space Was Prepared

The design space and rules described here were based on an extensive survey of existing user-interface systems. The space was formed by searching for classifications that brought systems with similar properties together. The rules were then prepared on the basis of observed correlations. We can compare this process to the development of biological taxonomies through natural history: the biologist also surveys and classifies existing forms and then looks for explanatory theories.

An obvious limitation of this approach is that it may not yield much insight about new structures (although the design space can call attention to untried combinations of known alternatives). However, for the purpose of codifying known practice this is not a major problem.

A more serious objection is that important dimensions may be overlooked. It seems difficult to demonstrate that a given design space covers everything that may be of interest at a particular level of abstraction. (Obviously a practical design space cannot cover all possible ways of looking at a software system, so some such restriction is necessary.) The experimental results suggest that functional (and perhaps also structural) dimensions associated with design methods may need to be added to the present space, so it is clear that the risk is real.

On the other hand, experience with this space suggests that getting rid of extraneous dimensions is just as important and difficult. For example, of the twenty-five functional dimensions originally defined for the space, it turns out that only about ten or twelve have significant impact; the other dozen seem to have considerably less influence, and perhaps should have been omitted entirely. In the structural dimensions, it proved possible to omit many design choices because they turned out to be closely correlated with choices that were retained. For example, the classification of application-interface abstraction level was sufficient to predict many properties of that interface, such as the nature of data types exchanged across it. Hence, those properties did not need to be represented by separate dimensions.

At present, refinement through practical use seems the only way to remove such bugs from a design space. When more experience has been gained with software design spaces, patterns will emerge that should lead to a more theoretical, rigorous way of creating spaces. A thought-provoking observation about the present space is that the top ten functional dimensions just alluded to show a strong bias towards measures of system flexibility. Of the example dimensions in Section 5.1.2 (all drawn from the top ten), user customizability, user-interface adaptability across devices, and application portability across user-interface styles each measure a different aspect of flexibility. Requirements of this kind turn out to substantially outweigh any specific system properties (such as the nature or speed of I/O devices). Perhaps this is an artifact of the methodology, or a unique characteristic of user interfaces; but perhaps flexibility will some day be recognized as a fundamental determinant of many kinds of software structures.

5.1.7   SUMMARY

This work attacks the problem of organizing software design knowledge to create routine design methods. Advances in this area promise not only to improve the basic process of software design, but to simplify a key task of software maintenance (namely understanding another person's design) and to provide a way of organizing the training of software engineers.

The underlying model of the design process is that one works from system requirements towards a completed design in several steps, or levels of abstraction. The particular design step considered here is the transition from high-level functional specifications to a gross system organization or architecture. We create a design space that describes the key functional specifications and the key structural choices to be made. Within this space, we formulate design rules that capture practical or theoretical knowledge about suitable choices for given requirements.

Since we view this technique as an engineering aid, the design rules need not be perfect to be useful. An informal set of rules (perhaps better called guidelines) can be useful simply by helping the designer to reject inferior choices quickly; this leaves more time available to consider and choose among the reasonable alternatives. In fact, even without rules the design space can be useful: it serves as a compact summary of different design approaches, and so can help the designer to avoid overlooking a good solution. Similarly, the functional side of the space reminds the designer of crucial considerations.

In the longer run, a reliable set of such design rules could serve as the basis for an automatic design assistant, or even for fully automatic system construction. The rule set experimented with here is a long way from that point, but seems already usable as a set of informal guidelines.

The present work has investigated only one domain of software design, namely, the architecture of user-interface systems. This was an essential limitation in order to create a design space of manageable size. Other researchers may undertake the task of building design spaces and rules for other domains—both other kinds of systems, and other levels of abstraction in the design process. Aside from being useful in their own right, such studies will show whether or not this approach really is a general-purpose method for organizing software engineering knowledge. Eventually, the combination of such studies may lead to the discovery of general principles about software design; for example, some kinds of design dimensions may be found to be universal.

5.2   The Quantified Design Space

by Toru Asada, Roy F. Swonger, Nadine Bounds, and Paul Duerig

5.2.1   Overview

Analysis of software artifacts has been studied and practiced for several decades. Theoretical and empirical measurements of system performance, complexity, reliability, testability, and other desirable qualities have become an integral part of the software engineering discipline. While these types of analysis are important, the software artifact is only the last step in the process of creating a product. It is now widely recognized that software can be only as good as the design from which it is produced.

The increasing attention paid to software design has not been accompanied by the development of tools to analyze these designs. Prototyping techniques can demonstrate feasibility or investigate particular questions about a design, and formal software inspections can find errors in a design before the process proceeds to a later stage of development [Hum90]. Formal specification languages allow designers to make assertions about a design [Hou91], but there is still no tool for the systematic and quantitative analysis of designs. Ideally, such a tool would obviate the need to actually construct a prototype, and would provide some measurement of the ability of a design to meet the requirements that the product must address. The tool should enable a designer to apply knowledge about the application domain and about software design and construction. Of course, to be useful the tool must provide timely feedback and results.

The quantified design space (QDS) was developed by the authors while working as a project team in the Master of Software Engineering (MSE) program at Carnegie Mellon University (CMU). The purpose of the QDS is to analyze and compare software designs in a specific application domain. The QDS is a structured encapsulation of design knowledge, implemented in a software spreadsheet, for use by system and software designers. Based on the concepts of quality function deployment (QFD) and design space, the QDS is a mechanism for translating system requirements into functional and structural design alternatives, and for analyzing these alternatives in a quantitative manner. The QDS can also be used to produce a model design for a desired system, analyze and compare existing designs, or suggest improvements for an existing product.

5.2.2   Background

The quantified design space is based on two foundation concepts, the design space and quality functional deployment.

DESIGN SPACE

The use of a design space for software system design was proposed by Lane (Section 5.1). As we have seen, a design space identifies the key functional and structural dimensions used to create a system design in a specific application domain. The design space is multi-dimensional, and each dimension describes a variation in one system characteristic or requirement. Values along a dimension correspond to different design alternatives. Rules are used to encapsulate design knowledge in the form of relationships between alternatives in different dimensions of the design space. Figure 5.1 shows two dimensions of a design space for user interfaces.

Dimensions. The dimensions of a design space may be functional or structural in nature. Functional dimensions describe aspects of the problem space as functional- and performance-related design alternatives, while structural dimensions describe the solution space as a set of alternative implementation characteristics. Lane's example was a design space for user interfaces.

Rules. Some dimensions of the design space are related to each other, and some are independent. Lane describes the relationships between dimensions as a set of rules that can be categorized as those linking functional to structural dimensions, and those interconnecting structural dimensions. The first category allows system requirements to drive a structural design, while the latter ensures the internal consistency of the design.

Lane also discusses automated application of the rules of a design space. Rules may be expressed as positive or negative weights assigned to a combination of design alternatives. Once a set of design choices is selected, we can calculate the score of the design by summing up the weights of the applicable rules. Lane prepared a set of rules which could be evaluated mechanically, and validated the design space and rules in an experiment using six different user-interface systems.

QUALITY FUNCTION DEPLOYMENT

Quality Function Deployment (QFD) is a quality assurance technique that helps translate customer needs into the technical requirements needed at each stage of product development—from requirements analysis through design, implementation, and into manufacturing and support. QFD has been used by Japanese automobile companies since 1977 with impressive results, and has since spread to other industries in both Japan and the U.S. [Sul86]. Fundamental to QFD is the goal that the "voice of the customer" must be manifested in each step of the product development process. The QFD philosophy focuses on achieving a common understanding among all stakeholders in the product development process. This approach brings the following benefits: [Bro91, Sul86]

- Issues in the development are raised in timely fashion, and can be dealt with before they become problems.
- Decisions are recorded in a structured framework, and can be traced when necessary.
- Requirements are less likely to be misinterpreted at any step in the development process.

- Rework is reduced, and the need for changes is minimized, resulting in shorter time to market.
- Product knowledge is captured in a defined structure, and is accessible both for the current product development and for future work.
- Customer needs are more closely matched by the final product.

The QFD Process. The QFD philosophy is supported by a specific graphical notation and a well-defined process for translating requirements to realization mechanisms at each stage of product development. The steps of the QFD process are described below [Bro91] and illustrated in Figure 5.4. The product being analyzed is a multiuser design system for cooperative engineering. The anticipated use of the system would include multiple, simultaneous users, each working with a different aspect of a single design:

1. The scope of the product or service being developed is established, and representatives from each stakeholder in the development process are recruited to participate in the QFD. Customer needs are gathered, as stated by the customers in their own language. A cross-functional team analyzes these requirements to reach a common understanding of terms and vocabulary. These requirements are entered in a column on the left side of a QFD chart, as shown in Figure 5.4.

2. The QFD team identifies realization mechanisms that will help meet the customer requirements. These realization mechanisms are entered across the top of the QFD chart, thus creating a matrix relating customer requirements to realization mechanisms.

3. Target values are established for each realization mechanism, and are entered along the bottom of the correlation matrix. These targets may be qualitative or quantitative goals, but in either case the target must be objectively verifiable.

4. The relationship between each mechanism and each customer need is established, to determine which mechanisms are most important in achieving customer needs. Each relationship is denoted by a graphical symbol indicating a strong, medium, or weak relationship between a requirement and a realization mechanism in the QFD matrix (where the realization mechanism does not help meet the requirement, the cell in the matrix is left blank). For example, the use of a database manager has a strong relationship to the performance of the system when working with large designs, but a weak relationship to the system's ability to apply expert knowledge. The relationships are given a numerical weight that is used in calculating the technical importance of each mechanism.

   The analysis of these relationships is one of the strengths of QFD. A realization mechanism such as the use of a database manager may originally be intended to help support cooperative design, but further analysis may show that an efficient database also helps realize the customer need for good performance when working with large designs. This type of "side benefit" is shown clearly by the QFD framework.

5. Any positive or negative correlation between realization mechanisms is determined. A positive correlation indicates that two realization mechanisms complement each other well, while a negative correlation denotes that one realization mechanism may interfere with the implementation of another. These correlations are expressed in the

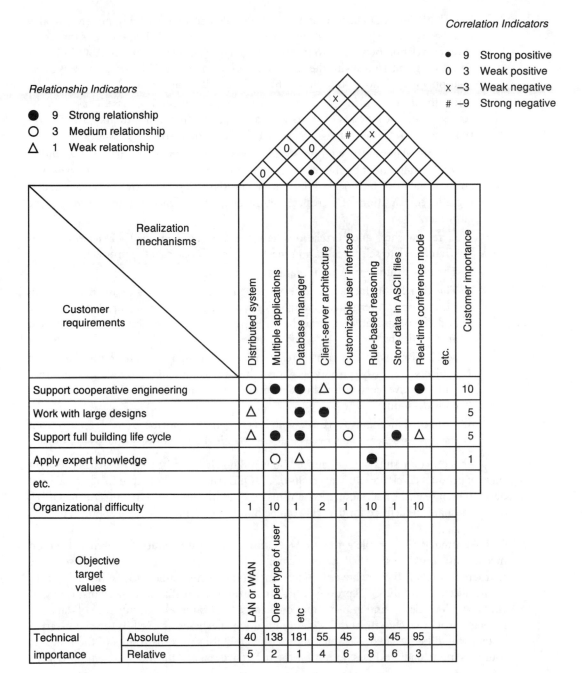

FIGURE 5.4   Sample QFD Framework

"roof" of the QFD chart by graphical symbols denoting strongly positive, weakly positive, weakly negative, or strongly negative correlations (a blank means that there is no correlation between two mechanisms). For example, the use of ASCII files for data storage interferes with the use of a database manager. This strong negative correlation will be factored into the analysis of the QFD chart in step 8.

6. The difficulty of implementing each realization mechanism is assessed, based on the strengths and weaknesses of the organization. The difficulty rating for each realization mechanism is recorded in a row just above the objective target values.

7. The technical importance rating is calculated by multiplying the customer weighting for each requirement by the relationship factor for each realization mechanism. The absolute value for technical importance is translated into a relative ranking, indicating the contribution of a realization mechanism to meeting the needs of the customer.

8. After relationships and correlations have been determined, the QFD team analyzes the framework to select realization mechanisms to be used in the product:

   a. The target value for each mechanism is finalized.

   b. The correlation factors may be inspected to spot conflicts between realization mechanisms. Alternatively, weights may be assigned to these correlation factors, and the organizational difficulty rating for each mechanism can be calculated arithmetically.

   c. Mechanisms with negative correlation factors or high difficulty ratings are good subjects for early prototyping or other risk-reduction strategies, and those with negative correlation but low importance may simply be removed from consideration.

   d. Unneeded mechanisms (those with low technical importance) are removed from the framework, and any needs that are not adequately addressed are reexamined.

This process results in an organized body of knowledge to be used at each subsequent stage of product development. The results of the QFD can be used as input to a later stage of development (e.g., the realization mechanisms may become input to a manufacturing QFD), or the mechanisms defined for the QFD can be directly implemented when appropriate.

QFD Summary. To complete this QFD example, the target values for each realization mechanism would be specified, and the columns for the realization mechanisms would be reordered to reflect their relative technical importance. This framework serves as input to the next iteration of the QFD process, which translates these realization mechanisms to specific lower-level design and implementation factors. For example, a specific type of database manager would be chosen, and the communication mechanisms used in the client-server system would be specified. Each iteration of the QFD thus uses the results of the previous round as input, and produces output for the successive stage in the development process.

5.2.3   QUANTIFIED DESIGN SPACE

As stated in Section 5.2.2, the QDS is based on the concepts of design space and QFD. QDS takes from the concept of design space the decomposition of a design into dimensions and alternatives, and the positive or negative correlation between design dimensions. The translation of requirements to realization mechanisms, the analysis of relationships between mechanisms and requirements, and the determination of correlations between mechanisms come from QFD. The implementation of the design space on the QFD framework is called the quantified design space.

IMPLEMENTING A DESIGN SPACE ON A QFD FRAMEWORK

The rules of the design space embody design knowledge in the form of positive and negative assertions about the relationship between different aspects of the product being developed. The QFD process captures design knowledge in the relationships between realization mechanisms and customer needs, and in the correlation factors among the mechanisms themselves. This common purpose—the capture of design knowledge—can be implemented by using QFD charts as a framework for the dimensions and alternatives of the design space.

The design space organizes the choices available for a particular design into a hierarchy of dimensions and alternatives. The result of a QFD process represents a particular set of these choices, one from each dimension of the design space. By explicitly including all alternatives of each dimension in the QFD framework, each alternative can be analyzed for its ability to meet the needs of the customer and for its correlation to alternatives in other dimensions.

The rules of the design space can then be captured in the relationships and correlation factors of the QFD framework. A rule stating that a particular system architecture "favors" a type of user interface, for example, indicates a positive correlation factor between those particular design alternatives. Similarly, a rule stating that a distributed system "cannot be implemented" with a monolithic program structure indicates a negative correlation. The designer determines the strength of these correlations according to his or her expertise, and this knowledge is captured in the QFD framework.

The number of dimensions and alternatives in the design space of any application domain is large, and the relationships between the many possible sets of design choices will probably be too complicated to be understood without automated assistance. Automation of a QDS is therefore a necessity. The matrix organization of both the design space and the QFD framework is handled well by software spreadsheets, as demonstrated by Figure 5.5.

Chart #1

Concepts	Customer weight	Functional #1			Functional #2			Functional #3			
		Alt #1	Alt #2	Alt #3	Alt #1	Alt #2	Alt #3	Alt #1	Alt #2	Alt #3	Alt #4
Requirement #1	10	1	9	0	9	3	1	0	0	0	0
Requirement #2	9	3	1	0	3	0	3	3	3	9	0
Requirement #3	2	1	3	0	3	0	0	1	1	3	0
Requirement #4	8	3	3	1	9	1	3	1	1	3	0
Calculated weight		63	129	8	195	38	61	37	37	111	0
Requirement #1		10	90	0	90	30	10	0	0	0	0
Requirement #2		27	9	0	27	0	27	27	27	81	0
Requirement #3		2	6	0	6	0	0	2	2	6	0
Requirement #4		24	24	8	72	8	24	8	8	24	0
Design decision			1		1					1	
Effective weight		0	129	0	195	0	0	0	0	111	0

FIGURE 5.5   Generalized Functional Design Space

Figure 5.5 depicts the functional level of a generalized quantified design space. The customer needs for the product are listed in the cells at the left of the spreadsheet, as in step 1 of the QFD process. The weights assigned to these requirements by the customers (in this case, the designer of the system) are placed in a separate column.

The functional dimensions and alternatives of the design space are placed along the top axis of the QDS, analogous to the realization mechanisms of the QFD. The relationship of each alternative to the customer requirements is entered in the corresponding cell of the spreadsheet, and a series of linear equations produces the calculated weight for each alternative. A higher weight indicates a greater contribution towards meeting the customer requirements. The calculated weight is further broken down by customer requirement, so the effect of an alternative on any single customer need can be readily deduced.

A binary design decision mask (1 or 0) represents the designer's choices. A "1" in the design decision mask indicates selection of an alternative from a dimension of the design space. The binary design decision mask filters the calculated weights, leaving an effective weight for each alternative. These effective weights serve as input to the structural design space shown in Figure 5.6.

Chart #2

Concepts		Effective weight	Structural #1				Structural #2		Structural #3			
Dimensions	Alternatives		Alt #1	Alt #2	Alt #3	Alt #4	Alt #5	Alt #1	Alt #2	Alt #1	Alt #2	Alt #3
Functional #1	Alt #1	0	1	1	1	3	1	0	9	3	0	3
	Alt #2	129	3	1	1	2	1	0	3	3	0	9
	Alt #3	0	3	1	1	2	1	0	3	9	0	9
Functional #2	Alt #1	195	3	3	0	0	1	1	9	0	0	9
	Alt #2	0	3	3	0	0	1	1	9	9	0	3
	Alt #3	0	1	1	0	0	1	1	9	0	0	3
Functional #3	Alt #1	0	0	0	1	0	0	0	3	3	1	3
	Alt #2	0	0	0	1	0	0	0	3	3	1	3
	Alt #3	111	0	3	0	0	1	0	3	3	1	3
	Alt #4	0	9	0	0	0	0	1	3	0	0	0
Calculated weight			972	1047	129	129	435	195	2475	720	111	3249
	Requirement #1		540	360	90	90	180	90	1080	270	0	1620
	Requirement #2		108	333	9	9	117	27	513	270	81	567
	Requirement #3		36	42	6	6	18	6	90	36	6	126
	Requirement #4		288	312	24	24	120	72	792	144	24	936
Design decision			1						1	1		1

FIGURE 5.6   Sample Structural Design Space

The structural design space is similar to the functional design space, but will generally be larger and more complex because of the larger number of inputs. In the example shown in Figure 5.6, the effective weights of the functional dimensions and alternatives are used in the same way as the customer weights in the functional design space of Figure 5.5.

The calculated weight for each structural design alternative can be further broken down by customer requirement. To do this, the effective weight for the functional alternatives is replaced by the calculated weight for each requirement from the functional design space depicted in Figure 5.5. This preserves traceability of structural alternatives to high-level design requirements.

Before the final score for a particular design is calculated, the calculated weights and design decisions of the structural design space are modified by the correlations between structural design choices. The spreadsheet in Figure 5.7 shows the correlation of all possible structural design alternatives for this particular domain. A correlation factor of 0.5 in a cell serves to average the scores of two alternatives, indicating that the alternatives are compatible in the same design. A correlation factor of 1 shows a strong positive correlation, and a factor of 0 indicates that two alternatives are mutually exclusive.

Root of chart #2

Concepts		Structural #1				Structural #2	Structural #3				
Dimensions	Alternatives	Alt #1	Alt #2	Alt #3	Alt #4	Alt #5	Alt #1	Alt #2	Alt #1	Alt #2	Alt #3
Structural #1	Alt #1		0	0.5	0.5	1	0.5	0.5	1	0.5	1
	Alt #2			0.5	1	0.5	1	1	1	0.5	0.5
	Alt #3				0	0.5	1	0	0.5	0	0
	Alt #4					0.5	0.5	0.5	0.5	0	0.5
	Alt #5						0.5	1	1	0.5	1
Structural #2	Alt #1							0	1	0.5	0.5
	Alt #2								0.5	0	0
Structural #3	Alt #1									0	0
	Alt #2										0
	Alt #3										

FIGURE 5.7   Correlation of Structural Design Alternatives

The correlation factors shown in Figure 5.7 feed into the final score of the design, shown in Figure 5.8. The following process is used to apply the correlation factors to each structural design selection:

1. Let $E_1 \ldots E_n$ be the effective weight of each selected structural design alternative.
2. Let C_{mn} be the correlation factor for alternatives m and n.
3. For each selected structural design alternative, add the effective weight of the design alternative to that of each other selected alternative, and multiply each term of the sum by the correlation factor from the matrix. The product sums are then added together, giving the final score for the design: Score $= SC_{ij} (E_i + E_j)$

The score for a set of design choices can be reported as a total, giving a score for the whole design. The score can also be broken down into partial scores for each customer need by selecting the effective weight separately for each requirement. Providing a partial score for each customer requirement may help identify areas for possible improvement in a design, or may highlight product strengths.

Score		5944.5
	Requirement #1	2970.0
	Requirement #2	985.5
	Requirement #3	225.0
	Requirement #4	1764.0

FIGURE 5.8 Sample Score of a Quantified Design Space

USING A QUANTIFIED DESIGN SPACE

Since the QDS is implemented on a spreadsheet, the user can select different alternatives and see the effect of these choices reflected immediately in the score of the design. However, the numbers and scores provided by a quantified design space are not an end in themselves. There is no absolute measure of the "goodness" of a design, so the scores produced by a completed quantified design space are unscaled numbers. Because the numbers have no units or dimensions, a QDS must therefore be carefully analyzed to be useful.

The most straightforward use of the QDS is to compare two existing designs and determine how well each meets a particular set of customer needs. The user can enter the choices represented by each design into the QDS spreadsheet, producing a set of scores broken down by customer need. By comparing these scores, the user can identify competitive advantages or disadvantages or analyze trade-offs between two or more designs in a development effort.

The QDS also serves as an exploratory tool for designers. The electronic spreadsheet was developed as a predictive analytical tool, and the QDS is a natural extension of this idea to the realm of design analysis. The QDS embodies a collection of design knowledge, and the spreadsheet mechanism provides rigorous checking of dependencies that would be very difficult for human designers. The user of the QDS can enter design choices and receive immediate feedback on those choices (in the form of numerical scores), experimenting with various combinations of design choices.

Though the QDS functions more naturally as an analytic or exploratory tool, it can also be used to design a model or ideal system in a particular application domain. This use of the QDS is an extension of exploratory design, with the expressed goal of achieving the highest possible score in a particular application domain. Selecting an ideal set of design choices is not easy—simply selecting the highest-scoring alternative in each functional and structural dimension may not work due to the complex relationships between structural alternatives. However, an intelligent designer working with a QDS can select a set of very good choices in a matter of hours. The QDS can also be used to design the worst possible system for an application domain. Such a set of design choices is useful for statistical analysis of a design, as explained in the statistical analysis below.

Producing a model or ideal system is most useful when using the QDS to identify possible improvements to an existing product or design. Since the scores produced by the QDS are dimensionless numbers, we need some sort of benchmark value to determine whether a number is relatively high or low. A model system serves well in this capacity. The scores for an existing design can be obtained from the QDS spreadsheet and compared against the scores for the ideal system. Categories in which the existing system scores relatively low are good candidates for improvement in future versions. This type of analysis may help guide resource allocation for a project.

Statistical Analysis Techniques. Statistical analysis techniques are useful when analyzing designs with a quantified design space. Four such techniques are spectrum analysis, contribution analysis, design selection analysis, and direct comparison analysis.

Spectrum Analysis: Spectrum analysis is based on the position of a particular set of design choices within the range between the best and the worst possible designs. This method can be used to evaluate the overall "goodness" of a particular set of design choices. The procedure for spectrum analysis follows:

1. Design a model system, as described above. Let S_b be the score of the model system.
2. Let S_w be the score of the worst possible set of design choices.
3. Let S be the score of the set of design choices to be analyzed.
4. The spectrum index I_s of S is calculated by the formula

$$I_s = \frac{S - S_w}{S_b - S_w} \times 100$$

The resulting spectrum index I_s is a percentile number indicating the overall score of a design. A spectrum index of 100 indicates that the set of choices is ideal—that the score for these choices matches that of the model system. Conversely, a spectrum index of 0 results from scores equal to those of the worst possible design. A better set of design choices will result in a higher index.

The advantage of spectrum analysis is that it directly evaluates a particular set of design choices in comparison to an ideal system. However, due to possible negative correlation between design choices, combining the highest choices of all dimensions will not necessarily yield the highest score. The same is true of combining the worst choices. Obtaining the best and worst set of design choices is thus a trial-and-error activity.

Contribution Analysis: Contribution analysis is used to identify the reasons that one set of design choices gets a lower score than another. This method can be used to identify possible improvements for a particular set of design choices.

Contribution analysis is based on the premise that the difference between two sets of scores comes from the differences between the individual choices of each design. The method identifies the amount of contribution from each difference to the final combined score. Contribution analysis is performed as follows.

1. Compare the best design choices with the design choices of a particular system, and identify the QDS dimensions where the choices of the two systems are different.
2. Perform the following for each dimension identified in step 1:
   a. In the dimension i of the ideal system, change the design choice from the best choice to the choice of the system being measured (all the other choices remain best).
   b. Calculate the new score of the design choices obtained in step 2a.
   c. The contribution factor of the dimension i (F_i) is the difference between the best score and the score obtained in step 2b.
   d. The contribution index of the ith dimension (C_i) can be calculated by the following equation, where n is the number of the dimensions.

$$C_i = \frac{F_i}{\sum_n F_n}$$

If C_i is large, this means that the system could be improved if the design choice of the ith dimension is changed to the best choice. Therefore, the dimensions with large contribution indices are good candidates for improvement.

The advantage of contribution analysis is that the contribution of each dimension to the final design can be evaluated separately and as a concrete number. However, since the score of a design depends on the combination of the design choices, it may be difficult to separate the dimensions from each other. Isolating a particular dimension from other dimensions has less meaning than considering all choices together. Further, identifying a dimension for possible improvement does not address the negative effect that a change in that dimension may have on the overall design of the system. The best design choice for a specific dimension may conflict with design choices in other dimensions of a system. Contribution analysis must therefore be used in the context of the overall system score.

Design Selection Analysis: Design selection analysis computes the number of dimensions where a particular system implements the best choices. This method can also be used to evaluate the overall "goodness" of a system. Design selection analysis is performed as follows.

1. Let N_s be the number of dimensions where a particular system implements the same choices as the ideal system.
2. Let N_a be the total number of dimensions in the design space.
3. The design selection index d is calculated by the following equation.

$$d = \frac{N_s}{N_a} \times 100$$

If the best choices and the worst choices are evaluated by this method, they will receive indices of 100 and 0, respectively. Therefore, the higher the index of a system, the better the system. This method is very simple and easy to understand. However, since it only considers the number of the design choices, it does not consider the importance of each choice.

Direct Comparison Analysis: Direct comparison analysis is based on spectrum analysis; it compares two sets of design choices to determine the amount by which one is an improvement over the other. Direct comparison is performed as follows.

1. Let I_1 and I_2 be the spectrum indices of the two systems to be compared.
2. The improvement index I_{mp} is calculated by the equation below:

$$I_{mp} = I_1 - I_2$$

In other words, the index is calculated by using the scores of the two systems, S_1 and S_2, and those of the best/worst system, S_b and S_w, as follows:

We define that system 1 has been improved by I_{mp} over system 2. If I_{mp} is a negative number, then system 1 has regressed from system 2.

This method can compare two different designs of the same application domain and evaluate how much one system has improved over or degraded from the other system. Since the method normalizes the improvement index into [0, 100] range, it does not consider the range of the scores for each customer requirement. This has the effect of weighting each customer need identically, which may not be desirable in every case.

For example, a system might be improved over another system by 30 in both response time and ease of use. This does not necessarily mean that the system has been improved proportionally by the same amount in both areas, because the actual score range of response time might be much bigger than that of ease of use. However, further analysis would highlight these differences.

5.2.4   CONCLUSION

The quantified design space is a powerful software engineering tool that facilitates the requirements elicitation, design, and evaluation phases of software development. The QDS combines the techniques of design space—a method of organizing the domain knowledge of an application domain—and quality function deployment, a quantitative method of breaking a goal down into weighted subgoals and calculating their priority for the project with a linear equation.

By combining these two techniques, the QDS provides its user with a software engineering tool that can be used in various ways. First, the QDS can be used to systematically organize the knowledge about an application domain. Second, once a well-organized QDS is established, it can be used to construct a model design by selecting the set of design choices which receives the highest score. Third, a well-organized QDS can be used to quantitatively evaluate existing designs and identify areas of improvement. The statistical methods described in Section 5.2.3 are used in these activities.

As software engineers acquire domain knowledge from various sources, such as interviewing domain experts, meeting with customers, or independent research, they can use the QDS and organize this domain knowledge in a consistent manner. The better the domain is understood, the more useful the QDS becomes. The advantages of developing a QDS are that it helps engineers to understand an application domain, and a well-organized QDS is a good way to communicate domain knowledge to other people.

The QDS is easy to implement on a spreadsheet, where different charts implement different types of rules. The advantage of implementing a QDS on a spreadsheet is that a user can interactively find the model design selection and evaluate existing designs. Users can also change the selections easily and get immediate feedback.

The QDS was used in a studio project for the Master of Software Engineering program at Carnegie Mellon University. The ARMILLA Prototype Evaluation and Development (APED) project team developed a QDS for the architectural computer aided design (CAD) system domain, implemented it on Microsoft Excel spreadsheets, and used it in the evaluation phase of the project. The team compared two prototypes based on the APED QDS, and identified possible improvements for each prototype. The results of the analysis were consistent with the intuition of the project team, and demonstrated this intuition in a quantitative manner. This case study effectively validates the QDS concept.

Although the QDS is a powerful tool, it does have some limitations. First, due to the way the QDS is organized, all rules must be broken down into relationships between two alternatives of different dimensions; rules that pertain to the combination of more than three alternatives cannot be directly defined on the QDS. For example, a rule such as "alternative x in dimension X and alternative y in dimension Y do not work together if alternative z in dimension Z is chosen" cannot be directly defined. Second, though the current QDS defines the relationship of structural design alternatives in a "roof," there is no similar correlation of functional alternatives. Including the functional correlations would provide a more accurate analysis of designs.

There are several topics for further research based on the QDS. First, as mentioned above, the correlation between functional alternatives needs to be analyzed using the same method as the structural alternatives, so that the relationship between the functional alternatives can be defined and can contribute to the score used to analyze designs. Second, the rules written in natural language are translated subjectively by the QDS developer, and will reflect the developer's biases. An objective method of translating the rules into numbers is needed. For example, the rule might translate adjectives and adverbs into numbers: strong or "very much" would be scored as a 9, "somewhat" would also be scored as a 3, and "little" might be scored as a 1.

Third, the effect of the correlation factors of the structural design roof is not fully understood in the formulas as currently defined. Study of these correlation factors may suggest changes in the range of values used to represent positive or negative correlations. Fourth, the cases where multiple alternatives are selected in one dimension have not been fully analyzed. Study of these cases may result in changes in the formulas of the roof, or in the range of the numbers in the roof. With some modifications and extensions, the QDS can be an even more powerful tool for software engineers in a wide range of applications: analyzing application domains, quantifying design knowledge, and comparing models to develop the optimal software design.

6

FORMAL MODELS AND SPECIFICATIONS

Good architectural design has always been a major factor in determining the success of a software system. However, while there are many useful architectural paradigms (such as pipelines, layered systems, and client-server organizations—outlined in Chapter 2), they are typically understood only in an idiomatic way and applied in an ad hoc fashion. Consequently, software system designers have been unable to fully exploit commonalities in system architectures, make principled choices among design alternatives, specialize general paradigms to specific domains, or teach their craft to others.

One important step towards a more scientific basis for design, therefore, is an appropriate formal foundation for software architecture. But what exactly does this mean? This chapter illustrates three approaches to formalizing software architecture. First, we briefly consider the nature of formal specification as it might apply to software architecture. Next we consider an example of an architecture for a specific system. This specification was produced as part of an industrial software development project. Then we illustrate a quite different use of formalism as a way to understand the meaning of an architectural style and its associated design space. We present formalisms for two different styles: the pipe-and-filter style and implicit invocation. For each of these formalisms we describe the advantages of each approach and speculate about the prospects of specifications that go beyond issues of functionality.

6.1 The Value of Architectural Formalism

It is generally agreed that formal models and techniques for formal analysis are cornerstones of a mature engineering discipline, but engineering disciplines use them in many different ways. Formalisms can be used to provide precise, abstract models and to provide analytical techniques based on these models. They can be used to provide notations for describing specific engineering designs. They are also useful for simulating behavior.

It is reasonable to expect that formalism will have a wide variety of uses in the area of software architecture as well. Indeed, we can enumerate several different things that might be formalized:

1. **The architecture of a specific system.** Formalisms of this kind allow the software architect to plan a particular system. Such formalisms can become part of the specification of the system, augmenting the informal characterizations of the system's architecture, and perhaps permitting specific analyses of the system.

2. **An architectural style.** Formalisms of this kind can be used to describe architectural abstractions for families of systems. Such formalisms have at least two purposes: (1) to make precise the common idioms, patterns, and reference architectures now used informally by designers; and (2) to elucidate a portion of the architectural space by showing how different architectures can be treated as specializations of a common abstraction.

3. **A theory of software architecture.** Formalisms of this kind can clarify the meaning of generic architectural concepts, such as architectural connection, hierarchical architectural representation, and architectural style. Ideally such formalisms would provide a deductive basis for analyzing systems at an architectural level. For example, such a theory might provide rules for determining when an architectural description is well formed.

4. **Formal semantics for architectural description languages.** This kind of formalism treats architectural description as a language issue and applies traditional techniques for representing the semantics of languages.

Simply recognizing that architectural formalisms may be useful in many ways does not, of course, provide much guidance for carrying out these different kinds of formalization or comparing their relative benefits. To help clarify these issues, we present three examples that illustrate some of the categories outlined above.

We use the Z specification language throughout the examples. The final section of this chapter summarizes the aspects of Z that we use. While a deep understanding of Z should not be necessary to appreciate the general ideas, the curious reader may wish to consult other references on the language [PST91, Spi89b].

6.2 Formalizing the Architecture of a Specific System

Many software systems start with an architectural design. These are typically described informally, since there may be no way to directly express the abstractions at this level of design in common notations for describing the structure of a software system. As we discuss in Chapter 7, module interconnection languages and the modularization facilities of programming languages are often inadequate because they require the system designer to translate architectural abstractions into low-level primitives provided by the programming language. Other notations may be appropriate for special kinds of architectural decomposition (e.g., object-oriented architectures), but may not apply to other situations and, again, may force the designer to use a lower level of abstraction than is appropriate.

To address this problem, we may use a formal specification language to describe the architecture of a specific system. To illustrate, we consider a formal architectural specification of an oscilloscope developed at Tektronix, Inc.[1] The purpose of this specification is to provide a precise characterization of the system-level functions that determine the overall product functionality.

Digital oscilloscopes and many other instrumentation systems are currently implemented by complex software systems, often involving multiple processors, sophisticated user interfaces, and an interface to external computing networks. A significant challenge in designing these systems is to find software organizations that permit rapid internal reconfiguration, exploitation of advanced signal-processing hardware and software, and flexible user interfaces.

The architectural framework that we developed to meet these requirements decomposes the overall processing of an instrumentation system into a graph of transformations. Analog signals enter the system, pass through a network of transformations, and emerge as pictures and measurements that are displayed to the user on the front panel of the instrument. In this respect, we can view the system as a instance of a pipe-and-filter architectural style (see Section 3.2).

However, in addition to processing data, each of the individual transformers has an interface that allows the user to tune the transformation by configuring it through parameter settings. For example, the transformation that determines how a waveform is displayed on a screen is parameterized by scaling and positioning factors that allow the user to zoom and pan the display over a signal. Similarly, a signal-acquisition transformation is parameterized by delay and duration, which partially determine how a given signal will be sampled for display.

To describe the architecture of a specific instrumentation system, one must specify each of the component transformations (or filters), how they are interconnected, and what data is communicated between them. Figure 6.1 illustrates the architecture of a small (and greatly simplified) portion of an oscilloscope. This corresponds roughly to the kinds of informal diagrams that an engineer might draw to describe the architecture of a particular system.

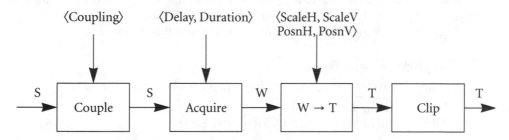

FIGURE 6.1   An Acquisition Channel of an Oscilloscope

To formalize this, we begin by characterizing the data that the system manipulates. We model *signals, waveforms,* and *traces* as functions over the primitive domains of time,

---

[1] This is the example we considered in Section 3.2. For a more detailed treatment of this specification, see [DG90, GD90].

volts, and screen coordinates. Signals (S) represent the inputs to the oscilloscope, waveforms (W) the data as it is stored internally, and traces (T) the pictures shown to a user.

$Signal == AbsTime \longrightarrow Volts$
$Waveform == AbsTime \rightarrowtail Volts$
$Trace == Horiz \rightarrowtail Vert$

For each of the components (represented by boxes in Figure 6.1) we provide a formal description that explains the configuration parameters, and for each configuration, what function is computed by the transformer. Formally we accomplish this by treating each component as a higher-order function: when we apply such a function to its configuration parameters, we get a new function that represents the resulting transformation.

To illustrate, consider the specification for the first component, called *Couple*. This transformer is used to subtract a DC offset from a signal. In this case the user has three choices of parameterization: DC, AC, and Ground. Choosing DC leaves the signal unchanged; AC subtracts the appropriate DC offset; GND produces a signal whose value is 0 volts at all times. As a higher-order function, the first parameter (of type *Coupling*) determines what the resulting function (of type $Signal \longrightarrow Signal$) will be.

$Coupling ::= DC \mid AC \mid GND$

> $Couple: Coupling \longrightarrow Signal \longrightarrow Signal$
> ___
> $Couple\ DC\ s = s$
> $Couple\ AC\ s = (\lambda\ t : AbsTime \bullet s(t) - dc(s))$
> $Couple\ GND\ s = (\lambda\ t : AbsTime \bullet 0)$

As a second example, a *Waveform* is obtained from a *Signal* by extracting a time slice. The waveform is identical to the signal, except that it is defined only over a bounded interval. That interval is determined by three things: two time values, called *delay* and *duration*, and a reference time, called a *trigger event*. The duration determines the length of the interval, while the delay determines when the interval is sampled relative to the trigger event. Again, we can use a higher-order function to model this component.

$TriggerEvent == RelTime$

> $Acquire: RelTime \times RelTime \longrightarrow TriggerEvent \longrightarrow Signal \longrightarrow Waveform$
> ___
> $Acquire\ (delay,dur)\ trig\ s =$
> $\{\ t : AbsTime \mid trig + delay \leq t \leq trig + delay + dur\ \} \lhd s$

We can provide similar descriptions of the other components of the architecture. However, we are not finished, since we still have to say how the pieces are put together. To do this, we interpret the connectors of the architecture as establishing input/output relationships between the components. Then we collect the individual components and compose them into a single subsystem.

As a first step, we package as a single "data structure" the parameters of the individual components: these become the collective parameters of the subsystem as a whole. The subsystem itself is then defined as the functional composition of the individual transformers.

ChannelParameters
_____

c : *Coupling*
delay, dur : *RelTime*
scaleH : *RelTime*
scaleV : *Volts*
posnV : *Vert*
posnH : *Horiz*

ChannelConfiguration : *ChannelParameters* $\longrightarrow$ *TriggerEvent* $\longrightarrow$ *Signal* $\longrightarrow$ *Trace*

ChannelConfiguration = (λ *trig* : *TriggerEvent* •
  Clip $\circ$ *WaveformToTrace* (*p.scaleH, p.scaleV, p.posnH, p.posnV*)
    $\circ$ *Acquire* (*p.delay, p.dur*) *trig* $\circ$ *Couple p.c*)

What have we gained by doing this? First, we have given a precise characterization of the system to be built. In this case the specification has been simplified considerably, but more realistic functions and configurations could have been defined. Second, and more importantly, we have exposed the architecture of the system as a configuration of components (here, parameterized data transformers) connected functionally through inputs and outputs. This characterization directly expresses the relevant architectural abstractions (of data transformations and stream connections) without requiring translation into the notation of any programming language. It also makes precise some architectural assumptions, such as the fact that components share data only via their connections, and the fact that external parameters must be evaluated before the components can perform their primary functions.

6.3 Formalizing an Architectural Style

While the specification outlined above has some nice properties, it also has a number of drawbacks. First, the underlying architectural style is not expressed explicitly; instead, it must be inferred from the description of the particular system. This leaves open some questions about possible elaborations on that design. For instance, in the previous example, is the absence of a cycle in the graph of transformations an accidental or essential feature of the specification? Second, the high level of abstraction avoids many important design issues, such as how data is actually transmitted between the filters or whether one should assume fair scheduling of the filters. A third problem is that architectural connection is implicit. Specifically, components were combined through functional composition. Thus, we cannot examine or reason about the system's topological properties independently of the system specification itself. In this section we show how to address some of these problems by explicitly formalizing an architectural style, in this case the pipe-and-filter style outlined in Section 2.2.

The components of a pipe-and-filter architectural style, *filters*, transform streams of data. Each filter has *input ports*, from which it reads data, and *output ports*, to which it writes results. A filter performs its computation incrementally and locally: a single computational step consists of reading a portion of the data available at its input ports, transforming that data, and writing it to the output ports. In addition, we usually think of the filters operating concurrently.

The connectors of the style, *pipes*, control the flow of data through the system. Each pipe links an output port to an input port, indicating the path that data will take and carrying out the transmission. Thus, a computational step in a pipe-and-filter system consists of either of two things: an incremental transformation of data by a filter or a communication of data between ports by a pipe.

To describe the pipe-and-filter architectural style formally we proceed in three steps. First, we define *filters*, the basic component of the architecture. Second, we define *pipes*, the basic connector of the architecture. Third, we show how pipes and filters are combined to form a complete system. For each of these three aspects of the architecture, we characterize both its static and its dynamic properties. To do this, we show how state is associated with each filter, pipe, or pipe-and-filter system. Then we show how a computation step can change that state.

In the following definitions, *FILTER*, *PORT*, *FSTATE*, and *DATA* are uninterpreted sets, and *Port_State* and *Partial_Port_State* are both defined as the partial function *PORT* $\rightarrowtail$ seq *DATA*.

6.3.1   FILTERS

A *Filter* ;is defined by its name, its ports, and its program. The ports of a filter are defined as a set of names. To model the idea that ports are directional, we partition them into a set of input ports and a set of output ports. We associate a type with each port. This represents the kind of data that the filter is prepared to process on that port. Note that this refines the informal model that filters and pipes operate over streams of data; in the formal model we see that these streams are actually *typed* data. In characterizing the types of data, we adopt a simple model: each type is a subset of *DATA*, the *alphabet* for the port.

Filter ───

filter_id : *FILTER*
in_ports, out_ports : **P** *PORT*
alphabets : *PORT* $\rightarrowtail$ **P** *DATA*
states : **P** *FSTATE*
start : *FSTATE*
transitions : (*FSTATE* × (*Partial_Port_State*)) $\longleftrightarrow$ (*FSTATE* × (*Partial_Port_State*))

───

start ∈ *states* ∧ *in_ports* ∩ *out_ports* = ∅ ∧ dom *alphabets* = *in_ports* ∪ *out_ports*
   $((c_1, ps_1), (c_2, ps_2))$ ∈ *transitions* ⇒ c_1 ∈ *states* ∧ c_2 ∈ *states* ∧
   dom ps_1 = *in_ports* ∧ dom ps_2 = *out_ports* ∧
   ($\forall$ *p* : *in_ports* • ran $(ps_1(p))$ ⊆ *alphabets*(*p*)) ∧
   ($\forall$ *p* : *out_ports* • ran $(ps_2(p))$ ⊆ *alphabets*(*p*))

───

The filter's program is defined in three parts: (1) a set of legal program states, (2) a start state, and (3) a mapping from inputs to outputs, with a change in state possible as a side effect. This provides a *state machine* view of a filter. The filter invariant includes predicates that act as consistency checks, ensuring, for example, that the filter program respects its port types and cannot put the filter in an illegal state.

The state of a filter during a computation (*Filter_State*) is composed of the current program state, *internal_state,* and the data that is either not yet read from an input port or that has been written to a port and has not yet been delivered to an input port at the other end of the pipe. The state of the filter's ports is represented by *pstate.*

Filter_State ————————————————————————————

f : *Filter*
internal_state : *FSTATE*
pstate : *Port_State*

---

internal_state $\in$ *f.states* $\wedge$ dom *pstate* $=$ *f.in_ports* $\cup$ *f.out_ports*
$\forall\ p$: dom *pstate* • ran $(pstate(p)) \subseteq f.alphabets(p)$

A computational step of a filter consists of reading some of the data from the inputs and writing data to the outputs. The relation between the two is based on those inputs, the internal state, and the program.

Filter_Compute ————————————————————————

$\Delta Filter\_State$

$f = f'$
$\exists\ ps_1, ps_2$: *Partial_Port_State* •
   $((internal\_state, ps_1), (internal\_state', ps_2)) \in f.transitions \wedge$
   $(\forall\ p : f.in\_ports •\ pstate(p) = ps_1(p) \ \widehat{}\ \ pstate'(p)) \wedge$
   $(\forall\ p : f.out\_ports •\ pstate(p) \ \widehat{}\ \ ps_2(p) = pstate'(p))$

These definitions formalize the intuition that a filter operates by transforming data incrementally. We see that the program defining the filter, *transitions,* is a local mapping from input data to output data: output can only depend on what is actually consumed, not on data yet to be consumed. This schema also clarifies the idea of "local" transformation: a filter *is* allowed to depend on computations it has performed in the past (*FSTATE* appears in the *transitions* relation), but it is not allowed to depend directly on anything outside the filter or on what it has written out (the "preconditions" of *transitions* are limited to *in_ports*).

6.3.2   Pipes

A pipe is simply a typed connection between two ports, one an output of a filter and the other an input to a filter.

Pipe _____

source_filter, sink_filter : Filter
source_port, sink_port : PORT
alphabet : **P** *DATA*

---
source_port ∈ source_filter.out_ports ∧ sink_port ∈ sink_filter.in_ports
source_filter.alphabets(source_port) = alphabet
sink_filter.alphabets(sink_port) = alphabet

The state of a pipe is divided into two parts: data that has been delivered to the sink and data that has not yet been delivered. We distinguish between these two sequences in order to model explicitly the transmission of data across the pipe. An important property of this model is that pipes are self-contained entities and can be reasoned about independently of filters.

Pipe_State _____

p : Pipe
source_data : seq DATA
sink_data : seq DATA

---
ran *source_data* ⊆ *p.alphabet* ∧ ran *sink_data* ⊆ *p.alphabet*

A consequence of this approach is that the same data is characterized in two places in the specification: at the ports of the filters and at the ends of the pipes. Although an implementation would be forced to treat the data either as part of the filters or as part of the pipes, in the mathematical model such redundancy is not a problem. When we combine pipes and filters into a unified system, we will simply identify the state on the two ends of the pipe with the state at the respective ports of the connected filters.

A computational step in a pipe delivers some of the data from its source to its sink. This definition clarifies several aspects of pipes that were not clear in the informal definition. First, data is not altered during transmission. Second, the order of the transmitted data is not changed. Third, a pipe connects exactly two ports. However, the amount of data transmitted is not specified. Here again, the model is intentionally abstract to allow different implementations to adopt different data-transmission policies.

Pipe_Compute _____

ΔPipe_State

---
p = p′
∃ *deliver : seq DATA | # deliver > 0 •*
    source_data = deliver ⌢ source_data′ ∧ sink_data′ = sink_data ⌢ deliver

---

6.3.3   PIPE-AND-FILTER SYSTEM

Next we describe how these objects are composed into a complete pipe-and-filter system. A system is defined as a collection of filters and a collection of pipes.

System

filters : $\mathbf{P}$ *Filter*
pipes : $\mathbf{P}$ *Pipe*

$\forall\ c_1, c_2$: filters $\bullet$ $c_1.filter\_id = c_2.filter\_id \Leftrightarrow c_1 = c_2$
$\forall\ p$: pipes $\bullet$ $p.source\_filter \in filters \land p.sink\_filter \in filters$
$\forall\ f$: filters; pt : $PORT\ |\ pt \in f.in\_ports$ $\bullet$
  $\#\{p$: pipes $|\ f = p.sink\_filter \land pt = p.sink\_port\} \leq 1$
$\forall\ f$: filters; pt : $PORT\ |\ pt \in f.out\_ports$ $\bullet$
  $\#\{p$: pipes $|\ f = p.source\_filter \land pt = p.source\_port\} \leq 1$

The consistency of a pipe-and-filter system is guaranteed by a number of requirements. First, each filter has a unique name. Second, there are no "dangling" pipes. This is an obvious requirement for being able to define a pipe-and-filter system without reference to other systems. It also clarifies that a pipe defines and is defined by the ports it connects; that is, pipes create the context within which filters operate. Third, we require that ports connect to no more than one pipe. This highlights the distinction between filters and pipes, and simplifies the model. If more complicated forms of data transmission are required—such as data broadcast—they must be modeled by the use of an intermediate filter.

The model does not, however, require that every port of a filter be connected to *some* pipe. This permits us to describe open pipe-and-filter systems by treating unbound input/output ports as system input/output channels. Further, this allows us to characterize systems that can later be combined with other pipe-and-filter systems by adding new pipe connections. Finally, as we discuss later, this approach allows us to treat systems hierarchically by encapsulating any pipe-and-filter system as an equivalent higher-level filter.

Just as a pipe-and-filter system is defined by its components, the state of a system is defined by the states of its components. States are defined for exactly those filters and pipes in the system. It is at this point that we identify the states of ports and pipes.

System_State

sys : *System*
filter_states : $\mathbf{P}$ *Filter_State*
pipe_states : $\mathbf{P}$ *Pipe_State*

$sys.filters = \{fs:filter\_states \bullet fs.f\} \land sys.pipes = \{ps$: $Pipe\_State \bullet ps.p\}$
$\forall\ fs_1, fs_2$: filter_states $\bullet$ $fs_1.f = fs_2.f \Leftrightarrow fs_1 = fs_2$
$\forall\ ps_1, ps_2$: pipe_states $\bullet$ $ps_1.p = ps_2.p \Leftrightarrow ps_1 = ps_2$
$\forall\ ps$: pipe_states $\bullet$ $\exists\ fs$: filter_states $\bullet$
  $ps.p.source\_filter = fs.f \land ps.source\_data = fs.pstate(ps.p.source\_port)$
$\forall\ ps$: pipe_states $\bullet$ $\exists\ fs$: filter_states $\bullet$
  $ps.p.sink\_filter = fs.f \land ps.sink\_data = fs.pstate(ps.p.sink\_port)$

A computational step in a pipe-and-filter system is either a computation step of a filter or a transmission of a pipe. The former is a straightforward extension of

Filter_Compute: the system nondeterministically executes a single filter, leaving the rest of the system unchanged.

_System_Filter_Step_

Δ*System_State*

$sys = sys'$
$\exists$ Filter_Compute •
 filter_states $\{\theta$ *Filter_State*$\} = $ *filter_states'* $\{\theta$ *Filter_State'*$\} \wedge$
 θ *Filter_State* $\in$ *filter_states* $\wedge$ θ *Filter_State'* $\in$ *filter_states'*

The definition of *System_Pipe_Step* is handled similarly. However, in this case it is somewhat more complicated to state that nothing changes but the executing pipe.

_System_Pipe_Step_

Δ*System_State*

$sys = sys'$
$\exists$ *Pipe_Compute* • θ *Pipe_State* $\in$ *pipe_states* $\wedge$ θ *Pipe_State'* $\in$ *pipe_states'* $\wedge$
 $(\forall$ *fs* : *filter_states*; *fs'* : *filter_states'*; *pt* : *PORT* | *fs.f* $=$ *fs'.f* •
  fs.internal_state $=$ *fs'.internal_state* $\wedge$
  $(pt \in$ *fs.f.in_ports* $\wedge$ *p.sink_filter* $\neq$ *fs.f* $\vee$ *p.sink_port* $\neq$ *pt* $\Rightarrow$
   fs.pstate$(pt) = $ *fs'.pstate*$(pt)) \wedge$
  $(pt \in$ *fs.f.out_ports* $\wedge$ *p.source_filter* $\neq$ *fs.f* $\vee$ *p.source_port* $\neq$ *pt* $\Rightarrow$
   fs.pstate$(pt) = $ *fs'.pstate*$(pt)))$

$$System\_Compute\_Step \;\hat{=}\; System\_Filter\_Step \vee System\_Pipe\_Step$$

We now define a pipe-and-filter system computation as a sequence of steps beginning with a start state and progressing through legal system computation steps. The start state of a system is one in which every filter is in its *start* state, every pipe empty, and every output port contains no data. We do not require unconnected ports to be empty since, as explained earlier, these ports are treated as system inputs and outputs.

CompleteComputation

trace : *seq System_State*

$\exists$ *sys* : *System* • $\forall$ *i* : dom *trace* • $(trace(i)).sys = sys$
$\exists$ *SystemStart* • θ *System_State* $= trace(1)$
$\exists$ *SystemFinal* • θ *System_State* $= trace(\#\,trace)$
$\forall$ *i* : 1 . . $(\#\,trace - 1)$ • $(\exists$ *System_State* ; *System_State'* | θ *System_State* $= trace(i)$
 $\wedge$ θ *System_State'* $= trace(i + 1)$ • *System_Compute_Step*$)$

A formal model such as this one provides a precise, mathematically based description of a family of systems. The model attempts to capture a class of systems that is otherwise understood only idiomatically, and to expose the essential characteristics of that family while hiding unnecessary details.

One of the benefits of doing this is that we can analyze various properties of systems designed in this style. Although we do not carry out the proof here, it is possible to demonstrate formally, for example, that such pipe-and-filter systems have the desirable property of hierarchy: connected subnets of pipes and filters can be encapsulated as a new filters.

Additionally the formalism allows us to consider specializations of the style. For example, a pipeline can be defined by adding a simple constraint to the basic architecture.

$$
\begin{array}{l}
\rule{0pt}{1em}\textit{Pipeline} \\[2pt]
\hline
\textit{System} \\[2pt]
\hline
\exists\ \textit{in, out} : \textit{PORT}; \ \textit{order} : (1 \mathinner{\ldotp\ldotp} \#\textit{filters}) \rightarrowtail \textit{filters} \bullet \\
\quad \#\textit{pipes} = \#\textit{filters} - 1 \wedge \\
\quad (\forall\ f : \textit{filters} \bullet f.\textit{in\_ports} = \{\textit{in}\} \wedge f.\textit{out\_ports} = \{\textit{out}\}) \wedge \\
\quad (\forall\ p : \textit{pipes} \bullet (\exists\ i : 1 \mathinner{\ldotp\ldotp} \#\textit{filters} - 1 \bullet \\
\qquad p.\textit{source\_port} = \textit{out} \wedge p.\textit{sink\_port} = \textit{in} \wedge \\
\qquad p.\textit{source\_filter} = \textit{order}(i) \wedge p.\textit{sink\_filter} = \textit{order}(i + 1)))
\end{array}
$$

6.4   FORMALIZING AN ARCHITECTURAL DESIGN SPACE

One of the difficulties in working with software architecture is that different designers may interpret an architectural idiom in different ways. For example, although two designers may both claim that their systems are built around a client-server paradigm, they may mean quite different things by that term [Ber92]. A related problem is that several systems may be designed with similar architectural structure, but the designers never recognize that these similarities exist. Consequently they miss opportunities to capitalize on the experience of other designers.

An architectural formalism can make relationships between architectures precise. To illustrate this, consider the problem of relating different systems built around the implicit invocation architectural style. As outlined in Section 2.4, implicit invocation systems are designed as systems in which components can announce events. Other components can be registered to receive announced events by associating one of the component's procedures with the event. When an event is announced, all procedures associated with it will be invoked automatically by the system; thus, an event announcement causes the "implicit" invocation of the components that have been registered for the event.

This simple description leaves many questions unanswered. What is the vocabulary of events? Can event announcements carry associated data? What is the level of concurrency in the handling of events? Different answers to these questions will lead to implicit invocation architectures with quite different properties [GS93a, NGGS93].

One way to formalize these relationships is to start with the simple architectural abstraction outlined above, and then show how specific systems refine that abstraction. We begin by assuming the existence of basic sets of events, methods, and component names.

Then we can model an architectural component (again using Z) as an entity that has a name and an interface consisting of a set of *methods* and a set of *events*.

[*EVENT, METHOD, CNAME*]

Component
name : *CNAME*
methods : **P** *METHOD*
events : **P** *EVENT*

A particular event (or method) is identified by a pair consisting of the name of a component and the event (or method) itself. In this way we can talk about the same event or method appearing in different components. (We use the type abbreviations *Event* and *Method* to refer to these pairs, respectively.)

$$Event == CNAME \times EVENT$$

$$Method == CNAME \times METHOD$$

An event system, *EventSystem*, consists of a set of components and an event manager. The event manager, *EM*, is a relation that associates events with methods that are to be invoked when that event is announced.

EventSystem
components: **P** *Component*
EM: *Event* $\longleftrightarrow$ *Method*

$\forall c_1, c_2$: *components* • $(c_1.name = c_2.name) \Leftrightarrow (c_1 = c_2)$
dom *EM* $\subseteq$ *Events components*
ran *EM* $\subseteq$ *Methods components*

The invariant of *EventSystem* asserts that the components in the system have unique names, and that the event manager relates events and methods that actually exist in the system.

This characterization of *EM* is extremely general. In particular, this model allows the same event to be associated with many different methods, and even with many methods of the same component. It also permits some events to be associated with no methods. Further, it leaves open the issue of what components can announce events, and whether there are any restrictions on the methods that can be associated with those events. (For further details about this model see [GN91].) To describe a more concrete architectural style, these (and other) issues would have to be resolved. Thus we have defined a generic, abstract architectural model that permits specialization to a variety of more specific architectural styles.

To illustrate how we can specialize this model to obtain a more concrete architectural style, we consider the implicit invocation mechanism that supports the Smalltalk-80 Model-View-Controller (MVC) paradigm [KP88]. This mechanism is based on the notion that any object can register as a "dependent" of any other object. When an object announces the *changed* event, the *update* method is implicitly invoked in each of its dependents. Thus, viewed as an implicit invocation system, the MVC provides a fixed, predetermined set of events (namely the *changed* event) and associated methods (namely the *update* method).

Formally, we first declare the *changed* event and *update* method to be elements of types *EVENT* and *METHOD*, respectively.

changed : *EVENT*
update : *METHOD*

We then model dependencies between objects as a relation between components. This dependency relation precisely determines the *EM* relation as follows: first, the events associated with each component are restricted to the set {*changed*}; and second, *EM* simply pairs *changed* events with the appropriate *update* methods.

ST80 ───

EventSystem
dependents : *Component* ⟷ *Component*

dom *dependents* ⊆ *components*
ran *dependents* ⊆ *components*
∀ *c* : *components* • *c.events* = {*changed* }
EM = { c_1, c_2: *components* | (c_1, c_2) ∈ *dependents* •
        ((c_1.*name*, *changed*), (c_2.*name*, *update*))}

A consequence of these definitions is that each dependent in the system must have *update* as one its methods. We could formulate this as a simple lemma to be proved about such a system. In its implementation, Smalltalk-80 supports this obligation by providing a default *update* method in the Object class, which is inherited by all other classes in the system.

A quite different application of an implicit invocation architectural style is the tool integration mechanism of the Field System [Rei90]. In a Field environment tools communicate by "broadcasting" interesting events. Other tools can register patterns that indicate which events should be routed to them and which methods should be called when an event matches that pattern. When an event is announced, a pattern matcher checks all registered patterns, invoking the associated method whenever a pattern is matched. For example, if a program editor announces when it has finished editing a module, a compiler might register for such announcements and automatically recompile the edited module.

To describe this behavior in terms of our basic model, we first define a new type of basic entity, *PATTERN*.

[*PATTERN*]

Next we associate a pattern matcher (*match*) with *EventSystem*, and a *register* relation that, for each component, associates patterns with the methods of that component. The register relation then determines *EM*.

Field

EventSystem
match : $EVENT \longleftrightarrow PATTERN$
register : $Component \longleftrightarrow (PATTERN \times METHOD)$

---

dom *register* $\subseteq$ *components*
$((c_1.name, e),(c_2.name, m)) \in EM \Leftrightarrow$
    $(\exists \, pat : PATTERN \bullet (c_2, (pat, m)) \in register \land (e, pat) \in match)$

The invariant guarantees that the Event/Method pairs in *EM* are those for which some registered pattern matches the event associated with the method.

What have we gained from this kind of formalization? First we have identified a common architectural abstraction (or style) shared by many systems. Second, we have exposed the similarities in two systems by showing how they are elaborations of the same basic formal architecture. Third, we have provided a template with which we can make other kinds of comparisons. (In other work, we have illustrated a number of these, including the implicit invocation mechanisms of Field, Forest, and APPL/A [GN91].) Moreover, the formal model is simple enough that students in a senior/masters-level course on software architecture are able to provide their own specializations to show how blackboard systems and spreadsheets can be characterized in this way [GSO+92, Gar94]. Third, as with the pipe-and-filter formalization, it is possible to provide a computational model associated with this style. Finally, the general pattern indicated in this and the pipe-and-filter models can be abstracted to provide a general framework for specifying such styles [AAG93].

6.5 TOWARD A THEORY OF SOFTWARE ARCHITECTURE

An important goal for researchers in software architecture is to clarify the basic nature of software architecture. What is a component? What is a connector? What might one mean by a *well-formed* architecture? What are reasonable rules for architectural decomposition, whereby a component or connector is itself represented by a subarchitecture?

Section 8.3 describes a first step towards answering these questions by presenting a formal language, called WRIGHT, for describing and reasoning about architectural interaction. Specifically, it provides a formal foundation for architectural connectors that allows one to characterize precisely many basic kinds of connectors: procedure call, event broadcast, pipes, and so on. Additionally, it allows one to describe connectors that represent more complex interactions, such as those defined by network protocols, database query protocols, and client-server protocols. Finally, it provides a way to check that an architectural description is well-formed, in the sense that components interact in ways consistent with the connector's specification.

6.6 WHAT NEXT?

As we have illustrated, different kinds of architectural formalism provide different benefits. A formal description of a specific system can precisely document a particular design and allow us to reason about the behavior of that system. A formal description of an architectural style allows us to characterize common architectural abstractions and idioms as well as to compare different uses of that idiom. A formal theory for software architecture can make clear the nature of architectural composition and provide analytical and mechanical leverage for characterizing and analyzing architectures.

Of course, these are not the only kinds of formalism that are possible and desirable. In particular, the specifications introduced thus far have focused primarily on issues of computational structure and behavior. However, many other properties are of concern to practical software designers, including performance (e.g., time and space costs), mathematical accuracy, security, and reliability.

The extension of formal specification techniques to include these properties should be done in such a way as to preserve the desirable characteristics of functional specifications. In particular,

- The generalized specifications should mesh with the abstract modular structure of the program; in this way they can be developed and studied along with functional specifications.
- The specification methods should allow as much or as little precision as may be appropriate; excessively precise specifications can be expensive to process and can constrain future evolution of the software.
- The specifications should be both precise and mathematically tractable; formal analysis is not always feasible, but it is more reliable than informal arguments.
- It should not be necessary to develop a new specification methodology for each additional property of interest; whenever possible, it is desirable to extend existing methods to new properties instead of developing new methods.

This suggests that the enterprise of developing formal underpinnings for software architecture will continue to be a multifaceted enterprise, and one ripe for further development. In this chapter we have briefly outlined several of those facets and expect others to emerge in the future.

6.7   Z NOTATION USED IN THIS CHAPTER

The Z notation is a mathematical language developed mainly by the Programming Research Group at the University of Oxford over the last fifteen years. The mathematical roots of Z are first-order logic and set theory. The notation uses standard logical connectives ($\land$, $\lor$, $\Rightarrow$, etc.) and set-theoretic operations ($\in$, $\cup$, $\cap$, etc.) with their standard semantics. Using the language of Z we can provide a model of a mathematical object. That these objects bear a resemblance to computational objects reflects the intention that Z be used as a specification language for software engineering. In this appendix, we describe the basics of the Z notation used in this chapter. The standard reference for practitioners of Z, and the basis for our use of Z, is Spivey's reference manual [Spi89b].

A Z specification consists of sections of mathematical text interspersed with prose. The mathematical text is a collection of types together with some predicates that must hold for the values of each type. Types in Z are sets of values. Z provides some fundamental types in its basic toolkit that are primitive, such as **N** for natural numbers and **Z** for integers. In addition, we can introduce further primitive types, called *given* types, by writing them in square brackets. By convention, given types are written in all capital letters. The construction of elements in a given type is not provided in a specification, usually because that level of detail is not necessary for the purposes of the specification. Prose surrounding the declaration of a given type should explain why the specifier has chosen to introduce the type rather than use an existing type. For example, we could introduce two given sets to represent all possible authors and papers that those authors might write. For use in this appendix, no further information about authors or papers needs to be explicit, so we write:

[*AUTHOR, PAPER*]

An element of a type is declared using a colon (:). So we would write *author : AUTHOR* and read this as "*author* is of type *AUTHOR*," meaning that *author* is an element in the set of values defined by *AUTHOR*. Since *AUTHOR* is a set, we could also write *author* ∈ *AUTHOR*, using the set membership function ∈. Z uses the : notation when a variable is declared and ∈ to express predicates over variables.

New types can also be defined by constructing them from primitive types, using the following type constructors:

- **P** X is the set of all subsets with elements from type X, also called the powerset of X.
- $X \times Y$ is the type consisting of all ordered pairs (x,y) whose first element is of type X and whose second element is of type Y, also called the cross-product of X and Y.
- seq X is the set of all sequences, or lists, of elements from X, including empty and infinite sequences.
- bag X is the set of all bags of elements from X.
- Relations and functions between types identify special subsets of the cross-product type. The ones used in this chapter follow:
  - $X \longleftrightarrow Y$ is the set of all relations between domain type X and range type Y. A relation is simply a subset of $X \times Y$.
  - $X \longrightarrow Y$ is the set of all partial functions between X and Y. A partial function does not have to be defined on all elements of its domain type.
  - $X \longrightarrow Y$ is the set of all total functions. Total functions are defined on all elements of the domain type.
  - $X \rightarrowtail Y$ is the set of all partial functions from X to Y whose inverse is a partial function from Y to X (also called 1-1 or *injective*).
  - $X \rightarrowtail Y$ denotes the total injective functions from X to Y.
  - $X \rightarrowtail Y$ denotes the bijective functions from X to Y, that is, the functions from X to Y that define a 1-1 correspondence (total, injective and surjective).

Z has a special type constructor, called the *schema*, an abstract version of the Pascal record or the C struct type constructors. A schema defines a binding of identifiers (or variables) to their values in some type. For example, we could specify the type *Proceedings* as a schema for a typical set of conference proceedings. The information we might want to specify about a set of proceedings would be the set of all authors and an index from authors to the papers they wrote. We represent this binding in the following boxed schema notation:

```
┌─ Proceedings ─────────────────────────────────────────────────────
│  authors : P AUTHOR
│  index : AUTHOR ⟷ PAPER
│
└───────────────────────────────────────────────────────────────────
```

A "dot" notation is used to select elements of a schema type; thus, we could refer to the authors in the proceedings of *sigsoft93* : *Proceedings* by writing *sigsoft93.authors*.

In addition to declaring the bindings between identifiers and values, a schema can specify invariants that must hold between the values of identifiers. In the following boxed notation, these invariants are written under a dividing line. All common identifiers below the line are scoped by the declarations above the line. If we wanted to model the invariant that the set of authors in type *Proceedings* can and must include only those authors appearing in the index, we could state that *authors* is the domain of the *index* relation. We would write this as follows.

```
┌─ EssentialProceedings ────────────────────────────────────────────
│  authors: P AUTHOR
│  index : AUTHOR ⟷ PAPER
│ ─────────────────
│  authors = dom index
│
└───────────────────────────────────────────────────────────────────
```

Z allows for schema inclusion to facilitate a more modular approach to a specification. In the above example, we could have introduced the invariant on the set of authors as

```
┌─ EssentialProceedings ────────────────────────────────────────────
│  Proceedings
│ ─────────────────
│  authors = dom index
│
└───────────────────────────────────────────────────────────────────
```

including the declarations and invariants of *Proceedings* in the new schema *EssentialProceedings*. Z defines a calculus of schema operations of which inclusion is just one example. We do not use many schema operations in this chapter, so we direct the interested reader to Spivey's reference manual.

In addition to the schema calculus for defining schema expressions, Z usage relies on some notational conventions for describing the behavior of state machines. The schema represents a binding from identifiers to values. We can view this binding as the static description of some state machine, that is, the view of the state machine at some point in time. Operations on the state machine are transitions from one legal state to another and can be described as a relationship between the values of identifiers before and after the operation. One of the most common conventions is the Δ convention for describing operations. If *Schema* is a schema type, then Δ*Schema* is notationally equivalent to two "copies" of *Schema*, one of which has all of its identifiers decorated with primes (′) to indicate the state after the operation. So, we could write

```
┌─ ProceedingsOp ──────────────────────────────────
│ ΔProceedings
│
└──────────────────────────────────────────────────
```

which is equivalent to

```
┌─ ProceedingsOp ──────────────────────────────────
│ Proceedings
│ Proceedings′
│
└──────────────────────────────────────────────────
```

or

```
┌─ ProceedingsOp ──────────────────────────────────
│ authors : P AUTHOR
│ index : AUTHOR ⟷ PAPER
│ authors′ : P AUTHOR
│ index′ : AUTHOR ⟷ PAPER
│
└──────────────────────────────────────────────────
```

Some other operations and notational conventions used in Z follow:

- $Point == \mathbf{N} \times \mathbf{N}$ introduces the type $Point$ as a type synonym for the cross-product. Type synonyms are a notational convenience.
- If f is a relation, function, or sequence, then dom f is the domain of f, and ran f is the range of f.
- If S is a set (or sequence), then $\# S$ is the size (or length) of S.
- $a \hat{\ } b$ is the concatenation of sequences a and b.
- If R is a relation, then $R\sim$ is its relational inverse and $R+$ is its transitive closure. If S is a set of elements in the domain type of R, then $R (\!|S|\!)$ is the image over R of the set of elements in S, that is, the set of elements in the range type of R that are related to elements in S under R.
- $\forall$ $decl \mid pred_1 \bullet pred_2$ is read "for all variables in $decl$ satisfying $pred_1$, we have that $pred_2$ holds."
- $\exists$ $decl \mid pred_1 \bullet pred_2$ is read "there exist(s) variable(s) in $decl$ satisfying $pred_1$ such that $pred_2$ holds."
- $\{ decl \mid pred \bullet expression \}$ is a set comprehension for the set of values $expression$ ranging over variables in $decl$ satisfying the predicate $pred$.

7

LINGUISTIC ISSUES

WE NOW CONSIDER THE ISSUE of architectural description languages. First, we consider the general linguistic nature of architectural description. We propose that architectural representation is an ideal candidate for description languages and enumerate six abstract properties that those languages should embody. We then argue that existing programming languages and their extensions as module interconnection languages are not adequate. Second we explore the nature of architectural connection. We argue that the abstractions embodied in the connecting lines of architectural diagrams require first-class treatment and indicate what form this might take in a language. Third, we consider the problem of augmenting existing languages to support certain architectural constructs. Specifically, we present an example in which an existing programming language (in this case Ada) was augmented to provide better treatment for new kinds of architectural connection (in this case implicit invocation). The main point of the example is to illustrate the kinds of semantic trade-offs that a language designer must resolve in order to embed a new architectural style in an existing programming language.

7.1   REQUIREMENTS FOR ARCHITECTURE-DESCRIPTION LANGUAGES

The use of software architectures is pervasive in the informal diagrams and idioms that people use to describe system designs. Unfortunately, diagrams and descriptions such as these are highly ambiguous. At best they rely on common intuitions and past experience to have any meaning at all. Moreover, system designers generally lack adequate concepts, tools, and decision criteria for selecting and describing system structures that fit the problem at hand. It is virtually impossible to answer with any precision the many questions that arise during system design. What is a pipeline architecture, and when should one pick it over, say, a layered architecture? What are the consequences of choosing one structural decomposition over another? Which architectures can be composed with others? How are implementation choices related to the overall performance of these architectures? And so on.

The problem of describing structural decompositions more precisely has traditionally been addressed by the modularization facilities of programming languages and module interconnection languages [PDN86]. These notations typically allow an implementor to describe software system structure in terms of definition/use or import/export relationships between program units. This supports many features for programming-in-the-large, such as separate compilation, well-defined module interfaces, and module libraries.

However, as we argue later, such language support is inadequate for architectural descriptions. In particular, descriptions at the level of programming language modules provide only a low-level view of interconnections between components, in which the only directly expressible relationships between components are those provided by the programming language. Moreover, they fail to provide a clean separation of concerns between architectural-level issues and those related to the choice of algorithms and data structures.

More recently a number of component-based languages have been proposed and implemented. These languages describe systems as configurations of modules that interact in specific, predetermined ways (such as remote procedure call, messages, or events [Pur88, Kra90, Pou89, Mak92, Bea92]) or enforce specialized patterns of organization [D+91, Ros85, L+88]. While such languages provide new ways of describing interactions among components in a large system, they too are typically oriented around a small, fixed set of communication paradigms and programming-level descriptions, or they enforce a very specialized, single-purpose organization. This makes them inappropriate for expressing a broad range of architectural designs.

In this section we examine the need for new higher-level languages specifically oriented to the problem of describing software architecture. First we show how ideas from "classical" language design apply to the task of describing software architectures. We then detail the characteristics that such languages should have in the areas of composition, abstraction, reusability, configuration, heterogeneity, and analysis. Finally, we show how existing approaches fail to satisfy these properties, thus motivating the need for new language design. In taking this general point of view, we do not propose a particular language—indeed, we believe that no single language will be sufficient for all aspects of architectural description. Rather, we intend to establish the framework within which architectural language design must take place.

7.1.1   THE LINGUISTIC CHARACTER OF ARCHITECTURAL DESCRIPTION

We now illustrate how the structure of the architectural task is amenable to treatment as a language problem and argue that the principles learned from the design of programming languages can serve us well in designing notations for software architecture. The argument is as follows:

- Analysis of commonly used architectures reveals common patterns, or idiomatic constructs.

- Those constructs rely on a shared set of common kinds of elements; similarly, they rely on a shared set of common intermodule connection strategies.

- Languages serve precisely the purpose of describing complex relations among primitive elements and combinations thereof.

- It makes sense to define a language when you can identify appropriate semantic constructs; we find an appropriate basis in the descriptions of architectures.

Common Patterns of Software Organization

Papers describing software systems often dedicate a section to the architecture of the system. This section typically contains a box-and-line diagram; boxes usually depict major components, and lines depict some communication, control, or data relation among the components. The boxes and lines mean different things from one paper to another, and the terms in the prose descriptions often lack precise meaning. Nevertheless, important ideas are communicated by these descriptions.

Some of the informal terms refer to common, or idiomatic, patterns used to organize the overall system. These are often widely used among software engineers in high-level descriptions of system designs, many of which were discussed in Chapter 2. Software developers would clearly benefit from having more precise definitions of these structures, including the forms in which they appear and the classes of functionality and interaction they provide.

Common Components and Interconnections

In the diagrams of architectural descriptions, the boxes usually have labels that are highly specific to the particular system: for example, "lexical analyzer," "alias table," or "requisition slip datafile." The lines (or sometimes adjacencies) that represent interactions are similarly specific: "identifiers," "update requests," or "inventory levels."

Examination of these descriptions shows that if the specific functionality of the elements (boxes) is set aside, the remaining structural properties often fall into identifiable classes. For example, here are some of the classes of components that appear regularly in architectural descriptions:

(Pure) computation	Simple input/output relations, no retained state. Examples: math functions, filters, transforms.
Memory	Shared collection of persistent structured data. Examples: database, file system, symbol table, hypertext.
Manager	State and closely related operations. Examples: abstract data type, many servers.
Controller	Governs time sequences of others' events. Examples: scheduler, synchronizer.
Link	Transmits information between entities. Examples: communication link, user interface.

The interactions among components are also of identifiable kinds. Some of the most common follow:

Procedure call	Single thread of control passes among definitions. Examples: ordinary procedure call (single name

space), remote procedure call (separate name spaces).

Dataflow

Independent processes interact through streams of data; availability of data yields control.
Examples: Unix pipes.

Implicit invocation

Computation is invoked by the occurrence of an event; no explicit interactions among processes.
Examples: event systems, automatic garbage collection.

Message passing

Independent processes interact by explicit, discrete handoff of data; may be synchronous or asynchronous.
Examples: TCP/IP.

Shared data

Components operate concurrently (probably with provisions for atomicity) on the same data space.
Examples: blackboard systems, multiuser databases.

Instantiation

Instantiator uses capabilities of instantiated definition by providing space for state required by instance.
Examples: use of abstract data types.

The significant thing about these classes of components and forms of interaction is that they are shared by many different architectural idioms—that is, the higher-level idioms are composed from a common set of primitives.

CRITICAL ELEMENTS OF A DESIGN LANGUAGE

Programming language design of the 1970s taught us that a language requires the following:

Components

Primitive semantic elements and their values

Operators

Functions that combine components

Abstraction

Rules for naming expressions of components and operators

Closure

Rules to determine which abstractions can be added to the classes of primitive components and operators

Specification

Association of semantics to the syntactic forms

For conventional programming languages, which deal with algorithms and data structures, the components include integers, floating-point numbers, strings, records, arrays, and so on. The operators include iteration and conditional constructs and type-specific operators such as +, –, *, /. Abstraction rules allow definition of macros and procedures. The closure rules of some languages, but not of others, make procedures first-class entities; in a data-abstraction language, user-defined types are supposed to be ratified by the closure rule, but this is usually incompletely carried out. The specification of semantics may be either formal or informal (e.g., the reference manual).

THE LANGUAGE PROBLEM FOR SOFTWARE ARCHITECTURE

Software architectures deal with the gross allocation of function to components in the system, with data and communication connectivity, and with overall performance and system balance. These are very different from the concerns of conventional programming languages. As a result, the specific forms of the various language elements are also different:

Components	Module-level elements (possibly but not necessarily compilation units of a conventional programming language); kinds of components suggested above; kinds of components can be characterized and used in many different ways.
Operators	Interconnection mechanisms as suggested above; most current systems now support only procedure call and perhaps shared data.
Patterns	Compositions (e.g, "client-server relation") in which code elements are connected in a particular way.
Closure	Conditions in which composition can serve as a subsystem in development of larger systems.
Specification	Not only of functionality, but also of performance, fault-tolerance, and so on.

These identifications of architectural components and techniques for combining them into subsystems and systems provide the basis for designing languages for architectural description. Such a language would support not only simple expressions defining connections among simple modules but also subsystems, configuration of subsystems into systems, and common paradigms for such combinations.

7.1.2   DESIDERATA FOR ARCHITECTURE-DESCRIPTION LANGUAGES

The broad outlines of a system to support architectural design are relatively clear from informal experience. Such a system must provide models, notations, and tools to describe architectural components and their interactions; it must handle large-scale, high-level designs; it must support the adaptation of these designs to specific implementations; it must support user-defined or application-specific abstractions; and it must support the principled selection of architectural paradigms.

In such a system there is clearly a close interplay between language and environment: a language is necessary to have precise descriptions, while an environment is necessary to make those descriptions usable and reusable. Focusing primarily on the linguistic issues, we can elaborate six classes of properties that characterize what an ideal architectural description language would provide: composition, abstraction, reusability, configuration, heterogeneity, and analysis.

COMPOSITION

It should be possible to describe a system as a composition of independent components and connections.

Composition capabilities allow us to combine independent architectural elements into larger systems. This has three important aspects: First, an architecture-description language must allow a designer to divide a complex system hierarchically into smaller, more manageable parts, and conversely, to assemble a large system from its constituent elements. Second, the elements must be sufficiently independent that they can be understood in isolation from the system in which they are eventually used. Third, it should be possible to separate issues at the implementation level (such as choice of algorithms and data structures) from those of architectural structure.

The need to handle large-scale systems at suitably high levels of abstraction implies both that an architectural description must be modular and that we can create new system elements by combining existing ones. Modularity is required to factor a complex description into smaller conceptual units. The language's closure rule must allow us to view entities of an architectural description as primitive at one level of description and as composite structures at a lower level of description. The need for independence of architectural elements—both components and connections—follows from the desire to represent these elements as stand-alone definitions. This not only makes it possible to reason about an architectural description in terms of its constituent parts, but also avoids preempting the use of those parts in many different contexts.

The need for explicit, abstract composition rules is evident in the use of common architectural idioms. For example, a pipeline architecture is modularized as a sequence of pipes and filters, while a layered architecture is modularized as a collection of abstraction layers that interact according to established rules. Moreover, a filter in a pipeline architecture might itself be internally represented as another pipeline system or even as an instance of a completely different architecture. A pipe, which can be viewed abstractly as a simple connection in a pipeline architecture, might be internally represented as a complex architecture such as a layered protocol. Independence of pipes and filters allows us to understand a given instance of the architecture in terms of the functional composition of the elements. Independence also allows us to use pipes and filters in contexts other than strict pipeline architectures. For example, a filter might be used in any system that requires a data stream transformation. Similarly, a pipe might be used wherever data transmission is required—for example, between a console and a command interpreter in a user-interface system.

ABSTRACTION

It should be possible to describe the components and their interactions within software architecture in a way that clearly and explicitly prescribes their abstract roles in a system.

Abstraction addresses the need to describe design elements at a level that matches the intuitions of designers. It is not sufficient to provide low-level mechanisms into which designers can translate their intuitions. In particular, it should be possible to represent as first-class abstractions new architectural patterns and new forms of interaction between architectural elements.

In all software systems abstraction is used to suppress unnecessary detail yet reveal important properties. For example, high-level imperative programming abstractions suppress issues such as register usage but reveal sequential control-flow abstractions (loops, exceptions, etc.). Similarly, programming language module interfaces suppress issues of implementation, but may reveal definition/use dependencies.

The architectural level of design requires a different form of abstraction to reveal high-level structure, so that the distinct roles of each element in the structure are clear. Such a description is needed to make explicit the kind of architectural elements that are being used and the relationships between those elements. It is not enough, for example, to describe a system simply as a set of modules whose interfaces are collections of procedure calls, because the structural relationships between modules is encoded in the low-level details of procedure semantics and definition/use dependencies.

For example, architectural abstractions should be able to indicate explicitly that components are related by a client-server relationship. While both the client and the server may be implemented as traditional modules, the "client-server-ness" of the architecture is not revealed simply by looking at the procedure call interfaces. In a similar way, it should be possible to describe a system of pipes and filters without having to rely on implicit coding conventions or unstated assumptions about the operating environment (e.g., that two processes will communicate through the Unix pipes).

REUSABILITY

It should be possible to reuse components, connectors, and architectural patterns in different architectural descriptions, even if they were developed outside the context of the architectural system.

While many languages permit reuse of individual components, few make it possible to describe generic patterns of components and connectors. Such patterns, or frameworks, should allow us to describe a family of system architectures as an open-ended collection of architectural elements, together with constraints on their structure and semantics. This form of reuse differs from the reuse of components from libraries, which supply complete closed or parameterized components whose identities are retained in the final systems. Architectural patterns, however, require further instantiation of substructure and indefinite replication of relations. That is, component libraries supply leaves of the "is-composed-of" structure of a system, whereas architectural patterns supply structured collections of internal nodes.

Systems are rarely conceived in isolation; they are usually instances of a family of similar systems that share many architectural properties. These shared properties may be structural—such as a specific topology of components and connectors. Or they may simply represent constraints on the use of certain kinds of architectural elements, without defining how they should be connected. An architectural language must permit the characterization of these shared properties.

The need for reusability goes considerably beyond the capabilities of most module constructs provided by programming languages. Such modules can usually be parameterized, as with Ada generics or SML functors, but few languages allow one to talk about parameterized *collections* of modules, or structural patterns. As a simple example, consider a pipeline architecture, which uses pipes and filters as its basic architectural elements, but also constrains the topology to be a linear sequence.

CONFIGURATION

> *Architectural descriptions should localize the description of system structure, independently of the elements being structured. They should also support dynamic reconfiguration.*

Properties of configuration permit us to understand and change the architectural structure of a system without having to examine each of the system's individual components. A consequence is that a language for architectural description should separate the description of composite structures from the elements in those compositions, so that we can reason about the composition as a whole.

Dynamic reconfiguration is needed to allow architectures to evolve during the execution of a system. This reflects common practice, in which new components can be created by other components, and new interactions between components can be initiated. In an object-oriented architecture, for example, it is essential to be able to create new objects; in a system of communicating processes it is often essential for processes to be created and killed.

HETEROGENEITY

> *It should be possible to combine multiple, heterogeneous architectural descriptions.*

There are two distinct aspects of heterogeneity. The first concerns the ability to combine different architectural patterns in a single system. For example, it should be possible to define a single component that communicates with some components through a pipe, but at the same time can access a shared database using an appropriate query protocol. Similarly, different levels of architectural description should be allowed to use different architectural idioms. For example, different layers in a layered architecture might be implemented by using different architectural organizations.

The second aspect of heterogeneity is the desirability of combining components that are written in different languages. Since an architectural description is at a higher level of abstraction than the description of the algorithms and data structures that implement the computations, there is no logical reason why these lower-level descriptions must use the same notation. Indeed, module connection systems that support interaction between distinct address spaces often provide this capability (e.g., Unix shell scripts, multiprocess message-passing systems, etc.).

ANALYSIS

It should be possible to perform rich and varied analyses of architectural descriptions.

The requirements of analysis address the ability to support automated and non-automated reasoning about architectural descriptions. Different architectures permit different kinds of analysis, and it should be possible to tailor the kind of analysis to the kind of architecture. This goes beyond the current support for analysis, which primarily consists of type checking.

A designer often uses a certain set of architectural elements to construct a system because this choice enables the analysis of specialized properties of that system. For example, in a pipe-and-filter architecture, it is possible to analyze properties of throughput, investigate questions of deadlock and resource usage, or infer the input-output behavior of a system from that of the component filters. It should be possible to tailor special-purpose analysis tools and proof techniques to these architectures.

Existing module-connection languages provide only weak support for analysis. At best they provide some form of type checking across component boundaries. They rarely permit more semantically based properties to be analyzed or even expressed. It is possible to add specification of input-output behavior and then reason via procedure-call proof rules. However, for many other forms of interaction, such as event broadcast, there are currently no corresponding systems of specification and analysis.

Enhanced forms of analysis are particularly important for architectural formalisms, since many of the interesting architectural properties are dynamic. For example, if a connector is associated with a particular protocol, it should be possible to determine whether the use of that connector is correct in its context of use. Similarly, issues such as timing, performance, and resource usage may play a significant part in reasoning about whether a given architectural description is adequate.

The variety of analyses that one might want to perform on an architectural description argues strongly that no single semantic framework will suffice. Instead, it must be possible to associate specifications with architectures as they become relevant to particular components, connectors, and patterns.

7.1.3   PROBLEMS WITH EXISTING LANGUAGES

Most existing notations for describing software architectures can be grouped into five broad categories: (1) informal diagrams, (2) modularization facilities provided by programming languages, (3) module interconnection languages, (4) support for alternative kinds of interaction, and (5) specialized notations for certain architectural styles. We now consider some of the ways in which each of these categories fails to satisfy the properties outlined earlier.

INFORMAL DIAGRAMS

Informal diagrams are typically used to convey a high-level view of system organization. They are frequently drawn as a diagram of boxes and lines, where the boxes represent components of many different kinds, and the lines represent interactions. The meanings of both boxes and lines vary considerably from diagram to diagram, and may even vary within one diagram. Different kinds of components in a single diagram are often distinguished with boxes of different shapes, but different kinds of connectives are rarely distinguished visually. For example, lines might represent dataflow, control flow, an inheritance relationship, a "contains" relationship, a type-instance relationship, a function call, asynchronous message passing, and so on.

The problems with such diagrams are relatively obvious. While they may offer a high level of abstraction, their informality is a serious drawback. Although they can convey intuitions effectively, it may be impossible to use them for analysis. Their relationship to implementations is tenuous at best, and they are typically constructed form scratch with each new application.

MODULARIZATION PROVIDED BY PROGRAMMING LANGUAGES

The second approach to architectural description is to use modularization facilities provided by a programming language. Representative examples include Simula classes, CLU clusters, Alphard forms, and Ada packages. These languages are based on the notion that a module defines an *interface*, which declares (1) the facilities that it provides to the system (its *exports*) and (2) the external facilities on which it depends (its *imports*). In this context *facilities* refer to the low-level entities (variables, functions, types, etc.) directly supported by the programming language used to define module implementations.

Modularization constructs were originally introduced to partition the code of a system so as to reduce complexity through abstraction, permit cooperative work, and allow incremental compilation of parts of a system. Programming language modules have had some success in raising software system construction to the level of "programming-in-the-large," but from the point of view of architectural description, they have some serious flaws.

Composition. Most modularization facilities permit hierarchical decomposition: modules may be declared within other modules. However, programming language modules provide poor support for independent composition of architectural elements, and they interfere with the separation of structural concerns from programming concerns.

The first problem is that intermodule connection is determined by name matching. It is common for a system to require that elements exported from one module be referred to by the same names in other modules. This is true, for example, for Ada and C. In Ada, modules (packages) are imported in their entirety via a "with" clause. Suppose package Foo declares functions f and g. Then package Baz would use f and g by including the line

> *with Foo*

at the beginning of the Baz package definition and referring to f and g, with name qualification, as Foo.f and Foo.g, respectively. In C, Foo would be defined by files Foo.c and Foo.h. Then Baz would include the line

#include Foo.h

in Baz.c (or possibly Baz.h) and refer to functions *f* and *g* without name qualification.

This scheme is good enough for the compiler to assure that addresses match at run-time, but it provides poor support for architectural description. In particular, name matching interferes with independent development of modules by requiring the importing module to use the name by which an element is exported, rather than using a name more appropriately determined by the context of its use.

The second problem is that the use of imports and exports in module interfaces forces system interconnection structure to be embedded in module definitions. Consequently, modules cannot easily be separated from the system in which they were originally defined.

Third, the use of imports and exports confuses algorithmic with architectural description. When facilities are imported from another module, this may indicate interaction between two components of a system. But it might also simply represent the inclusion of lower-level facilities to aid in the implementation of the importing module—for example, by importing a library module.

Abstraction. Programming language modules represent module interfaces as collections of independent procedures, data, and possibly other namable entities of the languages, such as types and constants. As a result, system structure must be expressed in terms of the primitive constructs of the programming language at hand.

Typically such modules provide only one or two forms of built-in interconnection mechanisms. Usually the mechanisms are procedure call and data sharing, but they may instead be pipes, message passing, or some other mechanism. While the use of a small set of mechanisms has the advantage of uniformity and simplicity, it also has the significant disadvantage that it preempts any other form of intermodule interaction.

Only rarely do existing systems support a richer vocabulary of architectural interconnection directly. The exceptions are usually in the form of support for one or a few additional simple connections, such as the Ada rendezvous. While these enlarge the vocabulary for architectural description, they do not provide a more general facility for user-definable interactions.

The problem is perhaps not particularly severe at the programming language level, where we generally prefer a simple, uniform computational model over a large collection of mechanisms. But the architectural level of design requires a diverse collection of abstractions to represent even the most common forms of component interconnection [Sha93a]. Indeed, the interactions represented by lines in informal diagrams are drawn from a much richer and more abstract vocabulary than the language-supported mechanisms. While most abstractions can usually be *implemented* by a mechanism such as procedure call or message passing, the inability to use more than the primitive programming-level forms of interaction in system definitions has three negative consequences. First, it tends to force system designers to think of an architecture solely in terms of those primitive constructs. Second, it limits reusability, since components that make different assumptions about module interconnection cannot be included. Third, it limits the level of abstraction that can be used to describe interactions.

The consequence is that a major part of the system design—the description of the high-level interactions between modules—is not explicit. It is encoded in individual procedures calls and shared data accesses; it is distributed through the code of multiple modules; it often remains undocumented; and it is exceedingly difficult to change.

Reuse. Programming modules provide poor support for reuse for many of the same reasons. Modules drawn from libraries include an explicit import statement (or set of import statements) rather than a requirement that they can provide certain specified additional capability. This interferes, first, with the implementor's ability to select alternative algorithms and representations and, second, with the possibility of packaging the required capability in different ways.

Further, even at their best, traditional schemes of module description support only reuse of the modules themselves. In particular, there is generally no support for reuse of patterns of composition.

Configuration. As we have indicated, the use of imports and exports leads to a situation in which the connectivity structure of the system is distributed through the module definitions. This makes it essentially impossible for a developer or maintainer to understand or analyze the structure as a whole.

The problem is mildly alleviated if build files, such as those used by *make* [Fel79], are used to show dependencies. However, these files are notoriously hard to read and write, they can easily diverge from the actual system, they may show indirect as well as direct dependencies, and they show only the *fact* of a dependency, not the nature of the connection or the designer's intention.

Finally, most module interconnection schemes allow only static configurations: dynamic reconfiguration is not generally supported. More recently, systems have been designed specifically to support dynamic reconfiguration.

Heterogeneity. Heterogeneity is poorly supported. In general, modules written in different programming languages cannot be combined or can only be combined with special tools for interlanguage procedure calls. Further, since only a few primitive forms of module interaction are supported, it is impossible to introduce new kinds of interaction without first encoding them in the primitives at hand. Even worse, conventional programming languages provide no means for distinguishing among different kinds of elements. Since they also fail to support abstractions for interactions, they have no way to express architectural paradigms, let alone ways to combine such paradigms.

Analysis. Programming language modules provide poor support for architectural analysis. This follows in part from the fact, mentioned above, that it is not easy to determine from imports and exports alone what the architectural structure of a system really is. Further, the use of name matching makes it difficult to check for consistency of interconnection. An intermodule-connection system should help to assure that the use of the imported element is consistent with the intentions of its exporter. Attempting to achieve this through name matching is insufficient, since name matching does not assure proper use. We should require at least correspondence among signatures of functions, structures of types, and so on. Even better, it would be desirable to require consistency among formal specifications.

Module Interconnection Languages

An alternative to the use of module interfaces to describe system interconnection is to use a special language. Such languages are sometimes called module interconnection languages. Representative examples include MIL75 and Intercol [DK76, Tic79, PDN86].

These languages partially separate the description of a system configuration from the parts of the system that are being composed. In that respect they satisfy some of the properties of composition and configuration better than programming language modules alone. However, they too are primarily concerned with resolving name bindings between the definitions and uses of low-level programming entities. In particular, they do not change the fact that only low-level interactions (such as procedure call) are supported. They also do not generally provide a way to indicate reusable patterns of composition. Thus, they share most of the shortcomings discussed in the previous section.

Languages That Support Alternative Forms of Interaction

Certain notations have been designed to make it easier to describe interactions beyond procedure call and data sharing. For example, Unix provides a shell language which supports direct definition of pipes as connectors [Bac86], and some systems support event broadcast by extending the facilities of a programming language [SN92, GS93a]. Ada supports intertask communication through rendezvous [DoD83].

Unfortunately, while all of these make it easier to describe *some* high-level interactions, none provides a more general facility for describing new abstractions for interaction. Hence, system builders must encode their intentions in terms of the specific primitives at hand.

Notations for Specialized Architectural Styles

A number of systems have been developed to support specific abstract paradigms. Some of these were mentioned in the introduction [Pur88, Kra90, Pou89, Mak92, Bea92, SEI90]. Each system works through a specific architectural style in detail. Most provide good high-level support for the paradigm of interest. However, heterogeneity is not among their design objectives, and we find so much need for heterogeneity in practice that we regard this as an important requirement.

Emerging Architectural Description Languages

Recently a number of languages have been proposed to explicitly address the concerns raised in this section. We consider three of them (and their supporting tools) in the next chapter. While they are still under development, they are good examples of linguistic frameworks that seek to satisfy the properties described earlier in this chapter. Among other languages that have been proposed are Rapide [LAK+95], an architectural description language based on event patterns; ArTek, a description language that focuses on the structure of architectural designs [T+94]; and a graphical language for architectural style developed by Dean and Cordy [DC95].

7.2   First-Class Connectors

Architectural descriptions treat software systems as compositions of components. They focus on the components, leaving the description of interactions among these components implicit, distributed, and difficult to identify. If the interfaces to the components are explicit, they usually consist of import/export lists of procedures and data. Interactions are expressed implicitly through include files or import and export statements, together with the documentation that accompanies various libraries. This view of software architecture organizes information around the components and ignores the significance of interactions and connections among the modules.

This section begins by discussing the limitations of the conventional approach to system configuration. It then argues that designers must attend as carefully to connections among components as to the components themselves. It closes by proposing a model of system composition in which connectors are first-class entities along with components. Section 7.2.1 summarizes current practice, and Section 7.2.2 describes some of the resulting difficulties. Section 7.2.3 gives a fresh view of system configuration, and Section 7.2.4 sketches a language to support that view.

7.2.1   Current Practice

When a designer writes a paper about a software system, the first section often includes a diagram and a few paragraphs of text labeled as the software architecture. The text refers informally to common software notions such as pipelines, client-server relations, interpreters, message-passing systems, and event handlers. The diagram usually consists of boxes and lines, but the semantics of the graphic elements varies substantially from one figure to another [GS93b]. Figure 7.1 is typical of these figures. It depicts a sequence of three processing steps in which the second step also uses four abstract data types and communicates in various ways with a satellite, an interactive workstation, and a database. The components depicted in the diagram may have substructure, but ultimately the implementations of the components must be written in conventional programming languages.

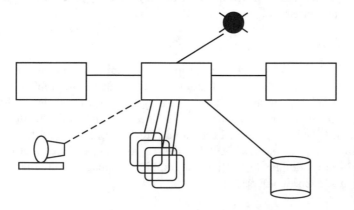

FIGURE 7.1 Typical Box-and-Line Depiction of a Software Architecture

Sometimes components have explicit interface definitions that define the external structure of the components. They usually consist of lists of procedures, exported data, and perhaps types, exceptions, and so on. Ada's specification parts and C's .h files are examples of such interface definitions. Interfaces do not aggregate these details to reflect the more abstract relations they implement. The specifications of functionality, if any, are generally written in prose; formal specifications that provide details beyond type and signature are relatively rare.

In these conventional designs, all modules have equal status. That is, they are undifferentiated collections of procedures, data, and other constructs of the underlying programming language. Nothing analogous to a type system indicates that a module has special properties, discriminates among different kinds of modules, or identifies specific kinds of analysis available. In the associated implementations, import and export statements in each module establish the dependencies among modules. In Ada these are *uses* clauses; in C they are *includes*. Specific associations—for example, between a procedure definition and its call—rely on matching the names at the definition and use sites. The models implicit in designers' architectural descriptions (both text and diagrams) do not match the actual realization of these models in code. Architectural models are rich, abstract, spontaneous, and almost wholly informal; however, the implementation languages, including module interconnection languages, are rigorous, precisely defined, and limited in expressiveness to the constructs of the underlying programming language. As a result of these mismatches, the code fails to capture designers' intentions for the software explicitly and accurately, and precise design documentation does not persist into maintenance. This impedes immediate checking and future guidance for development and maintenance activities. Even insofar as the code actually captures parts of the design, it does so in a highly distributed fashion, and it is hard for a reader to get a system-level overview. The need to address abstractions for system configuration is becoming widely recognized.

7.2.2   PROBLEMS WITH CURRENT PRACTICE

Current practice in architectural, or system-level, design focuses on components. For a system to work well, however, the relations among components, or connectors, require as much design and development attention as the components. Connectors are less obviously objects of design than are components. After all, the connectors often do not have code, and hence lack an identity of their own. They may be realized in distributed fashion by a variety of system mechanisms. Indeed, system mechanisms such as common scheduling and synchronization policies or the available communications protocols may constrain the designers' choices. Many of the problems with current techniques for architectural definition arise from the inadequacies of the mechanisms for defining component interconnection. This section reviews some of the problems with the conventional approach of embedding the interactions among components within those components.

INABILITY TO LOCALIZE INFORMATION ABOUT INTERACTIONS

Most current module interconnection techniques, including programming languages such as Ada, depend on import and export commands lodged in the code modules of the system [DK76, PDN86]. A link editor then connects the components by matching the names of exported and imported constructs, possibly with guidance from the import and export statements about the scope of names. This presents three major problems:

1. Forced agreement in spelling. The importer must use the same name as the exporter. Sometimes a reusable library cannot be used in a system because its names conflict with existing names of the system.

2. Dispersion of structural information. An import/export strategy distributes structural information throughout the system. This hides the system structure and impedes reuse by creating embedded references to other components.

3. Forced asymmetry of interaction. The import/export model assumes asymmetrical relations: there must be an owner and a user, or a master and a slave, or a source and a destination. Although many interactions are binary and asymmetrical, not all are: peer-to-peer communication is symmetrical, and client-server relations can have multiple components in each role.

Current practice is also unable to localize the related abstractions. There is no natural home for the definitions that govern a class of interactions. Interactions are provided and defined by the operating system, the programming language, subroutine libraries, embedded languages, and ad hoc user-defined mechanisms. Giving legitimate, uniform status to definitions of interactions would improve system understanding and analysis.

POOR ABSTRACTIONS

Boxes, lines, and adjacency don't have consistent meaning across system structure diagrams. They usually represent abstract interactions rather than the procedure calls and data declarations of the code. Practical systems have quite sophisticated rules about component interaction and shared representations. Existing definition mechanisms don't allow those design decisions to be captured in the code, so they can't be exploited for analysis or maintenance. The abstractions are hidden for several reasons:

- Inability to associate related elements and name the cluster. A module interface may export a large number of named elements. Apart from comments, which have no force, there is no good way to declare that a set of these elements behaves as a coordinated group. Further, there is no way to name the cluster for reference as a whole.

- Inability to specify relations among related elements. The ordering and state consistency requirements among a coherent set of calls are usually implicit. This is almost inevitable, for there is no logical place to state them.

- Inability to specify aggregate properties of a collection of elements. Even without explicit names, practical systems have quite sophisticated rules about protocols and shared representations. Individual procedure and data-element specifications localize information and are not adequate to express these relations.

In Figure 7.1, shapes help the reader differentiate among different kinds of components, even though the programming language and module interconnection language may not support the distinctions. However, all the connections in that figure are represented in the same way as simple lines.

Figure 7.2 shows an improved drawing, with different line textures denoting different kinds of interactions. Designers have abstract, sophisticated intentions for the relations

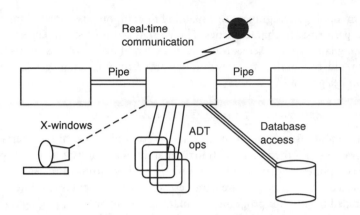

FIGURE 7.2 Revised Architecture Diagram with Discrimination among Connections

among components, but they have no reasonable way to capture these design intentions as a permanent part of the software. Even worse, the abstract relations are almost always realized as sequences of procedure calls embedded in modules whose ostensible function is something entirely different. Usual practice does not identify the abstract functions of the procedure calls, nor does it explain the rules about required order of operations.

Lack of Structure on Interface Definitions

As noted above, we lack a widely used notation for structuring interface definitions so that they cluster coherent subsets of operations. In practice, though, a module is likely to have interfaces for one or more sets of primary users (to provide the overt system function) and additional special operations for such special uses as audit trails, monthly reports, executive control (setpoints or system tuning), system initialization, monitoring, and debugging. Monolithic interfaces can neither clarify nor enforce these distinctions. Two levels of structure and abstraction are missing:

1. Abstractions for connections. Aggregation of primitive import/exports to show the intended abstract function of the connection.
2. Segmentation of interfaces. Decomposition of an interface into more or less conventional segments corresponding to different groups of users or different classes of functionality; each of these may involve several abstract connections.

Mixed Concerns in Programming Language Specification

Programming languages were designed to describe algorithmic operations on data. They are very good at defining data structures and algorithms that operate on those data structures. Extensions allow them to describe computational structures such as concurrency. They are not particularly good at describing reliability, absolute time, and a variety of extrafunctional properties. Nor are they good at defining interactions among other modules that are more abstract than procedure calls and shared data. Two problems result. First, all interactions not directly supported by the programming language must be encoded as sequences of procedure calls. Second, constructs for system composition have been grafted onto programming languages, with less than ideal results (e.g., *private* parts of Ada). The concerns of architectural design are not with algorithms and data structures, but rather with system topology, assignment of capability to components, interactions among components, and performance characteristics. Therefore it is unrealistic to expect conventional programming languages to serve. Much of the current awkwardness seems to arise from attempts to add capabilities to conventional programming languages that stretch them beyond their design limits.

POOR SUPPORT FOR COMPONENTS WITH INCOMPATIBLE PACKAGING

When multiple components are reused (e.g., from different libraries), their interfaces do not always mesh well, even if their computational capabilities are substantially compatible. For example, if a component is cast as a filter, it can't be used as a procedure because it does I/O via pipes instead of through procedure parameters. If a component is cast interactively, it often can't be called by another program. If semantics are suitable but packaging details such as name and parameter order differ, the user must write ad hoc conversions. Something akin to typing is going on here: to use a component, you need to know not only what it computes but also how it delivers that computation. In many of these cases, the incompatibilities can be overcome by introducing mediators that accommodate discrepancies between the protocol expected by the component and the protocol requested by the designer.

POOR SUPPORT FOR MULTILANGUAGE OR MULTIPARADIGM SYSTEMS

The connection between components is substantially independent of the programming languages of the components. For example, this is usually the case when the components run as separate processes. Connectors that work naturally in these cases include Unix pipes and many message systems. In other cases, the connection between components depends directly on the programming language. This is often true when components share assumptions about run-time systems such as representations of data types. The conditions under which components in different languages can interact must be detailed in such a way that a system development tool can tell which connections are allowable, which can be mediated, and which cannot be supported. Furthermore, tools intended to support one architectural paradigm—such as object management tools or Unix shells—offer little assistance in creating a system that mixes different architectural idioms.

POOR SUPPORT FOR LEGACY SYSTEMS

Most software development now involves modification of existing systems. Most of these systems evolved without configuration tools any more sophisticated than, say, *make*. Syntactic tools make it possible to extract the signatures (the names and types) of imported and exported entities. However, they offer no help in recovering the higher-level intentions, such as which set of procedures collectively implements a given abstract protocol. Over half of system maintenance effort goes into deciphering what the software already does, so the inability to record and retain the designers' higher-level intentions about component interactions is a major cost generator.

7.2.3   A Fresh View of Software System Composition

Systems are composed of identifiable components of various distinct types. The components interact in identifiable, distinct ways. Components roughly correspond to the compilation units of conventional programming languages. Connectors mediate interactions among components; that is, they establish the rules that govern component interaction and specify any auxiliary mechanisms required. Connectors do not in general correspond individually to compilation units; they manifest themselves as table entries, instructions to a linker, dynamic data structures, system calls, initialization parameters, servers that support multiple independent connections, and the like. It is helpful to think of the connector as defining a set of roles that specific named entities of the components must play. Software systems thus comprise two kinds of distinct, identifiable entities: components and connectors.

Components are the loci of computation and state. Each component has an interface specification that defines its properties, which include the signatures and functionality of its resources together with global relations, performance properties, and so on. Each is of some type or subtype (e.g., filter, memory, server). The specific named entities visible in the interface of a component are its interface points.

Connectors are the loci of relations among components. They mediate interactions but are not things to be hooked up (rather, they do the hooking up). Each connector has a protocol specification that defines its properties, which include rules about the types of interfaces it is able to mediate for, assurances about properties of the interaction, rules about the order in which things happen, and commitments about the interaction (e.g., ordering, performance, etc.). Each is of some type or subtype (e.g., remote procedure call, pipeline, broadcast, event). The specific named entities visible in the protocol of a connector are roles to be satisfied (e.g., client, server).

Components may be either primitive or composite. We usually code primitive components in the conventional programming language of our choice. Composite components define configurations in a notation independent of conventional programming languages. This notation must be able to identify the constituent components and connectors, match the connection points of components with roles of connectors, and check that the resulting compositions satisfy the specifications of both the components' interfaces and the connectors' protocols.

Similarly, connectors may be either primitive or composite. They are of many different kinds: shared data representations, remote procedure calls, dataflow, document-exchange standards, standardized network protocols. The set is rich enough to require a taxonomy to show relations among similar kinds of connectors. Primitive connectors may be implemented in a number of ways: as built-in mechanisms of programming languages (e.g., procedure calls associated by a linker); as system functions of the operating system (e.g., certain kinds of message passing); as library code in conventional programming languages (e.g., X/Motif); as shared data (e.g., Fortran COMMON or Jovial COMPOOL); as entries in task or routing tables; as a combination of library procedures and a single independent process for the connector (e.g., certain kinds of communication services); as interchange formats for static data (e.g., RTF); as initialization parameters (e.g., process priority in a real-time operating system), and probably in a variety of other ways. Composites may also appear in these diverse forms; we need (but do not yet have) ways to define them, as well. Connectors are properly treated separately from components for the following reasons:

- Connectors may be quite sophisticated, requiring elaborate definitions and complex specifications. In many cases, no single component is the appropriate location for a protocol specification.
- The definition of a connector should be localized. Just as good methodology requires a single location for the definition of a component, good methodology requires a single location for the definition of an interaction. This supports both design (especially analysis during design) and maintenance. Further, connectors can be rich enough for their definitions to deserve their own homes. For example, in a real-time system it may be appropriate for tasks to declare their needs and for a separate scheduler to satisfy them.
- Connectors are potentially abstract. They may be parameterizable. They may define classes of interactions that require additional scripting at the time of instantiation. Users may wish to define their own connectors, to make their own specializations of existing connectors, or to compose their own connectors. A single connector may be instantiated many times in a single system; for example, a multicast capability could support many distinct sets of communicating processes.
- Connectors may require distributed system support. The mechanism required by a connector is not always localized to individual uses. For example, a message-passing system may require exactly one server per processor for any number of communicating processes.
- Components should be independent. The interface specification of a component should provide a complete specification of the capabilities of that component but remain silent on how it is actually used.
- Connectors should be independent. A single (high-level) connector might mediate relations for a dynamically changing set of components. Wiederhold describes such a scheme [Wie92].
- Relations among components are not fixed. A component may be used differently by different kinds of connectors. For example, a client might be indifferent to whether its server is dedicated, shared, or distributed. In addition, system connectivity can change dynamically.
- Systems frequently reuse patterns of composition. Some of these patterns are commonly understood, at least intuitively: pipe/filter, client-server, layered system, blackboard. These common idioms can be defined as generic patterns that restrict the types of components and connectors to be used and describe how the pattern is implemented (cf. Chapter 2.) This may involve constraining the topologies of interconnection. Current module interconnection languages are wholly inadequate to this task for the reasons elaborated in Section 7.1.

7.2.4   AN ARCHITECTURAL LANGUAGE WITH FIRST-CLASS CONNECTORS

Software system composition involves different tasks from the writing of modules: the system designer defines roles and relationships rather than algorithms and data structures.

These concerns are sufficiently different to require separate languages. The architectural language must support system configuration, independence of entities (hence reusability), abstraction, and analysis of properties ranging from functionality to security and reliability. The design of such a language is not straightforward. In addition to having a syntax, it must do the following:

- Define semantics for connectors and their compositions.
- Generalize from import/export rules to rules with asymmetry, multiplicity, locality, abstraction, and naming.
- Establish type structures for system organizations, components, connectors, and the primitive units of association of these elements; this includes defining taxonomies for the types.
- Set out appropriate rules for architectural abstractions.

This section discusses these language-design problems and their solution.

LANGUAGE STRUCTURE

As suggested above, an architectural language needs separate (but parallel) constructs for components and connectors. It must provide notations for composition and a set of primitives (including primitives defined in conventional programming languages). For simplicity, the constructs for components and connectors can be similar.

Figure 7.3 suggests the essential character of the language. Each construct is typed. It has a specification part and an implementation part. The specification part defines specific units of association to be used in system composition.

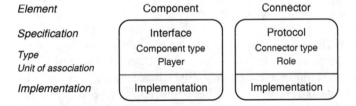

FIGURE 7.3   Gross Structure of an Architecture Language

It is sometimes useful to say explicitly that an element is primitive; this means that it is not further defined at the architecture level but is implemented in a programming language or with system-level mechanisms. For a nonprimitive element, the implementation part consists of a parts list, composition instructions, and related specifications. This establishes explicit associations and specification matches, thereby breaking free of name matching as the sole means of making connections. The specifications should be open with respect to construction and analysis tools. Many different approaches are available for specifying and verifying system properties of interest; the languages should be able to accept those as uninterpreted expressions and interact appropriately with the specialized tools.

CONNECTORS AND THEIR SEMANTICS

Most programming languages allow for some sort of intermodule connection, which usually supports only the primitive units of association of the language, such as procedure calls. Making the connectors first-class requires careful analysis of all the roles these constructs play in the definition of a system. A connector mediates the interaction of two or more components. It is not in general implemented as a single unit of code to be composed. The previous section describes a number of the implementation possibilities. Whatever the implementation of a connector (especially an abstract one), detail about the implementation technique is encapsulated when the connector is used. Moreover, many or all connectors of the same type may share the same code or data.

Like components, connectors require specifications, which are called *protocols*. Since protocols can be of many different kinds, languages should allow for flexible specifications. In particular, it is important to be able to characterize properties as diverse as the following:

- Guarantees about delivery of packets in a communication system
- Ordering restrictions on events, using traces or path expressions
- Incremental production/consumption rules about pipelines
- Distinguishing between the roles of clients and servers
- Parameter matching and binding rules for conventional procedure calls
- Restrictions on parameter types that can be used for remote procedure calls

One possibility is to use a formal notation that supports the definition of protocols. Section 8.3 describes one such approach based on the Hoares' CSP formalism. Another possibility is heavy use of property lists, with some standard attributes and some attributes specific to particular connector types. Sections 8.1 and 8.2 describe two approaches that adopt this strategy.

Primitive connectors include at least the ones directly supported by the programming language or operating system. These certainly include the procedure call and data accessors of each programming language; they also include language-specific process interactions such as the Ada rendezvous. Careful attention to the roles involved in primitive connectors shows the need to support asymmetry: a procedure has a definer and multiple callers; data has an owner and multiple users. On the other hand, in certain classes of event systems all entities are equally entitled to generate and recognize events, so it is also necessary to define symmetric roles in a protocol.

The usual import/export or provides/requires relation is too restrictive. The simplest kind of abstract connector is binary (its protocol has two roles, for example, definer and user). Some of these are direct analogs of the language-supported connectors, such as the procedure call. At the architecture level the relation is often more abstract. For example, it may be desirable to separate from the definition of a procedure the decision about whether it is to be a local or remote procedure call.

N-ary connectors that involve multiple components are also important. These may be symmetrical, with all connected components playing the same role (e.g., multicast). They may (probably more commonly) be asymmetrical, with different roles for different components or sets of components (e.g., client-server systems).

Connectors are often implemented as sets of procedures. A set of procedures frequently has an associated set of rules or assumptions about how the procedures will be used. These rules are often highly implicit; they may restrict the order in which procedures are called or require relations among parameter values. Such rules amount to protocols for the interaction. For example, the operations of an abstract data type are used as a bundle; they often have order restrictions, such as that initialize must be called before anything else, and push must be called at least as often as pop. Explicit restrictions may be expressed in various ways, as path expressions or traces for execution-order restrictions. Although it is not conventional, it is useful to think of abstract data types as having a protocol that guides the use of the operations. This not only captures essentials such as execution-order restrictions but also decouples the selection of the abstract type from the selection of an implementation. This is not unlike Larch's separation of abstract properties from actual implementations.

Figure 7.4 suggests the protocols required to construct the system of Figures 7.1 and 7.2. These protocols should exist as independent definitions in the computing environment. They may take parameters (including partial specifications) and may support several variants. When they are used, additional specifications may be needed to specialize the protocol or select a particular form.

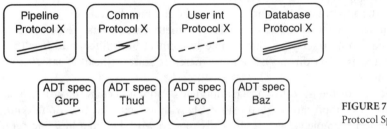

FIGURE 7.4 Constellation of Protocol Specifications

Figure 7.5 shows some of the information that should be in the interface of the central component of Figures 7.1 and 7.2. This syntax is suggestive rather than definitive. Annotations on the left side show correspondences to the line styles of the diagram. Each of the nine lines of the interface describes an interaction with some other component.

Note that in several cases the normal notion of exporting some resources and importing others does not apply well. For the pipes, additional specifications limit the type of information passing through the pipe. Similarly, a communication protocol may require additional specifications. The four abstract data types are all of the same general category of protocols; the bracketed names are the names by which the central component will call designated operations of the four types.

ARCHITECTURAL TYPE STRUCTURES

A problem akin to type checking arises at three points in an architectural language. Two appear in the preceding discussion: the types of components and of connectors. As with any type system, these express the designer's intent about how to use the element properly. To be useful, they must also have some enforcement power. Architectural types describe expected capabilities. They can limit the legitimate ways to use the construct, and they can

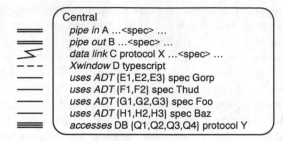

FIGURE 7.5 Interface Specification of
Central Component, Referring to Protocols

abbreviate restrictions on what can appear in the constructs specification. Examination of real systems shows that type hierarchies of this sort are useful. For example, there are many kinds of memories (components) and many kinds of event systems (connectors). Defining type structures for these elements requires the creation of taxonomies that catalog and structure the type variations.

The third place where something like type checking shows up is at the actual point of associating the interface points of components with the roles of connectors. Each of the named entities in the interfaces (of components) and protocols (of connectors) must have enough type and other specification to check on whether the connector definition allows the components to be associated as requested.

Furthermore, a component may be used differently by different kinds of connectors. For example, a client might be indifferent to whether its servers are dedicated, shared, or distributed. An abstract pipe may be able to connect both filters and files (but not processes that share data directly). We must therefore support flexible associations between players and roles.

Because of the need to reuse components and connectors in settings that aren't all quite alike, it is important to deal reasonably with associations that don't quite match. A very common example is the use of a Unix pipe to send data to a file. The definition of a Unix filter will probably say that it is intended to interact with other filters through pipes. However, it is often (but not always) well defined to substitute a file (passive component) for a filter (active component). The language must provide a way to define and control possible fix-ups, for example, by supporting such rules as "This pipe will accept a file in the role of filter under the following circumstances…" Other common examples include mismatches between the order and types of a library procedure's arguments and those of the procedure intended to call it, remapping data formats to support sharing, and the subtle differences between remote procedure calls and local procedure calls.

Some of the interesting alternatives follow:

- Associate anyhow: it will work without extra effort (some subtype relations).
- Rearrange or reformat information (data reformatters [Bea92], parameter remappers [PA91]).
- Wrap the component in a converter (a procedure wrapper for a filter would feed the input parameters to the input pipe of the filter and collect the result from the output pipe for delivery as a single value).
- Convert data to and from a shared form (interchange format).

- Convert data of one component to the form expected by another (pairwise compatibility; common message format, but data may need to be interpreted).
- Insert conversion module (buffer).
- Just say no.

The history of type coercion in conventional programming languages (especially PL/I) provides convincing evidence that this capability must remain firmly under control of the software designer at all times. A special case of compatibility checking and enforcement arises when components are written in different programming languages. The difficulty involved depends on the extent of the shared assumptions among the components.

Sometimes there is no problem. One common easy case occurs when two languages share run-time systems with common run-time representations, procedures, and protocols (Fortran/Snobol). A second common case involves explicit, loosely coupled interactions (Unix pipes with ASCII streams). Sometimes the problem can be resolved with mediation, as described above. Sometimes an external representation standard (RTF, PICT, SYLK) or an interlanguage procedure call can serve as a cross-language connector. Sometimes it is simply too hard (languages with essentially different assumptions: rule-based, static, imperative, dynamic).

ABSTRACTIONS FOR HIGHER-LEVEL CONNECTORS

The discussion so far has mentioned many different higher-level connectors. These include client-server relations, messages, event handlers, multicast communication, radio communication links, Unix pipes, shared data, interaction through X/Motif or SQL scripts, hierarchical layers, and blackboards. The example of Figures 7.1 and 7.2 might be instantiated with SQL, X/Motif, various data abstractions with usage restrictions, Unix pipes, and radio data links. The software development environment should provide the most common of these, either as part of the programming language, as basic operating system capability, or as part of the infrastructure (SQL, X/Motif). Protocols for this baseline collection should be primitive to the architectural language. It is still unclear exactly how to define the association of procedure calls with abstract protocols precisely, and the semantics of abstract connectors are also an open question at this time. However, it is clear that connectors have interesting internal structure, much as Unix pipes contain buffers.

As discussed in Section 7.2.2, component interfaces often have several distinct segments in order to establish different kinds of relations, and these often have corresponding protocols. An architectural language must support not only individual abstract connectors, but also high-level compositions that involve a number of connectors in specific relations to one another. For example, the language must be capable of capturing the high-level architectural idioms such as blackboards, interpreters, and various domain-specific architectures as abstractions. Nonprimitive connectors are probably the appropriate way to do this, but it has not yet been demonstrated.

7.2.5   THE PROMISE OF EXPLICIT ARCHITECTURAL NOTATIONS

What makes the construction of composable systems different from conventional programming? First, composing a system from subsystems is unlike programming the algorithms and data structures that lie within the primitive subsystems. The semantics of the components, the locality of reasoning, the character of interaction with other components, the properties of interest, and the nature of the reasoning are all different. Second, we are liberating ourselves from thinking of the task as simply programming. We are not merely building a program that receives inputs, executes, and terminates; we are building a system that has an enduring existence in some larger environment. Third, our units of manipulation are not simply conventional modules (which might export data, procedures, and perhaps tasks), but rather components and connectors.

Identifying connectors as first-class entities in a system can help to free us from the programming-language mindset for system composition languages. Legitimizing higher-level interactions among components allows us to understand the procedure call as one—perhaps the primary—primitive connector of pairs of modules. More significantly, it allows us to recognize higher-level connectors as critical to system design. We must learn to support higher-level connectors, composite components, and connectors whose properties, expressed in their interface and protocol specifications, are as understandable as their constituents. The view proposed in Sections 7.2.3 and 7.2.4 addresses the problems identified in Section 7.2.1.

- It specifically provides for localizing information about interactions. Nonprimitive components can invoke rich relations, and they concentrate structural information.
- It introduces abstractions for interactions and provides a starting point for user-defined abstractions and aggregations.
- It partially addresses the interface structure problem by using the roles of connectors to identify related operations as interface points for components.
- It separates architectural concerns from programming concerns by providing different language constructs with different semantics.
- It makes provisions for a type-checking system that can adapt to mild mismatches, thereby enhancing opportunities for reuse.
- It clarifies the conditions under which programming languages can be mixed.
- It offers prospects for improved support of legacy systems by making the architectural design of the system explicit.

7.3   ADDING IMPLICIT INVOCATION TO TRADITIONAL PROGRAMMING LANGUAGES

7.3.1   INTRODUCTION

Designers have traditionally constructed systems out of modules that interact with each other by explicitly invoking procedures provided in their interfaces. However, recently there has been considerable interest in an alternative integration technique, variously referred to as implicit invocation, reactive integration, and selective broadcast. The idea behind implicit invocation is that instead of invoking a procedure directly, a module can announce (or broadcast) one or more events. Other modules in the system can register an interest in an event by associating a procedure with the event. When the event is announced, the system itself invokes all of the procedures that have been registered for the event. Thus an event announcement "implicitly" causes the invocation of procedures in other modules.

There are numerous advantages to implicit invocation. One important benefit is that it provides strong support for reuse. Since modules need not explicitly name other modules, it is possible to integrate a collection of modules simply by registering their interest in the events of the system. A second important benefit is that it eases system evolution [SN92]. New modules may be added to an existing system by registering their interest in events. Similarly, one module may be replaced by another without affecting the interfaces of modules that implicitly depend on it. In contrast, in a system based on explicit invocation, whenever the identity of a module that provides some system function is changed, all other modules that import that module must also be changed.

Because of these desirable properties, many systems now use implicit invocation as their primary means of composition. While the use of the technique spans many application domains, these systems can be broadly grouped into two categories. The first category is tool-integration frameworks. Systems in this category are typically configured as a collection of tools running as separate processes. Event broadcast is handled by a separate dispatcher process that communicates with the tools through channels provided by the host operating system (such as sockets in Unix). Examples include Field, Forest, Softbench, and several other commercial tool-integration frameworks [Rei90, GI90, Ger89].

The second category is implicit invocation systems based on special-purpose languages and application frameworks. In these systems implicit invocation becomes accessible through specialized notations and run-time support. For example, many database systems now provide notations for defining active data triggers to database applications [Hew69]. Examples include APPL/A for Arcadia, daemons for Gandalf, relational constraints for AP5, and the "when-updated" methods of some object-oriented languages [SHO90, HGN91, KP88, Co89]. Other specialized applications that can be viewed as exploiting the paradigm include incremental attribute reevaluation, spreadsheet updating, and some blackboard systems [GKN92].

However, despite the successes of systems in these two categories, and despite the fact that the techniques are generally applicable to any modularizable system, the use of implicit invocation has been relatively limited. In particular, few applications can afford the overhead of separate processes used by tool-integration frameworks, and special-purpose languages are limited by their very nature.

In this section we show how to make implicit invocation more broadly available to the software engineering community by incorporating it into existing, general-purpose programming languages. The technique is simple: module interfaces of a procedure-oriented language are annotated to permit event declarations, announcements, and event-procedure bindings. The annotations are then preprocessed and compiled using traditional techniques. Dispatching of events is handled by a system-generated module, transparently to other modules, which can simply announce events as part of their normal code.

We begin by outlining the basic mechanism and illustrate its use in the context of the Ada programming language. While the ideas are straightforward, as we will see, attempts to add implicit invocation to standard languages require a number of design decisions that can have a significant impact on the properties of the mechanism and on its usability.

7.3.2   Adding Implicit Invocation to Ada

All of the ways to implement an implicit invocation mechanism are based on two funda-mental concepts. The first is that in addition to defining procedures that may be invoked in the usual way, a module is permitted to announce *events*. The second is that we may *regis-ter* a module to receive announced events by associating one of its procedures with each event of interest. When one of those events is announced, the implicit invocation mecha-nism is responsible for calling the procedures that have been registered with the event.[1]

Thus implicit invocation supplements, rather than supplants, explicit invocation. Modules may interact either explicitly or implicitly, depending on which mechanism is most appropriate. This feature makes it possible to view implicit invocation as a natural add-on to an existing explicit invocation system, such as one provided by a standard module-oriented programming language. What is required is a way to allow traditional modules to announce their own events and to register for the events of other modules. Let us now see how this can be done in the context of the Ada language.

Overview of the Implementation

In Ada the basic unit of modularization is the package [DoD83]. Packages have interfaces, which define (among other things) a set of exported procedures. We developed a small specification language to augment package interfaces. This language allows users to iden-tify events they want the system to support, and to specify which Ada procedures (in which package specifications) should be invoked on announcing the event. Figure 7.6 illustrates its use.

```
for Package_1
    declare Event_1
        X: Integer; Y: Package_N.My_Type;
    declare Event2
    when Event_3 => Method_1 B
end for Package_1
for Package_2
    declare Event_3 A,B: Integer;
    when Event_2 => Method_4
    when Event_1 => Method_2 X
end for Package_2 for Package_3
    when Event_2 => Method_3
    when Event_1 => Method_4 Y
end for Package_3
```

FIGURE 7.6   Event-Specification Language Example

In the specification language, for clauses identify the package under discussion. The declare clauses specify the events that this package will announce and the parameters asso-

---

[1] When multiple procedures have registered for the same event, the order of invocation is typically not specified. Thus users of implicit invocation must write their applications so that correctness does not depend on the existence or ordering of event registrations.

ciated with each event (if any). Each parameter has a type that may be any legal Ada type. For example, Package_1 declares two events. The first event, Event_1, has two parameters, X of type Integer and Y of type My_Type defined in Package_N.

The when clauses indicate which procedures in the package are to be invoked when an event is announced, and what event parameters are to be passed to the procedure. Any of the parameters may be listed, and in any order. This list indicates which parameters are to be passed to each procedure. For instance, in Figure 7.6, Package_1 declares its "interest" in Event_3. When Event_3 is announced (by Package_2), Method_1 should be invoked, passing only the second parameter, B.

Before compiling the Ada program, the user invokes a preprocessor that translates the specifications into an Ada package interface and body for a package called Event_Manager. (Although not illustrated in the figures here, the preprocessor assumes that the event-specification statements are delimited by the special comment mark "--!" so that they can easily be separated from normal Ada code.)

The generated interface of Event_Manager is illustrated in Figure 7.7. It provides the list of declared events as an Ada enumerated type, along with a record with a variant part that specifies the parameters for each event. In addition, the generated specification contains the signature of the Announce_Event procedure, which allows components to announce events.

```
with Package_N;
package Event_Manager is
        type Event is
        (Event_1,Event_2,Event_3);
    type Argument (The_Event: Event) is
        record
            case The_Event is
                when Event_1 =>
                    Event_1_X: Integer;
                    Event_1_Y: Package_N.My_Type;
                when Event_2 =>
                    null;
                when Event_3 =>
                    Event_3_A: Integer;
                    Event_3_B: Integer;
                when others =>
                    null;
            end case;
        end record;
    procedure Announce_Event(The_Data: Argument);
end Event_Manager;
```

FIGURE 7.7   Generated Specification for Event_Manager

The generated body of Event_Manager contains the implementation of Announce_Event. As illustrated in Figure 7.8, the procedure is structured as a case statement, with one case for every declared event. When a component wishes to announce an event, it invokes Announce_Event, as illustrated in Figure 7.9.

```
with Package_1;
with Package_2;
with Package_3;
package body Event_Manager is
procedure Announce_Event(The_Data: Argument) is
    begin
        case The_Data.The_Event is
            when Event_1 =>
                Package_2.Method_2(The_Data.Event_1_X);
                Package_3.Method_4(The_Data.Event_1_Y);
            when Event_2 =>
                Package_2.Method_4;
                Package_3.Method_3;
            when Event_3 =>
                Package_1.Method_1(The_Data.Event_3_B);
            when others =>
                null;
        end case;
    end Announce_Event;
end Event_Manager;
```

FIGURE 7.8   Generated Body for Event_Manager

```
Announce_Event(Argument'(Event_1, X_Arg, Y_Arg));
```

FIGURE 7.9   Event Announcement

KEY DESIGN QUESTIONS

This simple implementation provides many characteristics of more complex implicit invocation systems. However, it embodies a set of design choices whose consequences are important to understand because they help us to see how to use an implicit invocation system, and to be aware of the limitations of the implementation. The design decisions can be grouped into six categories:

1. Event definition
2. Event structure
3. Event bindings
4. Event announcement
5. Concurrency
6. Delivery policy

Event Definition. The first design decision concerns how events are to be defined. There are several related issues. Is the vocabulary of events extensible? If so, are events explicitly declared? If events are declared, where are they declared?

We considered four approaches to event extensibility and declaration.

1. **Fixed event vocabulary:** A fixed set of events is built into the implicit invocation system; the user is not allowed to declare new events.

2. **Static event declaration:** The user can introduce new events, but this set is fixed at compile time.

3. **Dynamic event declaration:** New events can be declared dynamically at run time; thus, there is no fixed set of events.

4. **No event declarations:** Events are not declared at all; any component can announce arbitrary events.

An example of a system with a fixed event vocabulary is Smalltalk-80, which provides a single changed event.[2] Active databases often have a fixed event vocabulary, where events are associated with primitive database operations, such as inserting, removing, or replacing an element in the database. At the other extreme, tool-integration frameworks, such as Field and Softbench [Rei90, Ger89], have no explicit event declarations at all. A tool can announce an arbitrary string, although tool builders typically describe the event vocabulary of each tool as externally documented conventions.

All four approaches can be implemented in Ada. In the first and second cases, events are naturally represented as enumerated types. In the third and fourth cases, events are often represented as strings.

We rejected the first alternative as too restrictive. When it came to deciding among the other approaches, there were arguments on each side. Static event declaration has an efficient implementation basis as an Ada enumerated type, and allows compile-time type checking of event declarations and uses. On the other hand, dynamic event declarations provide more flexibility, since they allow run-time reconfiguration. Moreover, since dynamic event systems do not use recompilation to maintain consistency between announcements and event bindings, a dynamic event system could be used to reduce recompilation overhead. A similar case can be made for nonexistent event declarations.

In the end, predictability through static checking won out. In particular, we felt that static interface declarations more naturally meshed with the spirit of Ada, led to more comprehensible programs, and offered better support for large-scale systems development, which requires predicatable behavior of the components.

Once we had decided on using static events, we were faced with the question of where the declaration of events should reside. In particular, since the events represent information shared between (at least) the announcing component and the event system, it is unclear which component "owns" the event, and thus where events should be declared. There were two obvious choices:

1. **Central declaration of events:** Events are declared at a central point and then used throughout the system.

2. **Distributed declaration of events:** Events are declared by each module, and each module declares the events it expects to announce.

Our implementation is neutral on this issue. Since the declarations are embedded within Ada comments, it is possible to declare events in the individual packages. However, an implementor can also place event declarations in a separate file.

---

[2] By convention, this event is announced by invoking the changed method on self. This causes the update method to be invoked on each dependent of the changed object. Other events could similarly be introduced by new methods that had a similar effect, but this is generally not done.

Event Structure. The next design issue is how events should be structured. We wanted a model of events that would make it easy to use them in system construction, and easy to understand the interactions between components. The choices we considered follow:

1. **Simple names:** Events are simple names without any parameter information.
2. **Fixed parameter lists:** All events have names and the same fixed list of parameters.
3. **Parameters by event type:** Each event has a fixed list of parameters, but the type and number of parameters can be different for different events.
4. **Parameters by announcement:** Whenever a component announces an event, it can specify any list of parameters. For example, the same event name could be announced with no parameters one time and with ten parameters the next.

Simple names are used in systems that use events as a kind of interrupt mechanism. In these systems there are typically only a few reasons for events to be raised. Fixed parameter lists are often used in combination with a fixed set of system-defined events. For example, in an active database events might require as a parameter the identity of the data that is being modified. At the other extreme, systems that use strings as events often allow arbitrary parameters: it becomes the job of the receiver to decode the string and extract parameters at run time.

We quickly settled on allowing parameters to vary by event type, because the first two approaches seemed unnecessarily restrictive. We also felt that letting parameters vary for each announcement could lead to undisciplined and unpredictable systems. Allowing parameters to vary by event type over a static list of events also solves a problem of parameter passing: with static events and static parameter lists, a record with a variant part becomes a natural way to represent parameters.

Event Bindings. Event bindings determine which procedures (in which modules) will be called when an event is announced. There are two important questions to resolve. First, when are events bound to the procedures? Second, how are the parameters of the event passed to these procedures?

With respect to the first issue, we considered two approaches to event binding:

1. **Static event bindings:** Events are bound to procedures statically when a program is compiled.
2. **Dynamic event bindings:** Event bindings can be created dynamically. Components *register* for events at run time when they wish to receive them, and *deregister* for events when they are no longer interested.

The decision to use static event bindings was largely forced on us by the language: Ada provides no convenient mechanism for keeping a pointer or other reference to a subprogram. It would have been possible to provide an enumerated type representing all procedures that might be bound to any event. Events could be bound to elements of this enumerated type dynamically and procedures would then be invoked through a large case statement. However, this conflicted with the desire to have a flexible parameter-passing mechanism (as described earlier), since the parameters would either have had to be fixed or encoded in the enumerated type.

Although Ada could be made to support dynamic event binding, it is not clear that this would be the right alternative. As with dynamic event declarations, dynamic event bindings decrease the predictability of a system. Moreover, dynamic event bindings can introduce race conditions at run time, because a newly registered binding may or may not catch an existing announced event, depending on the timing of the event and dynamic registration.

Having decided on static event bindings, we were faced with the question of how to translate the parameters from the event into the parameters for the invocation. The choices we considered follow:

1. **All parameters:** The invocation passes exactly the same parameters (in number, type and order) as are specified for the event.

2. **Selectable parameters:** As part of the event binding, the implementor can specify which parameters of the event are passed in the invocation, and in which order.

3. **Parameter expressions:** The invocation passes the results of expressions computed over the parameters of the announced event.

The transmission of all parameters to each procedure bound to an event requires some conspiracy between the designer of the procedure to be invoked and the designer of the events. We could easily imagine situations in which only some of the information in an event announcement would be useful to a component, and it seemed unnecessary to require the component to accept a dummy parameter just for that reason, or, conversely, to require two events to be announced—one with and one without the unneeded data.

We opted to provide selectable parameters, as this provided a balance between flexibility and ease of implementation. Selectable parameters allow more freedom in matching events to procedures, thereby promoting reusability. Moreover, it is straightforward to build the argument list from the event-binding declaration.

Although we did not implement it this way, we believe that expressions with no side-effects could provide increased flexibility. The ability to construct expressions as part of an event binding makes it easier to tailor a procedure to an event without modifying either the announcer or the recipient. The implementation becomes considerably more complex, however. In particular, we must ensure that operators used in parameter expressions are in scope and have the right type.

Event Announcement. Although announcing an event is a straightforward concept, there are several ways to do so:

1. **Single announcement procedure:** Provide a single procedure that would announce any event. Pass it a record with a variant part containing the event type and arguments.

2. **Multiple announcement procedures:** Provide one announcement procedure per event name. For example, to announce the Changed event, a component might call Announce_Changed. The procedure accepts exactly the same parameters (in number, type, order, and name) as the event.

3. **Language extension:** Provide an announce statement as a new kind of primitive to Ada and use a language preprocessor to conceal the actual Ada implementation.

4. **Implicit announcement:** Permit events to be announced as a side effect of calling a given procedure. For example, each time procedure Proc is invoked, announce event Event.

We decided on the single announcement approach for a number of reasons. First, in comparison to the multiple-procedure approach, it is simple: all event announcements look similar. Second, with respect to the third option, our users were fairly proficient with Ada, and we wanted to stay as close to pure Ada as possible. This discouraged us from modifying the language. We also wanted to avoid the extra complexity of a preprocessor that would have to process the full Ada language (and not just specially delimited annotations). Finally, we realized that instead of requiring the user to construct an Event_Manager.Argument record as a local variable and pass the variable to the procedure, the user could simply pass a record aggregate containing the desired information. This brought the syntax close enough to an announce statement to satisfy our desire for promoting events as first-class, without requiring any modification to Ada syntax.

The fourth approach, implicit announcement, has been used as a triggering mechanism for databases [DHL90] and some programming environments [HGN91]. It is attractive because it permits events to be announced without changing the module that is causing the announcement to happen. Although we could also have supported this form of announcement, we chose not to, largely because it would have required the preprocessor to transform procedures so that they would announce the relevant events. As noted above, we wanted to avoid having to process the full Ada language itself. However, this would be a reasonable extension in a future version of the system.

Concurrency. Thus far our enumeration of design decisions has left open the question of exactly what a component is. In our design, we considered three options:

1. **Package:** A component is a package, and an invocation is a call on a procedure in the package interface.
2. **Packaged task:** A component is a task (with an interface in a package specification), and an invocation is a call on an entry in the task interface.
3. **Free task:** A component is a task. An invocation is a call on an entry in the task interface. However, rather than providing an enclosing package, the task is built inside the Event_Manager package.

The first choice leads to a nonconcurrent event system: events are executed using a single thread of control. The second and third choices would permit concurrent handling of events. While we do not forbid tasks inside of packages, our implementation adopts the first approach.

Our decision was based primarily on the fact that, given the current understanding of event systems, it is much easier to develop correct systems using a single thread of control. For example, if we had adopted a concurrent approach, it would have been necessary either to require all recipients of an event to be reentrant, or to require the Event_Manager task to provide its own internal synchronizing task to ensure that invocations occurred only one at a time. A receiving task that attempted to announce another event while in its rendezvous could cause a deadlock.

Delivery Policy. In most event systems, when an event is announced all procedures bound to it are invoked. However, in some event systems this is not guaranteed. While delivery policy was not a major question in our development, there is enough variation in the way this is done in other systems to explore the design options. We considered the following:

1. **Full delivery:** An announced event causes invocation of all procedures bound to it.

2. **Single delivery:** An event is handled by only one of a set of event handlers. For example, this allows such events as "File Ready for Printing" to be announced, with the first free print server receiving the event. This delivery policy provides a form of "indirect invocation," as opposed to "implicit invocation."

3. **Parameter-based selection:** This approach uses the event announcement's parameters to decide whether a specific invocation should be performed. This is similar to the pattern-matching features of Field [Rei90] in that a single event can cause differing sets of subprograms to be invoked, depending upon exactly what data is transferred with the event.

4. **State-based policy:** Some systems (notably Forest [GI90]), associate a "policy" with each event binding. Given an event of interest, the policy determines its actual effect. In particular, the policy can choose to ignore the event, generate new events, or call an appropriate procedure. Policies can provide much of the power of a dynamic system while avoiding its complexities.

The single-delivery model did not match our interest in supporting implicit invocation, so it was quickly discarded. Although we considered the parameter-based policy model, we eventually decided on the full-delivery model, since it allowed the most straightforward analysis by our users. In a future implementation we would certainly consider adding policies to provide more flexibility.

7.3.3   EVALUATION

The system described in the preceding sections was initially developed for use in a masters-level software engineering course [GSO+92]. The students had an average of five years of industrial experience, and most were familiar with Ada. This early use of the system has resulted in both praise and criticism.

On the positive side, users of the system have had virtually no conceptual problems in transferring their abstract understanding of implicit invocation to the use of our implementation. The declarative nature of events apparently fit well with their abstract model. In addition, experienced Ada users found little difficulty in adapting their programs to an implicit invocation style. Our attempts to remain close to Ada syntax certainly contributed to this.

On the negative side, there appeared to be two limitations. The first was the common problem of debugging preprocessed source code. Since compiler errors are produced with respect to the preprocessed source, users had to translate between the output of the preprocessor and their initial source input. However, this problem was mitigated by the relative orthogonality of the language extensions, since the event-oriented extensions were largely isolated from normal code. The second limitation was the absence of dynamic event declaration and binding. While Ada programmers are used to strongly typed, static system designs, our users were also aware that other implicit invocation systems are more dynamic. (For example, some of them had used Softbench [Ger89].)

To these drawbacks we would add our own concern with the lack of support for concurrency in our design. As indicated earlier, we believe that it should be possible to exploit the tasking model of Ada; this is an opportunity for future work.

To sum up, in this section we have done two things. First, we have shown by example how to add implicit invocation to a statically typed, module-oriented programming language such as Ada. While some of the design decisions were constrained by the properties of Ada itself, many of those constraints are similar to those found in other programming languages (for example, strong typing). Second, we have elaborated the design space for this approach and shown how the decisions in this space are affected by the constraints of the programming language that is being enhanced. Ultimately this is the most important thing, since it serves as a checklist for those attempting to apply these techniques to other languages. Moreover, it indicates the kind of decisions that must be made when support for a new architectural paradigm is incorporated into an existing language.

8

TOOLS FOR ARCHITECTURAL DESIGN

As THE DESIGN OF SOFTWARE ARCHITECTURES emerges as a discipline within software engineering, it will become increasingly important to support architectural development with tools and environments. In this chapter we describe three research systems that aim to support architectural design and analysis. The first is UniCon, a language and set of tools for architectural description. UniCon supports compilation of architectural designs that use a wide variety of component and connection types. The second system is Aesop, a toolkit for constructing style-specific architectural design environments. Aesop makes it possible to define new architectural styles and then exploit those styles by enforcing their constraints and taking advantage of their specific properties. The third system is a language called WRIGHT, which supports architectural specification. WRIGHT focuses on the definition of connectors as protocols, and provides formal criteria and an associated tool for checking architectural consistency. All three systems embody many of the requirements for architectural description described in Chapter 7, and serve as good examples of an emerging class of architectural design languages.

8.1   UNICON: A UNIVERSAL CONNECTOR LANGUAGE

UniCon is an architectural-description language intended to aid designers in defining software architectures in terms of abstractions that they find useful, and in making a smooth transition to code. The long-term objective is to fully elaborate this model and to support it with notation and tools. Currently, we are more strongly motivated by the practical utility of the model than by formal foundations. At present, the model provides a framework for understanding our initial implementation, which is described in [SDK+95].

The model addresses several issues in novel ways:

- It supports abstraction idioms commonly used by designers—for example, explicitly distinguishing different types of elements and supporting type-specific analysis.

- It specifies packaging properties as well as functional properties of components—for example, distinguishing clearly between functionality delivered in the form of a filter from functionality delivered in the form of a procedure.

- It provides an explicit, localized home, called a *connector,* for information about the rules for component interactions, such as protocols, interchange representations, and specifications of data formats for communication.

- It defines an abstraction function to map from code or lower-level constructs to higher-level constructs. This is similar to Hoare's abstraction technique for abstract data types [Hoa72].

- It is open with respect to externally developed construction and analysis tools. It supports collection and delivery of relevant information to the tool and the return of results from the tool.

As we have argued in Chapter 7, software system composition is different from writing modules: the system designer defines roles and relationships rather than algorithms and data structures. These concerns are sufficiently different to require a separate language. The architectural language must support system configuration, independence of entities (and hence reusability), abstraction, and analysis of properties ranging from functionality to security and reliability. The model must be supported by a notation.

We will use three examples. The first example, shown in Figure 8.1, is a Unix-style pipe-and-filter system, with the wrinkle that the pipeline merges in a file of required standard data—a configuration that is difficult or impossible to describe in most shells. The system implements a KWIC indexer; we have used a very similar task as a class exercise in a software architecture class [GSO+92]. The challenge of this example is to make complex topologies as easy to describe as simple ones.

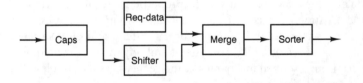

FIGURE 8.1 Pipe-and-Filter Example: The KWIC Indexer

The second example, shown in Figure 8.2, combines a pipe-and-filter architecture with a conventional procedural implementation of one of the filters. The challenge of this example is to compose architectural descriptions and to establish the correspondence between the abstraction of a pipeline and its implementation as calls on system procedures.

The third example, shown in Figure 8.3, involves coordinating real-time tasks. A simple, periodic real-time system has a number of tasks that must run on specified schedules. More challenging scheduling problems arise when tasks interact. We use an example with two schedulable tasks that interact through remote procedure calls. The challenge of this example is to incorporate an external analysis tool that determines the legality of the configuration (especially to make guarantees about schedulability) and to convert the code for the tasks into schedulable processes that run on a real-time operating system.

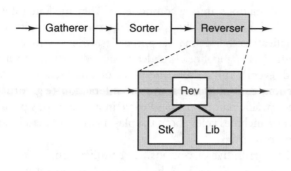

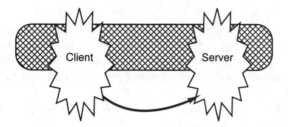

FIGURE 8.2 Heterogeneous implementation of a pipeline using both pipes and procedures. The lower diagram shows the implementation of the shaded component in the upper diagram.

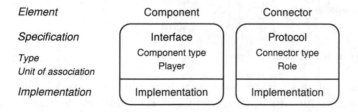

FIGURE 8.3 Real-Time Client-Server System

8.1.1 COMPONENTS AND CONNECTORS

We follow the model of Section 7.2.3, treating both components and connectors as major entities of first-class status.

Our model thus describes software systems in terms of two kinds of distinct, identifiable elements: components and connectors. Each element has a type, a specification, and an implementation. The specification defines the units of association used in system composition; the implementation can be primitive or composite. Figure 8.4 suggests the essential character of the model.

Element	Component	Connector
Specification	Interface	Protocol
Type	Component type	Connector type
Unit of association	Player	Role
Implementation	Implementation	Implementation

FIGURE 8.4   Gross Structure of an Architecture Language

Components are the loci of computation and state. Each component has an interface specification that defines its properties, which include the component's type or subtype (e.g., filter, process, server, data storage), functionality, guarantees about global invariants, performance characteristics, and so on. The specific named entities visible in a component's interface are its players. The interface includes the signature, functionality, and interaction properties of its players.

Connectors are the loci of relations among components. They mediate interactions but are not "things" to be "hooked up"; rather, they provide the rules for hooking up. Each connector has a protocol specification that defines its properties, which include its type or subtype (e.g., remote procedure call, pipeline, broadcast, shared data representations, document-exchange standard, event), rules about the types of interfaces it works with, assurances about the interaction, commitments about the interaction (e.g., ordering or performance), and so on. The specific named entities visible in a connector's protocol are roles to be satisfied. The interface includes rules about the players that can match each role, together with other interaction properties.

Components may be either primitive or composite. Primitive components could be coded in a conventional programming language, in shell scripts of the operating system, or as software developed in an application such as a spreadsheet. Composite components define configurations in a notation independent of conventional programming languages. This notation must be able to identify the constituent components and connectors, match the players of components with the roles of connectors, and check that the resulting compositions satisfy the specifications of both the components' interfaces and the connectors' protocols.

Connectors are in principle either primitive or composite. At the present time, UniCon supports only primitive (built-in) connectors.

The example of Figure 8.2, heterogeneous implementation of a pipeline, uses different types of components and connectors. It also shows a composite implementation of one of the filters. Figure 8.5 annotates its architectural diagram to point out these features.

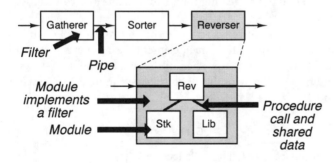

FIGURE 8.5   Abstractions in the Example of Figure 8.2.

The remainder of this section deals with three issues of particular interest for general-purpose architectural tools: abstraction and encapsulation (Section 8.1.2), the appropriate analog for types (Section 8.1.3), and the ability to provide access to externally developed tools (Section 8.1.4).

8.1.2   ABSTRACTION AND ENCAPSULATION

For a composite element, the implementation part consists of the following:

- A parts list (components and connectors)
- Composition instructions (association between roles and players)

- Abstraction mapping (relation between internal players and players of the composite)
- Other related specifications

This localizes and encapsulates information about the system structure rather than distributing it around the system in import/export statements. Since composition information is localized, global properties such as restrictions on topology or types of elements may be checked. Since the abstraction mapping is explicit, the responsibility for making sure the code correctly implements higher-level connectors can be assigned. Further, since the composition instructions make the matching of players and roles explicit, we can break free of name matching as the sole means of making connections.

Common system-composition idioms, such as pipeline, client-server, or blackboard, can be defined as idiomatic patterns, or styles, of components and connectors. These patterns describe the types of components and connectors that can be used and may constrain the interconnection topologies. Indeed, some such styles (e.g., pipe-and-filter) are described primarily in terms of the prescribed form for communication, data sharing, or other interaction. In practice, the rules for these styles are usually implicit. The combination of localized definitions and higher-level elements makes it possible to formalize rules for styles [AAG93,AG92,AG94c].

Abstract data types rely on an abstraction function to show the correspondence between the internal representation of a type and the abstract view that the user (and the specification) takes [Hoa72]. For software architectures, abstractions are required to implement higher-level components in terms of lower-level ones. When a component or connector is not directly implemented by a programming language, its definition must explain how the abstract properties will be implemented. This might take the form of a manual or informal guidance. Even better, it could be a code template, an automated generator, or a formalization. No matter how it is represented, the definition must set out the programmer's responsibility. When a number of components are connected to form a larger component, the players of the defined unit may be more abstract than the players of the implementation. In that case, the definition must explicitly indicate the correspondence among one or more external players (abstraction), one or more players of the constituent components, and the implementation rule. This is the abstraction mapping of the component. Similarly, abstraction mappings will be required for composite connectors. This differs from data abstraction chiefly in that it maps not simply data to an abstract value but rather data plus functions to a set of abstract player types.

8.1.3   TYPES AND TYPE CHECKING

As described in Section 7.2.4, a problem similar to type checking in a programming language arises at three points in an architectural language: the types of components and connectors, their adherence to a style, and the association of a component's player with a connector's roles. UniCon supports all three.

UniCon also addresses the problem of mismatch between the packaging of a component and the packaging needed. Our current implementation takes initial steps toward supporting adaptation in the face of mismatch.

8.1.4   Accommodating Analysis Tools

Architectural descriptions should be "open" with respect to construction and analysis tools. We must accommodate techniques that are applied at the systems level of design. These analysis tools will often be developed independently of the model. They may address such properties as functional correctness, performance, and temporal properties such as the allowable order of operations and real-time guarantees. The architectural notation should be able to record such system-level specifications as uninterpreted expressions and to interact appropriately with specialized tools.

Perhaps the most natural kind of system-level analysis is that of functional specification, which might use pre- and post-conditions to check procedure calls, for example. Perry suggested this as part of his software interconnection model [Per87]. Rather than building a theorem prover into the system, the system could collect the assertions from a procedure's definer and a potential caller and invoke an external theorem prover to decide whether to allow the call. This will provide a much stronger check than either name matching or signature comparison.

A second example is rigorous analysis of the real-time properties of a system. For certain classes of systems, correctness depends on the time at which computations are completed, not just on whether the computations themselves are correct. The designer of a system must account for the computation times of individual modules as well as the complex interactions within the composition of modules. Our implementation now supports the rate-monotonic analysis (RMA) technique, which is intended to address these concerns.

RMA originates from research in scheduling algorithms for real-time systems, when Liu and Layland [LL73] provided the theory for analyzing systems scheduled under the rate-monotonic scheduling (RMS) algorithm. A system scheduled with RMS could be formally analyzed to determine whether meeting real-time deadlines could be guaranteed. The theory has since been extended to handle more general types of systems, even those which are not scheduled using RMS. The Software Engineering Institute at Carnegie Mellon has grouped these extensions together and provided a handbook for their use [KRP+93].

Figure 8.6 revisits the real-time client-server example, a system with two competing processes organized in a client-server relation. They interact via remote procedure calls which are initiated by the client on the basis of a periodic timer. An analysis tool being developed at Carnegie Mellon performs rate-monotonic analyses of tasks in real-time

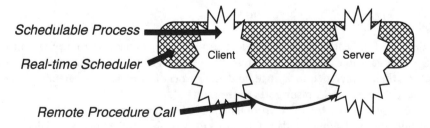

FIGURE 8.6   Abstractions for Real-Time Architecture Using RPC for Process Interaction

systems. This analysis tool expects a system characterization in a table format adapted from the "Implementation Table" format introduced in [KRP+93]. These tables describe the events, actions, and resources of the system. In this formulation, an event is an abstraction that consists of a stimulus and a set of responses that follow from it.

Table 8.1 characterizes the events as type Internal, Timed, or External (I, T, and E), specifies the relevant timing, and details the responses as a set of action ID's. Table 8.2 provides specific information for each action in the response list. An action must be assigned to one or more resources (CPU, bus, global data, etc.), flagged if it uses the resource atomically, given a user ID (usually the process name) and priority, and characterized in terms of total time required each time the action is invoked. Table 8.3 describes the resources required by the actions. The scheduling policy of a resource might be Fixed Priority, FIFO, or Priority Queue (or some other suitable policy), and allows the analysis tool to select the proper algorithm for determining schedulability.

Events					
Event name	Type	Mode name	Arrival pattern	Dead-line	Responses
client.external_interrupt1	T	n/a	1000	500	client.work_block1, server.work_block1, client.work_block2, server.work_block2, client.work_block3
client.external_interrupt2	T	n/a	1000	500	client.work_block1, server.work_block1, client.work_block2, server.work_block2, client.work_block3

TABLE 8.1   Event Table for Real-Time Analysis

Actions						
Action ID	Jitter	Resource ID	Atomic	User ID	Time used	Priority
client.work_block1	n/a	TESTBED.RT.XX.CMU.EDU	N	client	1	10
server.work_block1	n/a	TESTBED.RT.XX.CMU.EDU	N	server	10	9
client.work_block2	n/a	TESTBED.RT.XX.CMU.EDU	N	client	2	10
server.work_block2	n/a	TESTBED.RT.XX.CMU.EDU	N	server	20	9
client.work_block3	n/a	TESTBED.RT.XX.CMU.EDU	N	client	1	10

TABLE 8.2   Action Table for Real-Time Analysis

Resources		
Resource ID	Type	Scheduling policy
TESTBED.RT.XX.CMU.EDU	CPU	Fixed priority

TABLE 8.3   Resource Table for Real-Time Analysis

The architectural model should support a close relation between a tool that analyzes tables such as these and the tool that actually constructs the system. Indeed, the specifications given here were extracted automatically from the example of Figure 8.6.

8.2 Exploiting Style in Architectural Design Environments

As a discipline of software architecture becomes more established, it will become critical to support architectural description and analysis with development environments. Indeed, we are already beginning to see a proliferation of environments oriented toward specific architectural styles. These environments typically provide tools to support particular architectural design paradigms and their associated development methods. Examples include architectures based on dataflow [Mak92], object-oriented design [R+91], blackboard shells [Nii86], control systems [BV93], and reactive integration [Fro89].

Unfortunately each environment is built as an independent, hand-crafted effort—and at great cost. While development efforts may exploit emerging software environment infrastructure (persistent object bases, tool-integration frameworks, user-interface toolkits, etc.), the *architectural* aspects are typically redesigned and reimplemented from scratch for each new style. The cost of such efforts can be quite high. (For example, in the DSSA Program, some of the environments have taken over seven years to develop to a point that engineers can use them.) Moreover, once built, each environment typically stands in isolation, supporting a single architectural style tailored to a particular product domain.

In this section we focus on the issue of architectural style and describe an approach to adapting the principles and technology of generic software development environments to provide style-specific architectural support. Specifically, we show how to generate architectural design environments from a description of an architectural style. Like general-purpose environment technology, this approach is not committed to a particular architectural style or development method. But unlike general-purpose approaches, our approach provides specific mechanisms for defining new architectural styles and for using those styles to design new systems.

The remainder of this section describes a system—called *Aesop*—for developing style-oriented architectural design environments. The main features of Aesop are (1) a generic object model for representing architectural designs; (2) the characterization of architectural styles as specializations of this object model (through subtyping); and (3) a toolkit for creating an open architectural design environment from a description of a specific architectural style.

8.2.1 What Is Architectural Style?

It is possible to describe the architecture of a particular system as an arbitrary composition of idiosyncratic components. However, good designers tend to reuse a set of established architectural organizations—or *architectural styles*. Architectural styles fall into two broad categories.

1. **Idioms and patterns:** This category includes global organizational structures, such as layered systems, pipe-and-filter systems, client-server organizations, blackboards, and so on. It also includes localized patterns, such as model-view-controller [KP88] and many other object-oriented patterns [Coa92, GHJV95].

2. **Reference models:** This category includes system organizations that prescribe specific (often parameterized) configurations of components and interactions for specific application areas. A familiar example is the standard organization of a compiler into lexer, parser, typer, optimizer, and code generator [PW92]. Other reference architectures include communication-reference models (such as the ISO OSI 7-layer model [McC91]), some user-interface frameworks [K+91], and a large variety of domain-specific approaches in areas such as avionics [BV93] and mobile robotics [SLF90, HR90].

More specifically, we observe that architectural styles typically determine four kinds of properties [AAG93]:

1. They provide a *vocabulary* of design elements—component and connector types such as pipes, filters, clients, servers, parsers, databases, and so on.

2. They define a set of *configuration rules*—or topological constraints—that determine the permitted compositions of those elements. For example, the rules might prohibit cycles in a particular pipe-and-filter style, specify that a client-server organization must be an n-to-one relationship, or define a specific compositional pattern such as a pipelined decomposition of a compiler.

3. They define a *semantic interpretation*, whereby compositions of design elements, suitably constrained by the configuration rules, have well-defined meanings.

4. They define *analyses* that can be performed on systems built in that style. Examples include schedulability analysis for a style oriented toward real-time processing [Ves94] and deadlock detection for client-server message passing [JC94]. A specific, but important, special case of analysis is code generation: many styles support application generation (e.g., parser generators), or enable the reuse of code for certain shared facilities (e.g., user-interface frameworks and support for communication among distributed processes).

The use of architectural styles has a number of significant benefits. First, it promotes design reuse: routine solutions with well-understood properties can be reapplied to new problems with confidence. Second, using architectural styles can lead to significant code reuse: often the invariant aspects of an architectural style lend themselves to shared implementations. For example, systems described in a pipe-and-filter style can often reuse Unix operating system primitives to implement task scheduling, synchronization, and communication through pipes. Similarly, a client-server style can take advantage of existing RPC mechanisms and stub-generation capability. Third, it is easier for others to understand a system's organization if conventional structures are used. For example, even without giving details, characterizing a system as a client-server organization immediately conveys a strong image of the kinds of pieces involved and how they fit together. Fourth, use of standardized styles supports interoperability. Examples include CORBA object-oriented architecture [Cor91], the OSI protocol stack [McC91], and event-based tool integration [Ger89]. Fifth, as noted above, by constraining the design space, an architectural style often permits specialized, style-specific analyses. For example, it is possible to analyze a system built in a pipe-and-filter style for schedulability, throughput, latency, and deadlock-freedom. Such analyses might not be meaningful for an arbitrary, ad hoc architecture—or even one constructed in a different style. In particular, some styles make it possible to generate code directly from an architectural description. Sixth, it is usually possible (and desirable) to provide style-specific visualizations. This makes it possible to provide graphical and textual renderings that match engineers' domain-specific intuitions about how their designs should be depicted.

8.2.2   AUTOMATED SUPPORT FOR ARCHITECTURAL DESIGN

Given these benefits, it is not surprising that architectural styles have proliferated. In many cases styles are simply used as informal conventions. In other cases—often with more mature styles—tools and environments have been produced to ease the developer's task in conforming to a style and in getting the benefits of improved analysis and code reuse.

To take two illustrative industrial examples, the HP Softbench Encapsulator helps developers build applications that conform to a particular Softbench event-based style [Fro89]. This is done by "wrapping" applications with an interface that permits them to interact with other tools via event broadcast. Similarly, the Honeywell MetaH language and supporting development tools provide an architectural-description language for real-time, embedded avionics applications [Ves94]. The tools check a system description for schedulability and other properties and generate the "glue" code that handles real-time process dispatching, communication, and resource synchronization.

While environments specialized for specific styles provide powerful support for certain classes of applications, the cost of building these environments can be quite high, since typically each style-oriented tool or environment is built from scratch for each new style. An effective discipline of software architecture needs to facilitate automated support for defining new styles and incorporating those definitions into environments that can take advantage of them.

In order to do this, however, we need to answer a number of fundamental questions: How should we represent architectural descriptions? How can we describe architectural styles so that they can be effectively exploited in an environment? How can we accommodate different styles in the same environment? How can we ensure that support for architectural development dovetails with other software development activities? In the remainder of this section we provide one set of answers to these questions.

AESOP

Aesop is a system for developing style-specific architectural development environments. Each of these environments supports (1) a palette of design-element types (i.e., style-specific components and connectors) corresponding to the vocabulary of the style; (2) checking to ensure that compositions of design elements satisfy the topological constraints of the style; (3) optional semantic specifications of the elements; (4) an interface that allows external tools to analyze and manipulate architectural descriptions; and (5) multiple style-specific visualizations of architectural information together with a graphical editor for manipulating them.

Building on existing software development environment technology, Aesop adopts a "generative" approach. As illustrated in Figure 8.7, Aesop combines a description of a style (or set of styles) with a shared toolkit of common facilities to produce an environment, called a *Fable*, specialized to that style (or styles).

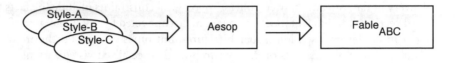

FIGURE 8.7   Generating Fables with Aesop

To give the flavor of the approach and to illustrate how different styles result in quite different environments, consider snapshots of three different Fables. Figure 8.8 illustrates the output of Aesop for the "null" style: that is, no style information is given. In this case the user can create arbitrary labeled graphs of components and connectors with the system-provided graphical editor. Both components and connectors can be described hierarchically (i.e., can themselves be represented by architectural descriptions). These descriptions are stored in a persistent object base. The user can also invoke a text editor to associate arbitrary text with any component and connector.

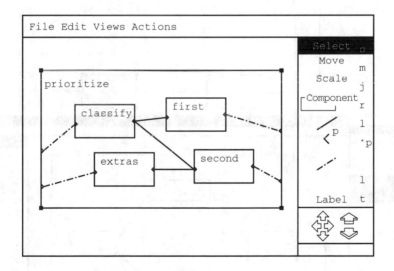

FIGURE 8.8   A "Style-less" Fable

In terms of the four stylistic properties outlined in Section 8.2.1, the design vocabulary is generic (components, connectors, etc.), the topologies are unconstrained, there is no semantic interpretation, and the analyses are confined to topological properties—such as the existence of cycles and dangling connectors. The associated tools consist of a graphical editor and a text editor for annotations. Hence, the resulting environment provides little more than informal box-and-line descriptions, such as one might find in any number of CASE environments.

In contrast, Figure 8.9 shows a Fable for a pipe-and-filter style. In this case, the style identifies (in ways to be described later) a specific vocabulary: components are filters and connectors are pipes. Filters perform stream transformations. Pipes provide sequential delivery of data streams between filters. Topological constraints include the facts that pipes are directional, and that at most one pipe can be connected to any single port of a filter. Filters can be decomposed into subarchitectures, but pipes cannot. Furthermore, the environment uses the semantics of the style to provide specialized visualizations, as well as to support the development of semantically consistent system architectures. A syntax-directed editor may be used to describe the computation of individual filters. Pipes are drawn as arrows to indicate the direction of dataflow. Color is used to highlight incorrectly attached pipes (not shown). Finally, the environment provides routines to check that correctly typed data is sent over the pipes, and a "build" tool uses the information present in the design database to construct the "glue code" needed to compile an executable instance of the system.

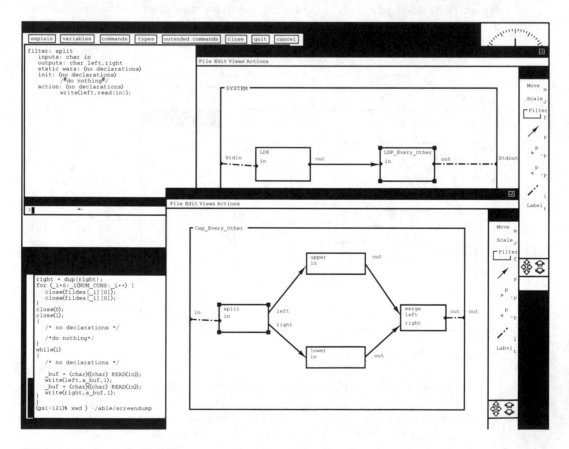

FIGURE 8.9   A Pipe-and-Filter Fable

As a third example, Figure 8.10 illustrates an environment for an event-based style similar to Field [Rei90] or Softbench [Ger89].[1] In this environment the components are active (event-announcing) objects, and the connectors are drawn as a kind of "software bus" along which events are announced and received by the components. In this case the connector can be "opened" to expose its underlying representation as an event dispatcher. This subarchitecture is described in a different style—namely, one in which RPC is used as the main connector, and the dispatcher acts as a server in a client-server style. This example illustrates the heterogeneous use of styles within a single Fable. That is, the style used to represent the internal structure of a component can differ from the style in which the component appears.

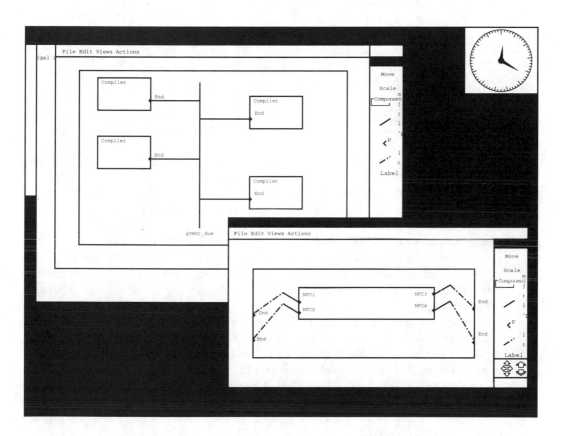

FIGURE 8.10   An Event-Based Fable

With this brief overview as background, we now turn to the technical design on which Aesop is based.

---

[1] The style shown in this example is only partially implemented in our current prototype.

THE STRUCTURE OF A FABLE

Aesop adopts a conventional structure for its environments. A Fable is organized as a collection of tools that share data through a persistent object base (Figure 8.11). The object base runs as a separate server process and provides typical database facilities: transactions, concurrency control, persistence, and so on. In the initial prototype the database was built by "serverizing" OBST, a public domain, C++-oriented database.[2]

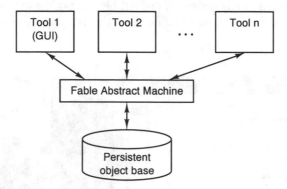

FIGURE 8.11 The Structure of a Fable

Tools run as separate processes and access the object base through an RPC interface called the Fable Abstract Machine (or FAM), which defines operations for creating and manipulating architectural objects. This interface is defined as a set of C++ object types that are linked with tools that intend to directly manipulate architectural data. Additionally, tools can register an interest in specific data objects, and will be notified when they change. Currently we use Hewlett Packard's Softbench [Ger89] for event-based tool invocation. This same mechanism also serves to integrate external tools. For example, in the pipe-and-filter environment described above, code is generated by announcing a message to a suitably encapsulated code-generation tool. Tools such as external editors are handled in the same way.

The user interface to a Fable is centered around a graphical editor and database browser provided by the Aesop system. As was illustrated in the examples earlier (and explained in more detail later), this tool can be customized to provide style-specific displays and views. The current graphical editor is based on the UniDraw framework of Inter-Views [LVC89], a C++-based GUI toolkit. While this editor is provided as a default, it is important to note that it runs as a separate tool, and can be easily replaced or augmented with other interface tools. (For example, we have recently added an alternative interface based on Tcl/Tk [Ous94].)

REPRESENTING ARCHITECTURAL DESIGNS

Given a persistent object base for architectural representation, we need to know what types of objects can be stored in the database. This information is critical, since, in effect, it answers the fundamental questions, What is an architectural design and how is it repre-

---

[2] In our most recent version, OBST has been replaced by the Exodus [C+90] storage manager.

sented? Our approach to architectural representation is based on a generic ontology of seven entities: components, connectors, configurations, ports, roles, representations, and bindings (see Figure 8.12).

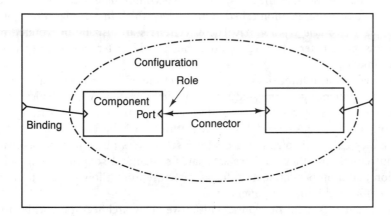

FIGURE 8.12 Generic Elements of Architectural Description

The basic elements of architectural description are *components, connectors*, and *configurations*. Components represent the loci of computation; connectors represent interactions between components; and configurations define topologies of components and connectors. Both components and configurations have interfaces. A component interface is defined by a set of *ports*, which determine the component's points of interaction with its environment. Connector interfaces are defined as a set of *roles*, which identify the participants of the interaction.

Because architectural descriptions can be hierarchical, we need a way to describe the "contents" of a component or connector. We refer to such a description as a *representation*. For example, Figures 8.9 and 8.10 illustrate architectural representations of a component and a connector (respectively).

For such descriptions there must also be a way to define the correspondence between elements of the internal configuration and the external interface of the component or connector. A *binding* defines this correspondence: each binding identifies an internal port with an external port (or, for connectors, an internal role with an external role).[3]

In the Aesop system this ontology is realized as fixed set of abstract class definitions: each of the seven architectural building blocks is represented as a C++ class. Operations supported by these classes include adding and removing ports, connecting a connector role to a component port, establishing a binding between two ports or two roles, adding a new representation to a component or connector, and so on. Collectively the classes define a FAM interface for the null-style environment.

In many cases representation of a component or connector is not architectural, per se. For example, a component might have a representation that specifies its functionality,

---

[3] Note that bindings are not connectors: connectors define paths of interaction, while bindings identify equivalences between two interface points. Moreover, connectors always associate a role with a port, while a binding associates a port with another port, or a role with another role.

or a code module that describes an implementation. Similarly, a connector might have a representation that specifies its protocol [AG94c]. That information is often best manipulated by external, nonarchitectural tools, such as compilers and proof checkers, and stored in an external database (such as the file system). To accommodate such external data, we provide a subtype of representation called *external_rep*, which in turn has other subtypes such as *text_file_rep, oracle_rep, ast_rep*. These references are usually interpreted by the tools that access them. External representations thus provide external data integration for Aesop environments.

Before leaving this outline of our generic object model for architectural representation, it is worth highlighting the unusual aspects of our approach. While the view of architecture as compositions of components and connectors appears to be gaining general acceptance, our approach has several distinctive features. First, we treat connectors as first-class entities: they have their own interfaces (as a set of roles); they may be decomposed into subarchitectures; and they can have associated semantic descriptions. This supports the conviction that a proper foundation for architecture must allow the creation of new kinds of "glue" for combining components.

Second is our treatment of representation: we allow architectural entities to have multiple descriptions representing alternative implementations, specifications, and views. This is unlike other approaches (such as in UniCon or Rapide) where an architectural element has a single implementation that defines its "truth." In our case, truth is in the eye of the tool that uses the architectural information to derive other related artifacts (such as executables).

Third, our *generic* interface is intentionally minimal: we provide only the bare framework for architectural description, leaving additional information to be added as stylistic elaborations. This is unlike other efforts that attempt to provide a single universal style, and therefore must build in many more primitive notions (such as event patterns, particular interface-specification languages, and richer vocabularies of connectors).

Defining Styles

The generic object model provides the foundation for representing architecture. However, to obtain a useful environment, that framework must be augmented to support richer notions of architectural design. In Aesop this is done by specifying a style.

The model adopted for style definition is based on the principle of subtyping: a style-specific vocabulary of design elements is introduced by providing subtypes of the basic architectural classes or one of their subtypes. Stylistic constraints are then supported by the methods of these types. Additionally, a style can identify a collection of external tools: some of these may be specifically written to perform architectural analyses, while others are links to external software development tools.

When proposing a subtyping discipline it is important to be clear about the underlying semantic model—specifically, about the ways in which subclasses can alter the behavior of their superclasses through overriding. In our system, the rule is that architectural subclasses must respect the semantic behavior of their superclasses. We use the term *respect,* however, in a nonstandard way. Rather than implying behavioral equivalence (as defined, for example, by Liskov and Wing [LW93]), we require a subclass to provide strict subtyping behavior for operations that succeed, although a subclass may introduce additional sources of failure.[4]

To see why this is useful (and necessary), consider the operation *addport*, which adds a port to a component. In the generic case any kind of port may be added to a component, so that when the list of ports is requested, the new port will be a member of the result. In the case of a filter in a pipe-and-filter style, however, we may want to allow a port to be added to a filter only if it is an instance of one of the port types defined in the style— namely, an input or output port. It is reasonable, therefore, to cause an invocation of *addport* to fail if the parameter is not one of these two types. On the other hand, if an input or output port *is* added, then the observable effect should be the same as in the generic case.

To provide more concrete detail on what sorts of styles can be built and how they behave, we now provide brief descriptions of four styles. For each style we (1) outline the design vocabulary, (2) characterize the nature of the configuration rules, (3) explain how semantics are encoded, and (4) describe the analyses carried out by tools in the environment.

A Pipe-and-Filter Style. As indicated earlier, a pipe-and-filter style supports system organization based on asynchronous computations connected by dataflow.

Vocabulary. Figure 8.13 illustrates the type hierarchy we used to define a pipe-and-filter style. *Filter* is a subtype of component, and *pipe* is a subtype of connector. Further, ports are now differentiated into *input* and *output* ports, while roles are separated into *sources* and *sinks*.

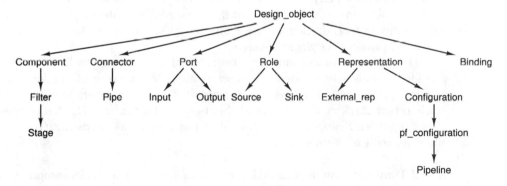

FIGURE 8.13   Style Definition as Subtyping

Configuration rules. The pipe-and-filter style constrains the kinds of children and connections allowed in a system. Besides the constraints on port addition described above, pipes must take data from ports capable of writing data, and deliver it to ports capable of reading it. Hence, source roles can only attach to input ports, and sink roles can only attach to output ports.

---

[4] Of course, this cannot be automatically enforced for C++.

Semantic interpretation. In the prototype pipe-and-filter system, the semantics of filters is given by a simple, style-specific filter language, as illustrated in Figure 8.9. The associated tool (based on Gandalf [HN86]) provides type checking and other static analyses. The semantics of pipes is described formally (but off-line) as in [AG94c].

Analyses. In addition to the static semantic checks just outlined, we incorporated a tool for generating code from filter descriptions. Hence, a pipe-and-filter description can be used to generate a running program, with the help of some style-specific tool and the external Gandalf tool.

A Pipeline Style. A pipeline style is a simple specialization of the pipe-and-filter style. It incorporates all aspects of that style except that the filters are connected in a linear order, with only one path of dataflow. (This corresponds to simple pipelines built in the Unix shell.) The pipeline style is an example of stylistic subspecialization.

Vocabulary. The pipeline style defines a new *stage* component as a subclass of filter. Its methods are identical, except that its initialization routine automatically creates a single input and output port, and the *addport* method is overridden so that it always fails.

Configuration rules. The configuration rules are the same as in the parent style, with the addition that the topology is constrained to be linear.

Semantic interpretation. The meaning of the pipes and filters is identical to the meaning given in the parent style. In particular, the same filter-description language can be used.

Analyses. The tools of the parent style can be reused in this style, as can the code written for the parent style's classes. Since we can substitute instances of subtypes for instances of their supertypes, code written for more generic styles will continue to work on their specializations. So the compiler for the pipe-and-filter system will still work on pipelines. Similarly, tools developed for the null style, like a cycle checker, will still work on instances of any of the styles in this section.

This example shows a number of benefits in using subtyping to define styles. First, it provides a simple way to extend the representation and behavior of building blocks for architectural descriptions. Second, it is supported by current methodologies and tools (such as type checkers, debuggers, and object-oriented databases). Third, it permits reuse of existing styles. New styles can be built by further subclassing of existing styles. Fourth, it allows for reuse of existing tools.

A Real-Time Style. An important class of system organization divides computations into tasks that communicate by synchronous and asynchronous messages. Within this general category are systems that must satisfy real-time scheduling constraints while processing their data. We created an Aesop environment for an architectural style developed at the University of North Carolina that supports the design of such systems [Jef93].

Underlying the architectural style is a body of theory for analyzing real-time systems [Jef92]. This theory allows one to determine the (scheduling) feasibility of a system from the processing rates of its component tasks, rates of inputs from external devices, and shared resource loads. The theory also leads to heuristics for improving the schedulability of a system that is not feasible. The style has been applied primarily to real-time, multimedia applications.

Vocabulary. The real-time style defines three subtypes of component: *devices*, which identify inputs to the system, *processes*, which compute over that data, and *resources*, which support shared resources such as disks, monitors, and so on. Components have associated style-specific information about rates of processing and computation loads. There are two new connector types, representing synchronous and asynchronous message passing.

Configuration rules. Configuration rules include the following: paths through the processing graph must originate with devices; there must be no dangling ports or connectors; communication with resources must be synchronous; and input devices may not have input ports.

Semantic interpretation. The semantic interpretation of a system is determined by the underlying semantics for the connectors, plus the code defined for the tasks. The task code is written in a stylized form which, like the pipe-and-filter style, provides syntactic guidance for reading and writing messages to ports. Our system checks that the types of information are consistent across the connectors, but code generation is supported by external tools.

Analyses. The new style enables two kinds of analyses. First, it is possible to detect whether there are resource conflicts. Such conflicts arise when the multiple processes try to access the same resource in such a way that one or more of the processes will not be able to maintain its processing rate. The second is an analysis of the scheduling feasibility of the system. This determines whether a single CPU can support the specific configuration of devices, processes, and resources. In addition to these analyses, a set of "repair heuristics" is incorporated in a tool that advises the user about possible ways to improve schedulability and resource usage. These heuristics center around decreasing the load on shared resources and/or reducing the rates of certain processes. Finally, a style-specific tool allows us to translate our architectural description into one that is readable by external tools for code generation and analysis. (Currently the code is targeted to Real-Time Mach.)

An Event-Based Style. In an event-based style, components register their interest in certain kinds of events, and then can announce events and receive them according to their interest.

Vocabulary. The event style defines a new *participant* component that registers for, announces, and receives events. An *event bus* connector is used to propagate the events between components.

Configuration rules. In this style, configuration rules simply state that the event bus connects only to components that announce events.

Semantic interpretation. Components are permitted to communicate events to each other only if they are connected to a common bus and the receiving component has registered an interest in the type of event announced by the sending component. An announced event can be received by zero or more components (in contrast to the pipe-and-filter style, where written data can only be read by one other component).

Analyses. A number of analyses are possible in event-based styles, such as identifying the flow of communication between components. As in the pipe-and-filter style, given a language for specifying the communication behavior of participant components, a compiler can be built to generate code for a particular event-based configuration [GS93a]. (We did not do this, however, in our prototype.)

User Interface

In addition to providing a representational model for tools to create and manipulate architectural descriptions, an environment must also provide a way for the user to view, edit, and use these descriptions. As we illustrated earlier, the default interface is a graphical editor, which is automatically provided by Aesop and which runs as a separate tool in the environment. To produce a style-specific environment, this editor (and potentially other interface tools) must also be specialized.

To accomplish this, each architectural class is associated with one or more visualization classes. New subclasses introduced by a style inherit the visualizations of their superclass, but may also define their own visualization classes. This induces a parallel hierarchy of visualization types, in which the root visualization types are defined by the default visualizations for the generic architectural types.

For example, to obtain the visualizations illustrated in Figure 8.9, the pipe subclass of connector would refer to an *arrow* visualization class, instead of the more generic *connector_line* class. Visualization classes can refer to external editors as well as to graphical objects. For example, there is a visualization class in the pipe-and-filter style that invokes a structure editor on filter code. The visualization classes are written in a highly stylized fashion and would be amenable to automatic generation, although we have not actually built such a tool.

Style-specific user interfaces also include object classes for user-oriented operations on the database in a particular style. These are subclasses of generic "action" classes. For instance, the user interface for a pipe-and-filter style may include actions to analyze the throughput of a particular configuration, or to generate code for a Unix-based implementation of the pipe-and-filter system. Typically these operations are carried out by external tools.

8.2.3   Observations about Environments for Architectural Design

Aesop was developed to investigate the hypothesis that style-specific architectural development environments can be produced at relatively low cost by specializing a generic architectural model. In our research thus far we have concentrated on the important initial steps of identifying an appropriate generic model, developing mechanisms for specializing the generic model to specific styles, and providing concrete infrastructure to support architectural development tools.

While we are only now starting to apply Aesop to industrial-strength architectural styles, over the past two years we have experimented with a number of common architectural paradigms (pipe-and-filter, events, client-server, etc.), as well as an abstract architectural style for Aesop itself. Our experience has made us optimistic about the ability of this approach to provide useful infrastructure for the architectural level of software system design.

First, we have found that the generic object model for architectural representation (Section 8.2.2) is a good starting point for architectural description. It provides a high enough level of abstraction that it can be specialized to the variety of architectural styles that we have encountered. At the same time it is concrete enough to provide both a solid conceptual structure and also associated automated mechanisms for developing new styles effectively.

Second, a subtyping model has been effective in structuring the task of developing new styles. In particular, the extension of the generic architectural model with new types provides a direct way to enrich the architectural vocabulary for design, and provide new functionality based on that design. However, as noted in Section 8.2.2, it is essential that the semantics of subtyping be flexible enough to allow subtypes to increase the failures associated with an inherited method.

Third, the approach is able to build on existing software environment building blocks: persistent object bases, tool-integration mechanisms, and user interface toolkits. This not only provides an interface to other tools and environments based on similar technology, but has simplified the effort of building Aesop itself.

More concretely, while the costs associated with developing a style or substyle vary greatly depending on the style, typically it takes a week to create a minimal environment for a style with the complexity of, say, the real-time style illustrated earlier. This includes defining the new design vocabulary, encoding the constraints, and developing any new visualizations. The task of cleanly integrating the Aesop environment with existing tools that support style-specific analyses takes a bit longer. For the tools that interact only loosely with the architectural design—such as source code compilers—tool integration involves little more than connecting them to our event-broadcast mechanism. The hard part is adapting the tools that need to directly manipulate our database of objects, since this typically requires a deeper understanding of the tool and its implementation.

On the negative side, we discovered that some desired capabilities of a style-oriented architectural design environment are difficult to handle with our approach to style definition and the technology on which Aesop is based. These capabilities fall into two categories.

The first category concerns the way in which styles are described, and includes the following:

- **Explicit representation of stylistic constraints.** Currently, the behavior associated with new styles—such as enforcing stylistic constraints, or enabling new kinds of analysis and tool support—must be encoded in the methods of the architectural types introduced by the style. These encodings tend to obscure the invariant properties of a style, because (1) they are bound into the imperative code of the methods, and (2) the responsibility for enforcement is often distributed over a number of different methods. This makes it difficult to reason about a style on the basis of its Aesop definition, to tell whether two styles have conflicting constraints, or to modify the policies associated with constraint enforcement and tool invocation. Approaches based on explicit rules (e.g., as in Darwin [MR88]) or interobject mediation (e.g., as in [SN92]) are attractive alternatives.

- **Control over supertype visibility.** When a new style is defined, the types of design elements should often be restricted to just those defined by the new style. For example, a pipe-and-filter style may restrict the possible port types to be only input and output ports (and therefore not allow creation of generic ports). This can be enforced as a constraint that is checked when a port is added to a component. But a much more natural solution would allow the style designer to restrict the accessibility of the type hierarchy.

The second category concerns the run-time behavior of style-oriented environments, and includes the following:

- **Dynamic incorporation of style descriptions.** In the current system our use of C++ requires us to compile style definitions at environment-creation time. This precludes incorporation of new styles during execution. However, in many situations a more dynamic scheme would be useful. For example, an externally developed repository of architectural building blocks might provide a component whose internal representation is characterized in terms of a new style.

- **Type migration.** Currently, as with most strongly typed object-oriented systems, an object's type is determined when it is created. However, we would like to be able to "promote" or "demote" the type of an object at run time. For example, if an object created as a *filter* happens to have a single input and output, it can be used as a *stage* (see Section 8.2.2) in a pipeline. To get the benefits of pipelines, however, we would need to change the type of the object from *filter* to *stage*. While such coersions can be handled on a case-by-case basis, a more uniform mechanism, such as one based on predicate types [Cha93], would be preferable.

These features suggest ways in which style-oriented architectural design raises new challenges for software support environments. First, allowing heterogeneity of styles is critical. Unlike software development environments centered on a single implementation language, architectural support must permit interoperability of many different design "languages." Second, requirements of reusability lead to an interest in dynamic regimes for style inclusion and for types of individual design objects. Unlike most programming environments, this one should allow us to introduce new types of objects and change the types of existing objects during execution. Finally, in a world of many interoperating and independently developed styles, it is important to have good formal mechanisms for specifying new styles and for detecting conflicts between existing ones.

8.3 BEYOND DEFINITION/USE: ARCHITECTURAL INTERCONNECTION

Large software systems require decompositional mechanisms in order to make them tractable. Breaking a system into pieces makes it possible to reason about overall properties by understanding the properties of each part. Traditionally, module interconnection languages (MILs) and interface definition languages (IDLs) have played this role by providing notations for describing (1) computational units with well-defined interfaces, and (2) compositional mechanisms for gluing the pieces together.

A key issue in the design of an MIL/IDL is the nature of that glue. Currently the predominant form of composition is based on definition/use bindings [PDN86]. In this model each module *defines* or *provides* a set of facilities that are available to other modules, and *uses* or *requires* facilities provided by other modules. The purpose of the glue is to resolve the definition/use relationships by indicating for each use of a facility where its corresponding definition is provided.

This scheme has a number of benefits. It maps well to current programming languages, since the kinds of facilities that are used or defined can be chosen to be precisely those that the underlying programming language supports. (Typically these facilities support procedure call and data sharing.) It is good for the compiler, since name resolution is an integral part of producing an executable system. It supports both automated checks (e.g., type checking) and formal reasoning (e.g., in terms of pre- and post-conditions).

Indeed, the benefits are so transparent that few question the basic tenets of the approach. However, we would argue that current MIL/IDLs based on definition/use have some serious drawbacks. As we will show, a significant problem is that they fail to distinguish between "implementation" and "interaction" relationships among modules. The former are useful (and necessary) for understanding how one module is built out of the facilities of others. However, the latter are needed to express architectural relationships—such as the nature of the communication between computational components.

To make this point concrete, we propose an alternative kind of glue. In this model computational *components* interact with other components along well-defined lines of communication, or *connectors.* Connectors are defined as protocols that capture the expected patterns of communication among modules. We show how this leads to a scheme that is much more expressive for architectural relationships, that allows the formal definition of module interaction, and that supports its own form of automated checks and formal reasoning.

8.3.1   IMPLEMENTATION VERSUS INTERACTION

At the level of system design the "implements" relationship between modules is an important one: a given module is defined in terms of facilities provided by other modules. For example, one module might import a string package that it uses to implement an internal data representation.

But this is not the only important kind of relationship. When people design systems, they typically provide an architectural description consisting of a set of computational components and set of intercomponent connections that indicate the interactions between those components. Often these descriptions are expressed informally as box-and-line diagrams, and the interaction relationships are described idiomatically with phrases such as *client-server interaction, pipe-and-filter organization,* or *event-broadcast communication.* These descriptions treat the components as independent entities that may interact with each other in complex ways.

The distinction between a description of a system based on "implements" relationships and one based on "interacts" relationships is important for three reasons. First, the kinds of description involve different ways of reasoning about the system. In the case of implementation relationships, reasoning typically proceeds hierarchically: the correctness of one module depends on the correctness of the modules that it uses. In the case of interaction relationships, the components (or modules) are logically independent of each other: the correctness of each module is independent of the correctness of other modules with which it interacts. Of course, the aggregate system behavior depends on the behavior of its constituent modules and the way that they interact.

Second, the two kinds of relationship have different requirements for abstraction. For implementation relationships it is usually sufficient to adopt the primitives of the underlying programming language (e.g., procedure call and data sharing). In contrast, interaction relationships often involve abstractions not directly provided by programming languages: pipes, event broadcast, client-server protocols, and so on. Whereas the implementation relationship is concerned with how a component achieves its computation, the interaction relationship is used to understand how that computation is combined with others in the overall system. Hence, the abstractions used reflect diverse and potentially complex patterns of communication, or protocols.

Third, they involve different requirements for compatibility checking. In the case of implementation relationships, type checking is used to determine if a use of a facility matches its definition. (Of course, this can be enhanced with reasoning about specifications [GH93].) With interaction relationships we are more interested in whether protocols of communication are respected. For example, does the reader of a pipe try to read beyond the end-of-input marker; or is the server initialized before a client makes a request of it.

Current MILs are well suited to describing systems in terms of their definition/use dependencies, and hence their implementation relationships. However, they are not adequate for describing architectural interactions. In the remaining sections we illustrate this point and provide an alternative model that is better suited to describing interaction relationships.

8.3.2 EXAMPLE

To illustrate the distinctions outlined above, we consider a simple system, *Capitalize*, that transforms a stream of characters by capitalizing alternate characters and lowercasing the others. Let us assume that the system is designed as a pipe-and-filter system that splits the input stream (using the filter *split*), manipulates each resulting substream separately (using filters *upper* and *lower*), and then remerges the substreams (using *merge*). In a typical implementation of this design we would probably find a decomposition such as the one illustrated in Figure 8.14. It consists of a set-up routine (*main*), a configuration module (*config*), input/output libraries, and modules for accomplishing the desired transformations. The set-up routine depends on all of the other modules, since it must coordinate the transfor-

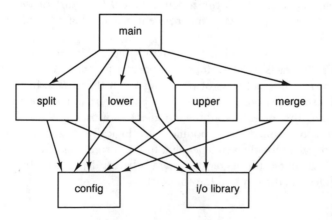

FIGURE 8.14 An
Implementation Description

mations and do the necessary hooking up of the streams. Each filter uses the configuration module to locate its inputs and outputs, and the I/O library to read and write data.

While it is useful, this diagram fails to capture the architectural composition of the system. It indicates what modules are present in the system, and to what modules their implementations refer.[5] But it fails to capture the overall system design, or architecture. Specifically the pipes in this pipe-and-filter system are not shown.

An alternative representation of the system is shown in Figure 8.15. In contrast to the previous description, the interaction relationships (i.e., the pipes) are highlighted, while implementation dependencies are suppressed. Of course, for the picture to have any meaning at all there must be a shared understanding of the meaning of the boxes and lines as filters and pipes.

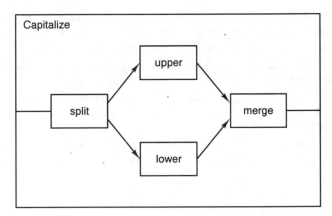

FIGURE 8.15 An Architectural Description

This second description clearly highlights the architectural design and suggests that in order to understand a system, we need diagrams that express not only the definition/use dependency relations between implementation "modules," but that also reflect directly the abstract interactions that result in the effective composition of independent components. In particular, to understand and reason about *Capitalize* it is at least as important to know that the output of *upper* is delivered to *merge* as it is to know that it is invoked by *main* and uses *I/O library*.

This example illustrates the three distinctions outlined above. In terms of reasoning about the system, the first description shows a hierarchical decomposition of the system functionality. A specification of the module *main* will be the specification of the behavior of the system as a whole. The first description indicates that the implementation of *main* refers to declarations in the other modules. To demonstrate the correctness of this module, the other modules' specifications must be used, and their correctness shown. In the second description the four filters are represented as logically separate entities that happen to be configured in a particular way. To determine that the overall system computation is correct one would have to consider the composition of the behaviors of the components together with the interactions indicated by the lines. In terms of the need for abstraction, the lines in the first description represent programming language relationships such as "calls" (in the case of the I/O library) or "shares data structure" (in the case of the configuration

---

[5] In this simple example we use the term *modules* loosely to represent separable coding units.

description). In terms of the need for checking, type checkers will make sure that the required I/O routines exist in the library and that those routines are called with appropriate parameters. For the second description, we are also interested in typing questions: Do the interacting filters agree on the type of data passing over the pipe. More important, we are concerned that the protocols of interaction are respected. For example, we would like to be able to check that a filter either reads or writes to a pipe, but not both; that the filters agree on conventions for signaling the end of data; and that the reader does not expect any more data than the writer will provide.

8.3.3   THE WRIGHT MODEL OF ARCHITECTURAL DESCRIPTION

Unfortunately, except in very specialized circumstances, the kind of architectural description given above is usually informal, and programmers must ultimately rely on concrete descriptions of implementation relationships to find the "truth" of the system.

In order to support more direct specification and analysis of architectural descriptions, we have developed the WRIGHT architectural-specification language. WRIGHT specifications are based on the idea that interaction relationships among components of a software system should be directly specifiable as protocols that characterize the nature of the intended interaction.

Figure 8.16 illustrates the use of the notation to describe the example system. As shown, a system description is divided into two parts. First, we specify both component

System Capitalize
    Component Split
        port In *[input protocol]*
        port Left, Right *[output protocol]*
        comp spec *[Split specification]*
    Component Upper
        port In *[input protocol]*
        port Out *[output protocol]*
        comp spec *[Upper specification]*
    ...
    Connector Pipe
        [Pipe specification]
Instances
    split: Split; upper: Upper; lower: Lower; merge: Merge;
    p1,p2,p3,p4: Pipe
Attachments
    split.Left **as** p1.Writer;
    upper.In **as** p1.Reader;
    split.Right **as** p2.Writer;
    lower.In **as** p2.Reader;
    ...
end Capitalize.

FIGURE 8.16   *Capitalize* in WRIGHT

and connector classes, indicating the interface and computation of components and the protocol that the connector class represents. Second, we describe the configuration of the system, using instances of these classes, and define the architectural topology as a list of attachments.

A WRIGHT specification describes a component interface as a collection of *ports*, or logical interaction points.[6] These ports factor the expectations and promises of the component into the points of interaction through which it will interact with its environment. The component may optionally further specify how the interactions on its ports are combined into a computation.

An example component specification (of the filter *Split*) is shown in Figure 8.17. Each port is defined in terms of a protocol written in a subset of CSP [Hoa85]. (We include a brief summary of CSP notation at the end of this chapter.) In this example the *In* port of *Split* repeatedly reads data until it encounters a *read-eof* event, at which point it terminates. Similarly, the *Left* and *Right* ports repeatedly write data until each chooses to *close*. The **comp spec** specifies that the pipe alternately passes its input to the *Left* and *Right* ports until a *close* event is encountered on its *In* port.

Component Split =
    port In = read?x → In $\square$ read-eof → close → √
    port Left, Right = write!x → Out $\sqcap$ close → √
    comp spec =
        let Close = In.close → Left.close → Right.close → √
        in Close $\square$
            In.read?x → Left.write!x → (Close $\square$ In.read?x → Right.write!x → **computation**)

FIGURE 8.17   The Filter *Split*

A connector class is defined by a set of *roles* and a *glue* specification. The roles describe the expected local behavior of each of the interacting parties. The glue specification describes how the activities of the roles are coordinated. The use of roles and glue allows us to separate the requirements on each component (filling a role in the interaction) from the details of how the roles interact with each other. As we will see in the next section, this allows us to use localized port-role compatibility checking when we attach an instance of the connector in a system description.

Consider the specification of *Pipe*, illustrated in Figure 8.18. This connector has two roles: *Writer* and *Reader*. The specification of the role *Writer* indicates that any participant at the source end of the pipe has two options: to write or to close the pipe, signaling the end of the communication. Because the writer is independent of the reader, the writer does not know or care that the data is delivered reliably to the reader using a FIFO discipline (as is indicated by the **spec** of the connector). Similarly, the *Reader* role indicates that this participant in the communication may decide to terminate the communication before all of the data has been delivered. The reader, however, must also account for the possibility that there may not be any more data to receive. This is indicated by the *Reader* role offering the connector a choice between the events *read* and *read-eof*.

---

[6] By using the term *port* we do not mean to imply that a port must be implemented as a port of a task in an operating system.

connector Pipe =
    role Writer = write!x → Writer ⊓ close → √
    role Reader =
        let ExitOnly = close → √
        in let DoRead = (read?x → Reader [] read-eof → ExitOnly)
        in DoRead ExitOnly
    glue = **let** ReadOnly = Reader.read!y → ReadOnly [] Reader.read-eof → Reader.close → √
                    [] Reader.close → √
        in let WriteOnly = Writer.write?x → WriteOnly [] Writer.close → √
        in Writer.write?x → **glue**
          [] Reader.read!y → **glue**
          [] Writer.close → ReadOnly
          [] Reader.close → WriteOnly
  spec ∀ Reader.read$_i$!y • ∃ Writer.write$_j$?x • $i = j \land x = y$
      ∧ Reader.read-eof ⇒ (Writer.close ∧ # Reader.read = # Writer.write)

FIGURE 8.18 A Pipe Connector

The *glue* specification of a connector is divided into two parts: a finite-state protocol and a predicate over the traces generated by this protocol. In combination, the two parts describe the nature of the interaction by constraining how the events in the roles are interleaved. The division into a "finite" part and an "infinite" part is analogous to the separation between a procedure's signature and its specification. As we indicate in the next section, the finite part allows us to check whether the connector is well formed, while the infinite part allows us to define its full behavior. For example, the *Pipe* specification in Figure 8.18 indicates that data is delivered in FIFO order and that all of the data will be delivered before *read-eof* is signaled to the *Reader*.

By comparing the protocols of the ports, such as those of *Split*, with the roles of *Pipe*, we can observe a number of important points about our specifications. The ports *Left* and *Right* both indicate that *Split* reserves the decision about how much data to produce at that port (via the nondeterministic choice generator ⊓). Also, *Split* promises to consume all of the data presented to it at the port *In*. Note how this differs from the specification of the role *Reader*, which will be instantiated by this port in the configuration *Capitalize*. The *Pipe* connector permits a component the freedom to decide how much of the data to consume, but the *Split* component chooses not to take advantage of this freedom.

8.3.4 Reasoning about Architectural Descriptions

An important property of any system-description language is its ability to support reasoning about system descriptions. Standard MILs typically support reasoning about certain forms of consistency (such as type checking) and (possibly) correctness.

In the case of architectural connection we are interested in richer forms of consistency. Specifically, we would like to know when it is legal to attach a given connector as a port in some system description. We refer to this as the "port-role compatibility" problem. (Recall that we use an instance of a connector by associating its roles with the ports of instances of components—see Figure 8.16.)

The most obvious and constrained form of compatibility checking would be to simply check that the port and role have identical protocols, but this is too restrictive. For example, we saw above that the ports of *Split* did not take advantage of the full flexibility provided by the *Pipe* roles. Similarly, we would like to be able to connect either end of a pipe to a file (as is done in Unix), even though files support both reads and writes while the end of a pipe supports only one. As another example, it should be possible to use a server port in a role that requires fewer services than the component provides. On the other hand, we would not like the client port to attempt to use more services than the server provides.

Informally, we would like to guarantee that the promised behavior of a role is respected by the port. In CSP terms, when a process provides a deterministic choice to its environment, the role should also do so. It turns out that this requirement is nicely captured by the notion of refinement in CSP (using the failures/divergences model), and with some straightforward modifications, we can use refinement in a definition of compatibility between roles and ports [AG94c]. Further, it is possible to show that this notion of compatibility is sound in the following sense: if a connector is deadlock free, then any compatible instantiation of an instance of that connector will remain deadlock free. An important practical consequence of this is that we can formally analyze a connector definition independent of its use and then perform simple local compatibility checks on each port-role attachment to determine if it is being used appropriately [AG94c].

However, a formal definition of compatibility is not enough by itself. We would also like to perform certain kinds of automatic checking of the property. To do this we need to have a sufficiently constrained description of the protocols. For this reason, we separated our connector role descriptions into two parts: a protocol (expressed as a CSP process) and a specification over the traces generated by that protocol. In a WRIGHT description the former is characterized with a "finite" subset of CSP.[7] The latter allows us to state more general properties.

The result of these choices is that it is possible to use existing commercial tools to perform automated compatibility checking on WRIGHT descriptions. In particular, we use the FDR System [For92], a tool that adapts model-checking techniques to determine various properties of CSP processes (e.g., deadlock-freedom and refinement assertions). Details on our use of FDR can be found in [AG94b].

8.3.5   A BRIEF EXPLANATION OF OUR USE OF CSP

While CSP has a rich set of concepts for describing communicating entities, we use only a small subset of these that includes the following:

- **Processes and Events:** A process describes an entity that can engage in communication events. Events may be primitive, or they can have associated data (as in e?x and e!x, representing input and output of data, respectively). The simplest process, STOP, is one that engages in no events. The event $\sqrt{}$ is used to represent the "success" event. The set of events that a process, P, understands is termed the *alphabet of P*, or αP.

---

[7] Essentially the expressive power is equivalent to that of finite state machines.

- **Prefixing:** A process that engages in event e and then becomes process P is denoted $e \rightarrow P$.

- **Alternative** (also called *deterministic choice*): A process that can either behave like P or Q, where the choice is made by the environment, is denoted $P \square Q$. (Here *environment* refers to the other processes that interact with the process.)

- **Decision** (also called *nondeterministic choice*): A process that can either behave like P or Q, where the choice is made (nondeterministically) by the process itself, is denoted $P \sqcap Q$.

- **Named Processes:** Process names can be associated with a (possibly recursive) process expression. Unlike CSP, however, we restrict the syntax so that only a finite number of process names can be introduced. We do not permit, for example, names of the form $Name_i$, where i can range over the positive numbers.

In process expressions, $\rightarrow$ associates to the right and binds tighter than either $\square$ or $\sqcap$. So $e \rightarrow f \rightarrow P \square g \rightarrow Q$ is equivalent to $(e \rightarrow (f \rightarrow P)) \square (g \rightarrow Q)$.

In addition to this standard notation from CSP we introduce three notational conventions. First, we use the symbol $\checkmark$ to represent a successfully terminating process. This is the process that engages in the success event and then stops. (In CSP, this process is called SKIP.)

Second, we allow the introduction of scoped names, as follows:

$$P = \textbf{let } Q = expr1 \textbf{ in } R$$

This subset of CSP allows one to define processes that are essentially finite state. It provides sequencing, alternation, and repetition, together with deterministic and non-deterministic event transitions.

9

EDUCATION OF SOFTWARE ARCHITECTS

IN THIS CHAPTER WE DESCRIBE a course that uses the material of this text, together with supplementary readings, to provide an introduction to architectural design. The semester-long course is intended for senior undergraduates and students in a professional master's program for software engineering. It has been offered each spring since 1992.

9.1 PHILOSOPHY AND COURSE OVERVIEW

9.1.1 OBJECTIVES

The primary purpose of the course is to teach students how to approach systems from an architectural point of view. Prerequisite skills for the course include exposure to systems development (such as that taught in an operating systems or compiler course), as well as some skill in mathematics for computer science (such as logic, set theory, and other discrete mathematics).

By the end of the course, students should be able to do the following:

- Recognize major architectural styles in existing software systems.
- Describe an architecture accurately.
- Generate reasonable architectural alternatives for a problem and choose among them.
- Construct a medium-sized software system that satisfies an architectural specification.
- Use existing definitions and development tools to expedite such tasks.
- Understand the formal definition of a number of architectures and be able to reason precisely about the properties of those architectures.
- Understand how to use domain knowledge to specialize an architecture for a particular family of applications.

9.1.2 APPROACH

We believe that important skills for designing complex systems can be provided by a course that examines systems from an architectural point of view. Specifically, our course considers commonly used software system structures, techniques for designing and implementing these structures, models and formal notations for characterizing and reasoning about architectures, tools for generating specific instances of an architecture, and case studies of actual system architectures. It teaches the skills and background that students need to evaluate the underlying architecture of existing systems and to design new systems in principled ways using well-founded architectural paradigms.

Since this is an entirely new course rather than a modification of an existing course, the major challenge in its development was to define and delimit its intellectual content. While the ability to recognize and use software architectures is essential for the practicing software engineer, there is currently no codified body of knowledge that deals specifically with this subject. Rather, relevant material is scattered over published case studies, standards reports, formal models, informal system documentation, and anecdotal experience. We have collected many of these sources, distilled them into a corpus of presentable knowledge, and discovered ways to make that knowledge directly usable by university students and the software engineering community at large.

Our approach focuses on developing four specific and related topic areas:

1. **Classification:** In order to use software architectures, we must first be able to recognize an architectural style and to describe a system in terms of its architecture. The tools required to describe and categorize common architectural models include notations for defining architectures and a taxonomy of existing models. In addition to introducing the student to these tools, this topic addresses the problem of architectural selection to solve a given software engineering problem. It covers both high-level architectural idioms (e.g., pipeline architectures) and specific reference models (e.g., the OSI layered model).

2. **Analysis:** Effective use of a software architecture depends on the ability to understand and reason about its properties (such as functional behavior, performance, developmental flexibility, evolvability, and real-time behavior). We can apply such analysis to many kinds of architectural description, but it is particularly effective in the context of formal descriptions, where we can exploit the power of mathematics. This topic therefore covers techniques for analyzing an architecture. It introduces students to formal and informal methods and illustrates how to use formal analysis to evaluate and select among architectural alternatives.

3. **Tools:** Some architectural styles have evolved to the point where there is system support for defining applications using them and for executing those applications once they are built. Examples include Unix support for single-stream pipeline architectures, compilers for module interconnection languages (such as Ada package specifications), and IDL (interface description language) readers and writers for shared data. Facility with such tools is a valuable skill for using the supported architectures in the context of current technology. Moreover, existing tools provide good illustrations of the kinds of automated support that we can expect to become pervasive as the field becomes more fully developed and populated with useful architectures.

4. **Domain-Specific Architectures:** Specific knowledge about an application domain can improve the power of the notations and tools for constructing systems in that domain. The same holds true for architectures, and there is active research and industrial development in the area of domain-specific software architectures. The course looks at a number of these to understand how to exploit domain knowledge in designing an architecture tailored to a specific application family.

We rely heavily on case studies in each of these topic areas. These are used to motivate the importance and scope of architectural approaches, illustrate what has been done so far, and give students models for creating architectural descriptions of their own. In addition we expect students to carry out a significant case study of their own. By doing so they practice applying the techniques of architectural description and analysis and contribute to the field by adding to the body of carefully documented architectural descriptions.

9.2 COURSE DESCRIPTION

In this section, we give an overview of each topic covered in the course. This information is summarized in Figure 9.1. Each row of the figure contains the lecture number, the major topic and subtopic covered in the lecture (as described below), and the readings that students should complete prior to attending the lecture. The "Text" readings refer to sections of this book. The homework assignments and project for the course are discussed in Sections 9.3.3 through 9.3.5.

INTRODUCTION (3 LECTURES)

- *Orientation.* What is the architectural level of software design, and how does it differ from intramodule programming? Overview of the course.
- *What Is a Software Architecture?* Constructing systems from modules. Some familiar kinds of architectures. Some common kinds of modules. Text Preface, Sec 1, 2.1, scan 2.3–2.10. Supplemental readings [PW92, Rec92, Jac94].
- *Classical MILs.* Historically, the earliest large systems were developed in procedural languages. The most common of the MILs reflect this in their emphasis on importing and exporting names of procedures, variables, and a few other constructs. Supplemental readings [DK76, PDN86].

PROCEDURE CALL (3 LECTURES)

- *Objects.* Information hiding, abstract data types, and objects. Organizing systems by encapsulating design decisions, or "keeping secrets." Text Sec 2.3. Supplemental readings [PCW85, Boo86].
- *Modular Decomposition Issues. KWIC.* Introduction of the KWIC problem used in the course assignments. Considering how to weigh the benefits of various decompositions for a system. Text Sec 3.1. Supplemental readings [Par72].
- *Formal Models.* Basic notation of the Z Specification Language. The schema calculus. Text Sec 6.1, 6.2. Supplemental readings [Spi89a, Sha85].

Lecture	Topic	Subtopic	Text	Supplemental Readings
1	Introduction	Overview and organization	Pref, Chapter 1, 2.1, scan 2.3–2.10	[PW92, Rec92, Jac94]
2		What is software architecture?		[DK76, PDN86]
3		Classical MILs		[PCW85, Boo86]
4	Proc Call	Information hiding and objects	Sec 2.3	[Par72]
5		Modular decomposition: KWIC	Sec 3.1	[Sha85, Spi89a, AAG93]
6		Formal Models	Sec 6.1, 6.2	
7	Data Flow	Batch sequential, pipeline systs	Sec 2.2, 3.4	
8		Tektronix case study	Sec 3.2	[Bac86]
9		Implementation using Unix pipes		
10		Formal models for data flow	Sec 6.2, 6.3	
11	Repositories	Databases and client-server systs	Sec 2.6	[GR93, Mul93]
12		Blackboard systems		[Nii86]
13	Events	Arch evolution, industry issues	Chapter 4	[Eco93, MF93]
14		Models of event systems	Sec 2.4, 6.4–6.7	[GKN92]
15		Implementation of event systems	Sec 7.3	[Rei90]
16	Processes	Communicating process archs		[And91]
17		Formal models for processes	Sec 8.3	[Hoa85]
18	Other	Interpreters, proc control, heter	Sec 2.7–2.10, 3.4, 3.5	
19	Design	Design assistance	Chapter 5	
20		Classification of arch constructs		
21		Interface matching	Sec 7.1, 8.2	[PA91, N+91, Bea92]
22		Aesop	Sec 7.2, 8.1	
23		UniCon		
24		Heterogeneity and mismatched parts		
25		Info architectures for cyberspace		[GAO95]
26		Architectural languages		[ODL93]
27		Patterns and pattern languages		[A+77, Ker95, Mul95]
28	Projects	Final presentations		
29		Final presentations		

FIGURE 9.1 Summary of Course Topics

DATAFLOW (4 LECTURES)

- *Batch Sequential and Pipeline Systems.* Systems where data flows linearly through a sequence of discrete processing steps. Contrasts executing to completion at each step with continuous flow through a system and incremental processing. Text Sec 2.2, 3.4.
- *Tektronix Case Study.* Specific example of a pipeline system used as part of a larger application. Example of formally modeling components and connectors. Text Sec 3.2.
- *Implementation Using Unix Pipes.* The Unix paradigm connects independent processes by dataflow. The organization of the processes, and the style and tools for connection are substantially different. Supplemental readings [Bac86].
- *Formal Models for Dataflow.* Formal model of pipes and filters. Use of formalism to explain what a software architecture is and to analyze its properties. Text Sec 6.2, 6.3.

REPOSITORIES (3 LECTURES)

- *Databases and Client-Server Systems.* Databases and client-server systems use a centralized, persistent store of information. This contrasts with dataflow architectures. Text Sec 2.6. Supplemental readings [GR93, Mul93]
- *Blackboard Systems.* Sharing complex knowledge about a problem; making progress when you can't tell in advance what order to impose on the subproblems. Supplemental readings [Nii86].
- *Architectural Evolution and Industry Issues.* Historically, the requirements of users coupled with advancing technology have produced an architectural evolution from batch sequential systems through pipelines to repositories. Consideration of how industry deals with the choices. Text Chapter 4. Supplemental readings [Eco93, MF93].

EVENTS (2 LECTURES)

- *Models of Event Systems.* Distinguishing implicit invocation from client-server communication and point-to-point message passing. Using formal models to define a general architecture which can be further specified as needed. Text Sec 2.4, 6.4–6.7. Supplemental readings [GKN92].
- *Implementations of Event Systems.* Examines and compares two implementations which enable components to communicate via events. Presents alternatives for the underlying implementation of implicit invocation mechanisms. Text Sec 7.3 [Rei90].

PROCESSES (2 LECTURES)

- *Communicating Process Architectures.* Topologies and techniques for orchestrating multiple, independent but communicating processes to collectively solve a problem. Supplemental readings [And91]
- *Formal Models for Processes.* Introduction to CSP for modeling sequences of execution. Comparison between CSP and Z schema calculus. Text Sec 8.3. Supplemental readings [Hoa85]

OTHER ARCHITECTURES (1 LECTURE)

- *Interpreters, Process Control, and Heterogeneity.* Two examples of architectures frequently found in practice. Examples of how "pure" architectures often appear combined in implemented systems. Text Sec 2.7–2.10, 3.4, 3.5.

DESIGN (9 LECTURES)

- *Design Assistance.* The selection of a software architecture should depend on the requirements of the application. This example of a system shows how to make the structural design of a user interface explicitly dependent on the functional requirements. Text Chapter 5.
- *Classification of Architectural Constructs.* Presentation of a partial taxonomy for architectural styles, components, and connectors.
- *Interface Matching.* Supplemental readings [PA91, N+91, Bea92].
- *Aesop.* Text Sec 7.1, 8.2.
- *UniCon.* Text Sec 7.2, 8.1.
- *Heterogeneity and Mismatched Parts.* Supplemental reading [GAO95].
- *Information Architectures for Cyberspace.* Supplemental reading [ODL93].
- *Architectural Languages.*
- *Patterns and Pattern Languages.* Identifying patterns in the use and combination of architectural styles and components, as well as recording and communicating the patterns in useful ways. Supplemental readings [A+77, Ker95, Mul95].

9.3   ASSIGNMENTS

9.3.1   PURPOSE

The purpose of the assignments, as in any course, is to help students master the material. Assignments serve the additional purpose of demonstrating their mastery of the material, thereby establishing a basis for evaluation.

Students begin by examining and understanding existing work in the area. Then they apply what they've seen and heard, first by trying to emulate it and then by performing analysis. Three kinds of assignments lead students through these activities.

First, the course is organized around written papers and lectures that present and interpret this material. We believe that the lectures are most useful if they provide interpretation, explanation, and additional elaboration of material students have already read and thought about. In addition to assigning readings, we provide guidance about the important points to read for and questions to help students focus on the most significant points in the reading.

Second, four two-week assignments ask students to apply the lecture material. Three of these assignments require students to develop small software systems in specific architectural styles. The fourth is a formal analysis task, which allows them to work with a specific architectural formalism.

Third, students examine existing software systems to determine their architectures. We identified several systems of about twenty modules. For the final project of the course, each student team analyzes the actual system structure of one of these and interprets the designer's architectural intentions.

We organize the students into teams of three. This encourages students to enhance their understanding through discussions with other students, reduces the amount of overhead required of any one student to get to the meat of a problem, and allows us to partially compensate for differences in programming language and other related experience. The course includes both undergraduate students and students in the CMN Master of Software Engineering program; to the extent possible we pair undergraduates with graduates so that their experiences would complement each other.

Since students often tend to spend most of their attention and energy on the components of a course that contribute to the final grade, we use the allocation of credit as a device to focus them on the most important activities. To this end, we include four factors in the grading basis. Here is the description of these factors as stated in the initial course handout:

- *Readings: (25%)* Each lecture will be accompanied by one or more readings, which we expect you to read *before* you come to class. To help you focus your thoughts on the main points of the reading, we will assign a question to be answered for each of the reading assignments. Each question should be addressed in less than a page, due at the beginning of the class for which it is assigned. Each of these will be evaluated on a simple ok/not-ok basis and will count for about 1% of your grade.

- *Homework Assignments: (40%)* There will be four homework assignments. Each will count 10% of your grade. The first three will be system-building exercises. Their purpose is to give you some experience using architectures to design and implement real systems. You will work in groups of three to carry out each assignment. To help clarify your designs, we will hold a brief, ungraded design review for each assignment during class a week before it is due. Groups will take turns presenting their preliminary designs and getting feedback from the class and instructors. The fourth assignment will give you some practice in using formal models of software architectures.

- *Project: (25%)* There will be a course project, designed to give you some experience with the architecture of a substantial software system. You will analyze an existing software system from an architectural point of view, document your analysis, and present the results to the rest of the class. Your grade will depend both on the quality of your analysis and also on the presentation of that analysis.

- *Instructors' Judgment: (10%)*

9.3.2   READINGS

In addition to this text, background material for the course includes readings, primarily from professional journals, selected to complement the lectures and discussions. The objective is for every student to complete all readings before the corresponding class lecture.

To ensure this, a short homework assignment is set for each class, each consisting of a few questions to be answered about the readings. These assignments are due at the beginning of the corresponding lecture and discussion. Though the single grade attached to a particular assignment does not significantly affect the course grade, the cumulative effect of these individual grades result in significant weight being placed on the readings.

A beneficial side effect of this policy is that it obviated the need for examinations. The incremental learning process is monitored and reinforced by the assignments, so there is no need for a final exam to measure student progress. As a result, end-of-semester energy can be productively directed to the course project.

Each reading is accompanied by hints which identify points to look for in each paper and give advice on parts to ignore. These hints help students to focus on the important concepts in each paper, and are particularly important because of the wide variety of notations and languages introduced in the readings.

Here are some examples of the hints we give:

- In these readings you will be exposed to many different languages. You should not try to learn the specific syntax of each language, nor should you memorize the specific features of each language. Rather, you should try to get a feel for the design space of Module interconnection languages—what it is possible to represent and what it is desirable to represent.
- First and foremost, read to understand the blackboard model and the kinds of problems for which it is appropriate. Study Hearsay and HASP to see how the model is realized in two rather different settings. Look at the other examples to see the range of variability available within the basic framework.

The questions for each assignment also played an important role in focusing the intellectual energies of the students. The questions are structured to lead students to an understanding of the concepts involved, rather than simply to get them to complete the homework. Since the reading and homework combined are intended to take only a couple of hours, the questions deal with major points and do not require deep thought or analysis.

Here are some examples of the questions we ask:

- What are the essential differences between the architectural style advocated by Parnas and that advocated by Garlan, Kaiser, and Notkin?
- What abstract data type does a pipe implement? What common implementation of that abstract data type is used to implement pipes?
- What is the problem addressed by sharing specifications in SML? Why doesn't this come up with Ada generics?
- What are the major abstractions of an interconnection model? How are these specialized in the unit and syntactic models?

9.3.3   ARCHITECTURAL DEVELOPMENT TASKS

Believing that one must constructively engage a style to understand it, we assign programming tasks in three different architectural idioms. For each task, we supply an implementation in the required idiom that uses several components from an available collection. The assignment requires students to extend the implementation *in the same style* by reconnecting parts, using other components, or minimally changing components. The choice of this format is driven by two guiding principles:

- The attention of the students should be focused at the architectural level rather than at the algorithms-and-data-structures level. (Students should already know how to do the latter.)
- It is unreasonable to expect the accurate use of an unfamiliar idiom without providing illustrative sample code employing that idiom.

A pleasant side effect of this choice of format is that problems more closely resembled software maintenance/reuse than building a system from scratch. In addition, we are faced with a considerable diversity of programming language background among the students. It's easier to work in an unfamiliar language if you have a starting point.

To encourage cooperation and to balance unfamiliarity with particular programming languages and systems, students work in pairs on the programming tasks. However, each task has a set of questions to be answered individually.

A major objective of this course is for students to gain an understanding of the essential features of a given problem that make a particular architectural choice appropriate or inappropriate. To this end, we assign variations of a single core problem for all three tasks, differing primarily in the features related to the choice of idiom. By assigning the same basic problem for each architectural idiom, we avoid the risk of students associating problem class *X* with architectural idiom *Y*, instead promoting understanding of the features of each problem that should lead the designer to choose that idiom. By varying the features related to the architectural choice, we also discourage students from leaving each solution in the same basic architectural idiom, adding only the superficial trappings of the second idiom. For example, by changing the system requirements, we ensure that an event-driven solution will not merely be a pipe-and-filters solution "dressed up" to look like an event-driven system.

Because the problems involve not only the production of a working system but also the analysis of an architectural style, we hold design reviews halfway through each assignment. The students present their reviews in class, with each team making one presentation sometime during the semester. The reviews are not graded; thus they provide a means for the class to engage in discussions about the architectural style and for the instructors to guide the student solutions (both those being presented and those of the students watching the presentation) by asking pointed questions. The schedule for these presentations appears in Figure 9.1.

In past versions of the course the core task chosen was the KWIC indexing problem [Par72]. In this problem, a set of lines (sequences of words) is extended to include all circular shifts of each line, and the resulting extended set is alphabetized. This core problem was varied in each architectural idiom as follows:

- **Object-Oriented:** This variation was *interactive*: a user enters lines one at a time, interspersed with requests for the KWIC index. Students were supplied with a system which generated the KWIC index without the circular shifts (i.e., a line alphabetizer) and asked to include the shifts. In addition, students were asked to omit lines which began with a "trivial" word (e.g., *and* or *the*).

- **Pipes & Filters:** In this variation, students were asked to generate a batch version which generated KWIC indices of login and user names (as generated by the *finger* command). Students carried out two tasks. In one task, students used the Unix shell to connect "modules" such as the common Unix commands *finger, sort,* and *uniq*. A second task required them to connect the same modules in a pipe organization too complex to describe in the shell, so that they had to use raw pipes from within C. As before, they began with solutions which alphabetized lines but did not generate circular shifts.

- **Event-Driven (implicit invocation):** This variation extended the problem for the object-oriented architecture with a *delete* command. Students were required to reuse existing modules, augmenting them with event bindings to establish how they communicated.

9.3.4   FORMAL MODELING

To develop skill in understanding and manipulating formal models, we assigned a task that require students to extend an existing formal model of a software architecture. As with the architectural development tasks, the formal modeling task builds on an existing base—in this case the formal model developed by Garlan and Notkin of event systems [GN91]. In this work the authors show how a simple model of systems based on event broadcast can be specialized for a number of common systems, including Smalltalk MVC, Gandalf programming environments, the Field programming environment, and APPL/A.

The students are asked to perform similar specializations for two different architectures: spreadsheets and blackboard systems. In addition, they are asked to provide a commentary that answered the following questions:

1. What important aspects of the modeled architectures are (intentionally) left out of the model?

2. For the blackboard system, would it be possible to model some notion of "non-interference"?

3. For the spreadsheet system, is the *Circular* property defined in the events paper a useful concept? Why or why not?

4. Based on the formal models, briefly compare each of the two new systems with the other ones that were formally modeled. For example, you might explain which of the other systems they are most similar to.

9.3.5   ANALYSIS AND INTERPRETATION OF A SYSTEM

In addition to the assignments described above, students also examine and describe the architecture of a nontrivial system. About midway through the semester we ask each group of students to select a system from a list of candidates that we supply. Alternatively, students can volunteer a system of their own, provided it meets the criteria outlined below.

The students' task is to complete an architectural analysis of the chosen system by the end of the semester. Their analysis has to include the following components:

1. **Parts catalog:** A list of the modules in the system, making the interfaces explicit, together with an explanation of what each one does.

2. **Interconnections catalog:** A list of the connections between modules and a description of each.

3. **Architectural description:** A description of the system's architecture, using the vocabulary developed in the course.

4. **Critique:** An evaluation of how well the architectural documentation for the system matches the actual implementation.

5. **Revision:** Suggestions for improvements to the system architecture.

In addition to a written analysis, students are expected to present their analysis to the class. We allotted three days at the end of the semester for this. The grade on the project was determined both by the written analysis and the presentation.

In selecting candidate systems, we attempt to find systems that are tractable but challenging. Specifically, we apply the following criteria for selection:

- **Size:** Ten to twenty modules containing between 2,000 and 10,000 lines of code.

- **Documentation:** Enough system documentation that students did not need to start from raw code to do their analysis.

- **Resident guru:** There should be someone in the local environment who knows the system and can answer questions about its design and implementation.

9.4   EVALUATION

9.4.1   LESSONS FROM THE INITIAL OFFERING

The first offering of the course ran during the spring semester of the 1991–1992 academic year at Carnegie Mellon University. Four undergraduate students and seven Master of Software Engineering students took the course. There were also half a dozen regular auditors. The lessons we learned as a result of that offering are based upon the students' progress in learning the course material and on evaluation of the course by the students themselves.

CONTENT

It is clear that a sufficiently large body of knowledge exists to support a course in software architecture. When we designed this version, we were unable to include all the topics of interest, and we made some hard decisions among alternative materials for the topics we did include.

The specific topics of the course had varying success. The treatment of architectural idioms was particularly valuable. The use of formal methods worked out well, but for students with no exposure to Z, it required considerably more effort than the other sections. (Almost all of the master's level students had already had a course in formal methods.) The lecture on design was reasonably successful, but suffered because there is relatively little material directly applicable to software architectures.

The assignments that involved construction and analysis of systems were generally quite valuable, as they gave students practice in applying the principles of the course. However, we felt that we could have chosen more challenging tasks focused on some of the more important issues of architectural design.

Chosing good practical problems is one of the most difficult (and important) parts of developing such a course. Part of the problem centers around finding systems that are of the right size and complexity. On the one hand, it is important to find systems that are large enough to represent nontrivial architectures. On the other hand, there is a limit to the size of system that students can handle, especially since we wanted students to have experience with several architectures.

Our approach to the problem was to give students a working system and a collection of parts that they could reuse and modify in adapting the system to the task assigned. Overall this was a good approach, although it takes a lot of preparation to make it successful. We attempted to use Booch components [Boo87] for the first and third assignments, and standard Unix tools for the second assignment. However, much of the software needed in the solutions to the problems could not be found in these standard collections. As a result we developed most of the code in the starting frameworks from scratch. For example we used only one Booch component package (a total of 200 lines), but wrote 1400 lines of Ada and 300 lines of C for the frameworks provided to the students.

Another aspect of chosing good assignments is to find problems that exploit the target architecture but do not have a single solution. Our assignments were not sufficiently rich to accomplish this. Moreover, time constraints prevented us from making more parts available than were absolutely required for the assignments, so the students did not face the challenge of selecting an architectural solution from a rich parts kit.

One issue involving the assignments was the use of multiple programming languages. We wanted to avoid giving the impression that there is a one-to-one mapping between programming languages and architectures. However, our parts kit (the Booch components) was in Ada, and our version of the Ada compiler did not provide a library for manipulating Unix pipes. This led us to use Ada for the first and third assignments, and C for the second.

FORMAT

Assigning questions on the class readings was a good idea. It served both to focus students' attention and to encourage them to do the reading in advance. This worked well enough that we could plan lectures that elaborated on and interpreted the material rather than repeating it.

The task formats worked well in terms of the amount of time allotted and overall structure of the assignments. However, one challenge lay in the diversity of language experience among the students. In particular, Ada was familiar to some students, but new to others. While this course was not intended to be a "programming course," we found it necessary to provide a brief Ada help session for students without Ada experience. This session's effectiveness was limited because it was held outside normal class hours and was not graded. Ideally in an architectures course, however, all students should know the programming languages to be used for the assignments prior to entering the class.

Using groups to accomplish the assignments had generally positive results. Mixing graduate and undergraduate students on each team formed a balanced collection of strengths which enabled teams to grasp the essentials of the programming assignments quickly. Also, the team environment allowed students to discuss the architectural issues among themselves in a more structured format than might otherwise have been available. We believe this would have been even more effective with a more challenging set of problems.

COMMENTS FROM STUDENTS

We distributed two course evaluations to students: one midway through the course and one at the end. Overall student responses were quite positive. Typical comments were, "I've noticed that I'm viewing problems in other classes from a different perspective," and "I now finally understand what we were doing when we built that system in the way we did."

At a more detailed level the students felt that the study of architectural idioms was most important, and that it provided a foundation for a body of knowledge to which they had not been exposed. They also said that the course encouraged a new perspective on software systems. Some students wanted more emphasis on the process of architectural design and guidance in choosing an architectural idioms. The general opinion was that more could be added to the course, but not at the expense of current material.

The readings were generally viewed as a valuable part of the course. Students appreciated the incentive to read them regularly, and they particularly appreciated the absence of a final exam. They also liked having lectures serve to elaborate the readings rather than repeating them—something that is only possible when the instructor can assume that students have actually read the readings.

The course required a significant amount of work, but the students thought it was worth the effort. They noted that, unlike most courses, the load is fairly level. They had to pay attention to the course regularly, but they didn't wind up with massive deadline crunches.

The team organization was also judged favorably. We received no complaints about unequal workload within a team, although some team members commented that getting a consensus, even on a small team, took time.

9.4.2   CONCLUSIONS ABOUT TEACHING SOFTWARE ARCHITECTURE

Software architecture is worth teaching, and it can be taught in many ways. From our experience with the present course and previous experience with four semesters of graduate reading seminars in the area, we can draw some conclusions about teaching software architecture in any format.

- Architecture provides a bridge between theory and coding. In any program teaching system design, there are high principles of program construction which are difficult to relate to the small programming assignments that comprise the majority of the undergraduate experience. A course that presents students with the terminology of software architecture and that gives them concrete examples of systems to relate to specific architectural styles allows the students to relate these two disparate bodies of information more readily and concretely.

- Students seem capable of rapidly developing an aesthetic about architectures. They can identify systems in their own experience which match specific styles, and they can also identify flawed designs as examples of poorly formed or poorly understood architectures. They are quite capable of answering open-ended questions about the appropriateness of a specific architecture to a problem and defending their positions rationally and powerfully. Unity does not evolve among the students, however. Different students will promote different architectures for the same problem, depending upon their particular points of view.

- There is little concrete material available in any form to guide design decisions. Without such material, students get little help in resolving point-of-view differences. Instructors should make every effort to present techniques for selecting among architectural alternatives, including even simple rules of thumb such as "consider an interpreter when you're designing for a machine that doesn't actually exist."

- There is enough substantive material to fill a course. The selection we made for this offering was based on the coverage of our graduate reading seminars. However, we recognize that there were a number of difficult choices in our selection which might well have gone another way. In our opinion, the field of software architectures is moving from a point where finding enough papers is difficult to one where the challenge is to select the appropriate complement of papers.

- We wish there were more organized surveys of the material than are currently present. Currently, the fragmented nature of the material requires that the students be carefully instructed on exactly which information within a given paper is appropriate to the subject at hand. This is compounded by the sheer size and disorganization of the current software architectures field. There are few papers which view problems from a purely architectural perspective, and the boundaries between architectural idioms are not always clear. We would like to see more papers presenting architectural analysis techniques, and more worked examples in specific architectures. We would also like to see more mature distributed systems architectures and more papers like Nii's [Nii86] that survey a class of systems against a single architectural paradigm. We think this will come with a better understanding of the idioms that comprise software architecture.

- It is tempting to treat the subject of software architectures abstractly and present only idealized views of the various architectural idioms. Resist this. Students have weak intuitions about the high-level architectural abstractions. Every formal or abstract model must be related to a real example, so that the student not only learns the abstract view of the architecture, but also the characteristics of a concrete instance of that architecture.

- Practice in using models is important. Analyzing existing architectures without working within the specific architectural framework does not allow the student to recognize the strengths and weaknesses of individual architectural styles. It is not sufficient for students to be able to recognize a specific idiom; they must also be able to decide which idiom to apply to a particular problem. For that skill, analysis alone is not enough.

BIBLIOGRAPHY

[A+77] Christopher Alexander et al. *A Pattern Language: Towns, Buildings, Construction.* Oxford University Press, New York, 1977.

[A+91] Rafi Ahmed et al. The Pegasus heterogeneous multidatabase system. *IEEE Computer,* 24(12):19–27, December 1991.

[AAG93] Gregory Abowd, Robert Allen, and David Garlan. Using style to give meaning to software architecture. In *Proceedings of SIGSOFT'93: Foundations of Software Engineering,* Software Engineering Notes, 118(3):9–20. ACM Press, December 1993.

[ACM90] Vincenzo Ambriola, Paolo Ciancarini, and Carlo Montangero. Software process enactment in Oikos. In *Proceedings of the Fourth ACM SIGSOFT Symposium on Software Development Environments,* SIGSOFT Software Engineering Notes, 183–192. Irvine, California, December 1990.

[Ado85] *Postscript Language Reference Manual,* Adobe Systems, Inc. Addison-Wesley, 1985.

[AG92] Robert Allen and David Garlan. A formal approach to software architectures. In Jan van Leeuwen, ed., *Proceedings of IFIP'92.* Elsevier Science Publishers B.V., September 1992.

[AG93] Joanne M. Atlee and John Gannon. State-based model checking of event-driven system requirements. *IEEE Transactions on Software Engineering,* 19(1):24–40, January 1993.

[AG94a] Robert Allen and David Garlan. Beyond definition/use: Architectural interconnection. In *Proceedings of the ACM Interface Definition Language Workshop,* 29(8). SIGPLAN Notices, August 1994.

[AG94b] Robert Allen and David Garlan. Formal connectors. Technical Report CMU-CS-94-115. Carnegie Mellon University, 1994.

[AG94c] Robert Allen and David Garlan. Formalizing architectural connection. In *Proceedings of the Sixteenth International Conference on Software Engineering,* May 1994.

[And91] Gregory R. Andrews. Paradigms for process interaction in distributed programs. *ACM Computing Surveys,* 23(1):49–90, March 1991.

[ASBD92] Toru Asada, Roy F. Swonger, Nadine Bounds, and Paul Duerig. The quantified design space: A tool for the quantitative analysis of designs. Technical Report CMU-CS-92-213. Carnegie Mellon University, November 1992.

[Bac86] Maurice J. Bach. *The Design of the UNIX Operating System*, chap. 5, pp. 111–119. Software Series. Prentice Hall, 1986.

[Bal86] Robert M. Balzer. Living with the next generation operating system. In *Proceedings of the 4th World Computer Conference*, September 1986.

[BAS89] J.C. Browne, M. Azam, and S. Sobek. Code: A unified approach to parallel programming. *IEEE Software*, July 1989.

[Bea92] Brian W. Beach. Connecting software components with declarative glue. In *Proceedings of the Fourteenth International Conference on Software Engineering*, 1992.

[Ber92] Alex Berson. *Client/Server Architecture*. McGraw-Hill, 1992.

[Bes90] Laurence J. Best. *Application Architecture: Modern Large-Scale Information Processing*. Wiley, 1990.

[BG88] Nathaniel S. Borenstein and James Gosling. UNIX EMACS: A retrospective (lessons for flexible system design). In *Proceedings of Symposium on User Interface Software*, pp. 95–101. ACM Press, October 1988.

[BN71] C. Gordon Bell and Allen Newell. *Computer Structures: Reading and Examples*. McGraw-Hill, 1971.

[BO92] Don Batory and Sean O'Malley. The design and implementation of hierarchical software systems with reusable components. *ACM Transactions on Software Engineering and Methodology*, 1(4):355–398, October 1992.

[Boo86] Grady Booch. Object-oriented development. *IEEE Transactions on Software Engineering*, SE-12(2):211–221, February 1986.

[Boo87] Grady Booch. *Software Components with Ada: Structures, Tools and Subsystems*. Benjamin/ Cummings, Menlo Park, California, 1987.

[Bro91] P.G. Brown. QFD: Echoing the voice of the customer. AT&T Technical Journal, March/April 1991:18–32.

[BS92] Barry Boehm and William Scherlis. Megaprogramming. In *Proceedings of Software Technology Conference, DARPA*. ARPA, 1992.

[BSS84] David R. Barstow, Howard E. Shrobe, and Erik Sandewall, eds. *Interactive Programming Environments*. McGraw-Hill, 1984.

[BV93] Pam Binns and Steve Vestal. Formal real-time architecture specification and analysis. In *Tenth IEEE Workshop on Real-Time Operating Systems and Software*. New York. May 1993.

[BW93] David Barstow and Alex Wolf. Design methods and software architectures track. In *Proceedings of the 7th International Workshop in Software Specification and Design*. IEEE Press, 1993.

[BWW88] M.R. Barbacci, C.B. Weinstock, and J.M. Wing. Programming at the processor-memory-switch level. In *Proceedings of the 10th International Conference on Software Engineering*, pp. 19–28. IEEE Computer Society Press, April 1988.

[C+90] M. Carey et al. The EXODUS extensible DBMS project: An overview. In S. Zdonik and D. Maier, eds., *Readings in Object-Oriented Database Systems*. Morgan Kaufmann, 1990.

[CBCD93] Lee Champeny-Bares, Syd Coppersmith, and Kevin Dowling. The Terregator mobile robot. Technical Report CMU-RI-TR-93-03. Carnegie Mellon University, Robotics Institute, Pittsburgh, Pennsylvania, 1993.

[CE78] Ivan M. Campos and Gerald Estrin. SARA-aided design of software for concurrent systems. In *Proceedings of National Computer Conference*. ACM, 1978.

[Cha93] Craig Chambers. Predicate classes. In *Proceedings of ECOOP '93*, 1993.

[CN92] Minder Chen and Ronald J. Norman. A framework for integrated CASE. *IEEE Software*, 9(2):18–22, March 1992.

[Coa92] Peter Coad. Object-oriented patterns. *Communications of the ACM*, 35(9):153–159, 1992.

[Coh89] D. Cohen. Compiling complex transition database triggers. In *Proceedings of the 1989 ACM SIGMOD*, pp. 225–234. Portland, Oregon, 1989.

[Coo79] Lee W. Cooprider. *The Representation of Families of Software Systems*. Ph.D. thesis, Technical Report CMU-CS-79-116. Carnegie Mellon University, April 1979.

[Cor91] The Common Object Request Broker: Architecture and Specification. OMG Document Number 91.12.1, December 1991. Revision 1.1 (Draft 10).

[D+91] Doubleday et al. Building distributed Ada applications from specifications and functional components. In *Proceedings of TRI-Ada'91*, pp. 143–154. ACM Press, October 1991.

[DC95] Thomas R. Dean and James R. Cordy. A syntactic theory of software architecture. *IEEE Transactions on Software Engineering*, Special Issue on Software Architecture, 21(4), April 1995.

[DG90] Norman Delisle and David Garlan. Applying formal specification to industrial problems: A specification of an oscilloscope. *IEEE Software*, 7(5):29–37, September 1990.

[DHL90] Umeshwar Dayal, Meichun Hsu, and Rivka Ladin. Organizing long-running activities with triggers and transactions. In *Proceedings of the 1990 ACM SIGMOD International Conference on the Management of Data*, pp. 204–214. ACM Press, May 1990. Special issue of SIGMOD Record 19(2), June 1990.

[Dij89] Edsger W. Dijkstra. On the cruelty of really teaching computing science. *Communications of the ACM*, 32(12):1398–1404, December 1989.

[DK76] Frank DeRemer and Hans H. Kron. Programming-in-the-large versus programming-in-the-small. *IEEE Transactions on Software Engineering*, SE-2(2):80–86, June 1976.

[DoD83] *Reference Manual for the Ada Programming Language*. United States Department of Defense, January 1983.

[Eco93] The computer industry. Editorial article in *The Economist*, February 1993.

[Elf87] Alberto Elfes. Sonar-based real-world mapping and navigation. *IEEE Journal of Robotics and Automation*, (3):249–265, 1987.

[F+90] S.J. Fenves et al. An integrated software environment for building design and construction. *Computer-Aided Design*, 22(1):27–36, 1990.

[Fel79] Stuart I. Feldman. Make—a program for maintaining computer programs. *Software—Practice and Experience*, 9:255–265, November 1979.

[Fis89] PROVOX plus Instrumentation System: System overview. Fisher Controls International, 1989.

[FO85] Marek Fridrich and William Older. Helix: The architecture of the XMS distributed file system. *IEEE Software*, 2(3):21–29, May 1985.

[For92] *Failures Divergence Refinement: User Manual and Tutorial*. Formal Systems (Europe) Ltd., Oxford, England, 1.2β edition, October 1992.

[Fro89] Brian Fromme. HP Encapsulator: Bridging the generation gap. Technical Report SESD-89-26, Hewlett-Packard Software Engineering Systems Division, Fort Collins, Colorado, November 1989.

[GAO94] David Garlan, Robert Allen, and John Ockerbloom. Exploiting style in architectural design environments. In *Proceedings of SIGSOFT'94: Foundations of Software Engineering*. ACM Press, December 1994.

[GAO95] David Garlan, Robert Allen, and John Ockerbloom. Architectural mismatch, or, why it's hard to build systems out of existing parts. In *Proceedings of the 17th International Conference on Software Engineering.* Seattle, Washington, April 1995.

[Gar93] David Garlan. Formal approaches to software architecture. In David Alex Lamb and Sandra Crocker, eds., *Proceedings of the Workshop on Studies of Software Design,* no. ISSN-0836-0227-93-352, in External Technical Report. Queen's University Department of Computing and Information Science, May 1993. To be reprinted in [Lam96]

[Gar94] David Garlan. Integrating formal methods into a professional master of soft-ware engineering program. In *Proceedings of the Z Users Meeting.* Springer-Verlag, June 1994.

[Gar95a] David Garlan, ed. *Proceedings of First International Workshop on Architectures for Software Systems,* CMU Technical Report CMU-CS-95-151, April 1995. Summary reprinted in ACM Software Engineering Notes, July 1995.

[Gar95b] David Garlan. What is style? In *Proceedings of the First International Workshop on Architectures for Software Systems,* April 1995. CMU Technical Report CMU-CS-95-151, April 1995.

[GD90] David Garlan and Norman Delisle. Formal specifications as reusable frameworks. In *VDM'90: VDM and Z—Formal Methods in Software Development,* pp. 150–163. Kiel, Germany, Springer-Verlag, LNCS 428, April 1990.

[Ger89] Colin Gerety. HP Softbench: A new generation of software development tools. Technical Report SESD-89-25. Hewlett-Packard Software Engineering Systems Division, Fort Collins, Colorado, November 1989.

[GH93] John V. Guttag and James J. Horning. *Larch: Languages and Tools for Formal Specification.* Springer-Verlag Texts and Monographs in Computer Science, 1993.

[GHJV95] Erich Gamma, Richard Helm, Ralph Johnson, and John Vlissides. *Design Patterns: Elements of Reusable Object-Oriented Design.* Addison-Wesley, 1995.

[GI90] David Garlan and Ehsan Ilias. Low-cost, adaptable tool integration policies for integrated environments. In *Proceedings of the Fourth ACM SIGSOFT Symposium on Software Development Environments.* SIGSOFT '90, Irvine, California, December 1990.

[GKN92] David Garlan, Gail E. Kaiser, and David Notkin. Using tool abstraction to compose systems. *IEEE Computer,* 25(6), June 1992.

[GN91] David Garlan and David Notkin. Formalizing design spaces: Implicit invocation mechanisms. In *VDM'91: Formal Software Development Methods,* pp. 31–44. Noordwijkerhout, The Netherlands, October 1991. Springer-Verlag, LNCS 551.

[GPT95] David Garlan, Frances Newberry Paulisch, and Walter F. Tichy, eds. *Summary of the Dagstuhl Workshop on Software Architecture,* February 1995. Reprinted in ACM Software Engineering Notes, pp. 63–83, July 1995.

[GR93] Jim Gray and Andreas Reuter. *Transaction Processing: Concepts and Techniques.* Morgan Kaufmann, 1993.

[GS93a] David Garlan and Curtis Scott. Adding implicit invocation to traditional programming languages. In *Proceedings of the Fifteenth International Conference on Software Engineering,* Baltimore, Maryland, May 1993.

[GS93b] David Garlan and Mary Shaw. An introduction to software architecture. In V. Ambriola and G. Tortora, eds. *Advances in Software Engineering and Knowledge Engineering,* pp. 1–39, 1993. World Scientific Publishing Company. Also appears as SCS and SEI technical reports: CMU-CS-94-166, CMU/SEI-94-TR-21, ESC-TR-94-021.

[GSO+92] David Garlan, Mary Shaw, Chris Okasaki, Curtis Scott, and Roy Swonger. Experience with a course on architectures for software systems. In *Proceedings of the Sixth SEI Conference on Software Engineering Education*, pp. 23–43. Springer Verlag, LNCS 376, October 1992.

[Har87a] D. Harel. Statecharts: A visual formalism for complex systems. *Science of Computer Programming*, 8:231–274, 1987.

[Har87b] William Harrison. RPDE[3]: A framework for integrating tool fragments. *IEEE Software*, 4(6), November 1987.

[Hew69] Carl Hewitt. Planner: A language for proving theorems in robots. In *Proceedings of the First International Joint Conference in Artificial Intelligence*, 1969.

[HGN91] A. Nico Habermann, David Garlan, and David Notkin. Generation of integrated task-specific software environments. In Richard F. Rashid, ed. *CMU Computer Science: A 25th Commemorative*, Anthology Series, pp. 69–98. ACM Press, 1991.

[HK91] I. Houston and S. King. Experiences and results from the use of Z in IBM. In *VDM'91: Formal Software Development Methods*, Lecture Notes in Computer Science, no. 55, pp. 588–595. Springer-Verlag, October 1991.

[HN86] A. Nico Habermann and David S. Notkin. Gandalf: Software development environments. *IEEE Transactions on Software Engineering*, SE-12(12):1117–1127, December 1986.

[Hoa72] C.A.R. Hoare. Proof of correctness of data representations. *Acta Informatica*, 1(4):271–281, October 1972.

[Hoa85] C.A.R. Hoare. *Communicating Sequential Processes*. Prentice Hall, 1985.

[Hov92] Haig Hovaness. Price war: There's fierce combat ahead over the cost of client-server databases. *Corporate Computing*, 1(6):45–46, December 1992.

[HR85] Fredrick Hayes-Roth. Rule-based systems. *Communications of the ACM*, 28(9):921–932, September 1985.

[HR90] Barbara Hayes-Roth. Architectural foundations for real-time performance in intelligent agents. *The Journal of Real-Time Systems*, Kluwer Academic Publishers, 2:99–125, January 1990.

[HRPL+95] Barbara Hayes-Roth, Karl Pfleger, Phillippe Lalanda, Phillippe Morignot, and Marko Balabanovic. A domain-specific software architecture for adaptive intelligent systems. *IEEE Transactions on Software Engineering*, Special Issue on Software Architecture, 21(4):288–301, April 1995.

[HSL85] Philip J. Hayes, Pedro A. Szekely, and Richard A. Lerner. Design alternatives for user interface management systems based on experience with Cousin. In *Proceedings of CHI '85*, pp. 169–175. ACM, 1985.

[Hum90] W.S. Humphrey. *Managing the Software Process*. The SEI Series in Software Engineering. Addison-Wesley, 1990.

[IW95] Paola Inverardi and Alex Wolf. Formal specification and analysis of software architectures using the chemical, abstract machine model. *IEEE Transactions on Software Engineering*, Special Issue on Software Architecture, 21(4):373–386, April 1995.

[Jac94] Michael Jackson. Problems, methods, and specialisation (a contribution to the special issue on software engineering in the year 2001). *IEEE Software Engineering Journal*, November 1994. A shortened version of this paper also appears in *IEEE Software*, 11(6), November 1994.

[JC94] G.R. Ribeiro Justo and P.R. Freire Cunha. Deadlock-free configuration programming. In *Proceedings of the Second International Workshop on Configurable Distributed Systems*, March 1994.

[Jef92] Kevin Jeffay. Scheduling sporadic tasks with shared resources in hard-real-time systems. In *Proceedings of the 13th IEEE Real-Time Systems Symposium,* pp. 89–99. Phoenix, Arizona, December 1992.

[Jef93] Kevin Jeffay. The real-time producer/consumer paradigm: A paradigm for the construction of efficient, predictable real-time systems. In *Proceedings of the 1993 ACM/SIGAPP Symposium on Applied Computing,* pp. 796–804. ACM Press, Indianapolis, Indiana, February 1993.

[K+91] Rudolf K. Keller et al. User interface development and software environments: The Chiron-1 System. In *Proceedings of the Thirteenth International Conference on Software Engineering,* 1991.

[Kah74] G. Kahn. The semantics of a simple language for parallel programming. *Information Processing,* 1974.

[Ker95] N.L. Kerth. Caterpillar's fate: A pattern language for the transformation from analysis to design. In James Coplein and Douglas Schmidt, eds., *Pattern Languages of Program Design,* pp. 293–320. Addison-Wesley, 1995.

[KG89] Gail E. Kaiser and David Garlan. Synthesizing programming environments from reusable features. In Ted J. Biggerstaff and Alan J. Perlis, eds., *Software Reusability,* vol. 2. ACM Press, 1989.

[Knu73] Donald E. Knuth. *Fundamental Algorithms,* vol. 1 of *The Art of Computer Programming.* Addison-Wesley, Reading, Massachusetts, 1973.

[KP88] G.E. Krasner and S.T. Pope. A cookbook for using the model-view-controller user interface paradigm in Smalltalk-80. *Journal of Object Oriented Programming,* 1(3):26–49, August/September 1988.

[Kra90] Jeff Kramer. Configuration programming—A framework for the development of distributable systems. In *Proceedings of the IEEE International Conference on Computer Systems and Software Engineering.* IEEE Press, Israel, May 1990.

[KRP+93] M.H. Klein, T. Ralya, B. Pollak, R. Obenza, and M.G. Harobur. *A Practitioner's Handbook for Real-Time Analysis: Guide to Rate Monotonic Analysis for Real-Time Systems.* Kluwer Academic, 1993.

[KS91] Won Kim and Jungyun Seo. Classifying schematic and data heterogeneity in multidatabase systems. *IEEE Computer,* 24(12):12–18, December 1991.

[L+88] K.J. Lee et al. An OOD pardigm for flight simulators. 2nd ed. Technical Report CMU/SEI-88-TR-30, Carnegie Mellon University, Software Engineering Institute, September 1988.

[LAK+95] David C. Luckham, Larry M. Augustin, John J. Kenney, James Veera, Doug Bryan, and Walter Mann. Specification and analysis of system architecture using Rapide. *IEEE Transactions on Software Engineering,* Special Issue on Software Architecture, 21(4):336–355, April 1995.

[Lam96] David A. Lamb. *Proceedings of Workshop on Studies of Software.* Lecture Notes in Computer Science. Springer-Verlag, To appear, 1996.

[Lan90a] Thomas G. Lane. Studying software architecture through design spaces and rules. Technical Report CMU/SEI-90-TR-18 ESD-90-TR-219 and CMU-CS-90-175. Carnegie Mellon University, November 1990.

[Lan90b] Thomas G. Lane. *User Interface Software Structures.* Ph.D. thesis. Carnegie Mellon University, May 1990.

[LFW90] R. Lumia, J. Fiala, and A. Wavering. The NASREM robot control system and testbed. *International Journal of Robotics and Automation,* (5):20–26, 1990.

[Lin87] Mark A. Linton. Distributed management of a software database. *IEEE Software,* 4(6):70–76, November 1987.

[LK77] J. Richard Landis and Gary G. Koch. The measurement of observer agreement for categorical data. *Biometrics*, 33:159–174, March 1977.

[LL73] C.L. Liu and J.W. Layland. Scheduling algorithms for multiprogramming in a hard real-time environment. *Journal of the ACM*, 20(1):46–61, January 1973.

[LP90] Tomas Lozano-Perez. Preface, *Autonomous Robot Vehicles*. Springer-Verlag, New York, 1990.

[LS79] Hugh C. Lauer and Edwin H. Satterthwaite. Impact of MESA on system design. In *Proceedings of the Third International Conference on Software Engineering*, pp. 174–175. IEEE Computer Society Press, Atlanta, Georgia, May 1979.

[LVC89] Mark A. Linton, John M. Vlissides, and Paul R. Calder. Composing user interfaces with InterViews. *IEEE Computer*, 22(2), February 1989.

[LW93] Barbara Liskov and Jeannette Wing. A new definition of the subtype relation. In *Proceedings of ECOOP '93*, July 1993.

[M+79] James G. Mitchell et al. *Mesa Language Manual*. Xerox Palo Alto Research Center, Systems Development Department, April 1979.

[Mak92] Victor W. Mak. Connection: An inter-component communication paradigm for configurable distributed systems. In *Proceedings of the International Workshop on Configurable Distributed Systems*. London, UK, March 1992.

[Mar87] Lionel S. Marks. *Mark's Standard Handbook for Mechanical Engineers*. McGraw-Hill, 1987.

[McC91] Gary R. McClain, ed. *Open Systems Interconnection Handbook*. Intertext Publications McGraw-Hill, New York, 1991.

[MF93] Charles R. Morris and Charles H. Ferguson. How architecture wins technology wars. *Harvard Business Review*, 71(2), March–April 1993.

[MG92] Erik Mettala and Marc H. Graham. The domain-specific software architecture program. Technical Report CMU/SEI-92-SR-9. Carnegie Mellon Software Engineering Institute, June 1992.

[MQR95] M. Moriconi, X. Qian, and R. Riemenschneider. Correct architecture refinement. *IEEE Transactions on Software Engineering*, Special Issue on Software Architecture, 21(4):356–372, April 1995.

[MR88] Naftaly H. Minsky and David Rozenshtein. A software development environment for law-governed systems. In *Proceedings of the ACM SIG-SOFT/ SIGPLAN Software Engineering Symposium on Practical Software Development Environments*, November 1988.

[Mul93] Sape Mullender. *Distributed Systems*. Addison-Wesley, 1993.

[Mul95] D.E. Mularz. Pattern-based integration architecture. In *Languages of Program Design*, pp. 441–452. Addison-Wesley, 1995.

[N+91] G.S. Novak et al. Negotiated interfaces for software reuse. *IEEE Transactions on Software Engineering*, SE-18(7):646–653, July 1991.

[NAT69] Software engineering: report on a conference sponsored by the NATO science committee. Meeting of 1968, published 1969.

[New82] Allen Newell. The knowledge level. *Artificial Intelligence*, 18:87–127, 1982.

[New90] Allen Newell. *Unified Theories of Cognition*. Harvard University Press, 1990.

[NGGS93] David Notkin, David Garlan, William G. Griswold, and Kevin Sullivan. Adding implicit invocation to languages: Three approaches. In S. Nishio and A. Yonezawa, ed., *Proceedings of the JSSST International Symposium on Object Technologies for Advanced Software*, p. 489–510. Springer-Verlag, LNCS, 742, November 1993.

[Nii86] H. Penny Nii. Blackboard systems. *AI Magazine*, 7(3):38–53 and 7(4):82–107, 1986.

[Nis91] NIST/ECMA reference model for frameworks of software engineering environments. NIST Special Publication 500-201, December 1991.

[NS91] Allen Newell and David Steier. Intelligent control of external software systems. *AI in Engineering*, 1991. To appear. (Was Carnegie Mellon University, Engineering Design Research Center Report EDRC 05-55-91).

[ODL93] Katia Obraczka, Peter B. Danzig, and Shih-Hao Li. Internet resource discovery services. *IEEE Computer*, pp. 8–22, September 1993.

[Ous94] John K. Ousterhout. *Tcl and the Tk Toolkit*. Addison-Wesley, 1994.

[P+84] Robert H. Perry et al. *Perry's Chemical Engineers' Handbook*. McGraw-Hill, New York, 1984.

[PA91] James Purtilo and Joanne Atlee. Module reuse by interface adaptation. *Software: Practice and Experience*, 21(6):539–556, June 1991.

[Par72] D.L. Parnas. On the criteria to be used in decomposing systems into modules. *Communications of the ACM*, 15(12):1053–1058, December 1972.

[Par79] David L. Parnas. Designing software for ease of extension and contraction. *IEEE Transactions on Software Engineering*, 5:128–138, March 1979.

[Par90] David Lorge Parnas. Education for computing professionals. *IEEE Computer*, 23(1):17–22, January 1990.

[Pau85] Mark C. Paulk. The ARC Network: A case study. *IEEE Software*, 2(3):61–69, May 1985.

[PCW85] David L. Parnas, Paul C. Clements, and David M. Weiss. The modular structure of complex systems. *IEEE Transactions on Software Engineering*, SE-11(3):259–266, March 1985.

[PDB84] Gregg Podnar, Kevin Dowling, and Mike Blackwell. A functional vehicle for autonomous mobile robot. Technical report, Carnegie Mellon University, Robotics Institute, Pittsburgh, Pennsylvania, 1984.

[PDN86] Ruben Prieto-Diaz and James M. Neighbors. Module interconnection languages. *The Journal of Systems and Software*, 6(4):307–334, November 1986.

[Per87] Dewayne E. Perry. Software interconnection models. In *Proceedings of the Ninth International Conference on Software Engineering*, pp. 61–68, Monterey, California, March 1987. IEEE Computer Society Press.

[Pou89] D. Pountain. Occam II. *Byte*, 14(10):279–284, October 1989.

[Pre95] Wolfgang Pree. *Design Patterns for Object-Oriented Software Development*. Addison-Wesley, ACM Press, 1995.

[PST91] Ben Potter, Jane Sinclair, and David Till. *An Introduction to Formal Specification and Z*. Prentice Hall, 1991.

[Pur88] James M. Purtilo. A software interconnection technology. Technical Report UMIACS-TR-88-83 CS-TR-2139. University of Maryland, College Park, November 1988.

[PW92] Dewayne E. Perry and Alexander L. Wolf. Foundations for the study of software architecture. *ACM SIGSOFT Software Engineering Notes*, 17(4):40–52, October 1992.

[R+91] James Rumbaugh et al. *Object-Oriented Modeling and Design*. Prentice Hall, Englewood Cliffs, New Jersey, 1991.

[Rec92] Eberhardt Rechtin. The art of systems architecting. *IEEE Spectrum*, October 1992.

[Rei90] Steve P. Reiss. Connecting tools using message passing in the Field Environment. *IEEE Software*, 7(4):57–66, July 1990.

[RMP+82] David S.H. Rosenthal, James C. Michener, Gunther Pfaff, Rens Kessener, and Malcolm Sabin. The detailed semantics of graphics input devices. *Computer Graphics*, 16(3):33–38, July 1982.

[Ros85] Frederick Rosene. A software development environment called STEP. In *Proceedings of the ACM Conference on Software Tools*, April 1985.

[RW80] Brian K. Reid and Janet H. Walker. *Scribe User's Manual*. Third Ed. Unilogic, Ltd., 1980.

[S+87] Alfred Z. Spector et al. Camelot: A distributed transaction facility for Mach and the Internet—an interim report. Technical Report CMU-CS-87-129. Carnegie Mellon University, June 1987.

[S+88] V. Seshadri et al. Semantic analysis in a concurrent compiler. In *Proceedings of ACM SIGPLAN '88 Conference on Programming Language Design and Implementation*. ACM SIGPLAN Notices, 1988.

[S+94] Mary Shaw et al. Candidate model problems in software architecture. Draft Publication, 1994.

[SBH+83] Mary Shaw, Ellen Borison, Michael Horowitz, Tom Lane, David Nichols, and Randy Pausch. Descartes: A programming-language approach to interactive display interfaces. *Proceedings of SIGPLAN '83: Symposium on Programming Language Issues in Software Systems*, ACM SIGPLAN Notices, 18(6):100–111, June 1983.

[SDK+95] Mary Shaw, Robert DeLine, Daniel V. Klein, Theodore L. Ross, David M. Young, and Gregory Zelesnik. Abstractions for software architecture and tools to support them. *IEEE Transactions on Software Engineering*, 21(4):314–315, April 1995.

[Sed88] Robert Sedgewick. *Algorithms*. Addison-Wesley, Reading, Massachusetts, 1988.

[SEI90] *Proceedings of the Workshop on Domain-Specific Software Architectures*, Software Engineering Institute, Hidden Valley, Pennsylvania, July 1990.

[SG86] Robert W. Scheifler and Jim Gettys. The X window system. *ACM Transactions on Graphics*, 5(2):79–109, April 1986.

[SG94] Mary Shaw and David Garlan. Characteristics of higher-level languages for software architecture. Technical Report CMU-CS-94-210. Carnegie Mellon University, School of Computer Science, 1994. Also printed as CMU Software Engineering Institute Technical Report SEI-94-TR-23, ESC-TR-94-023.

[Sha85] Mary Shaw. What can we specify? Questions in the domains of software specifications. In *Proceedings of the Third International Workshop on Software Specification and Design*, pp. 214–215. IEEE Computer Society Press, August 1985.

[Sha88] Mary Shaw. Toward higher-level abstractions for software systems. In *Proceedings of Tercer Simposio Internacional del Conocimiento y su Ingerieria*. October 1988. Available from author.

[Sha90] Mary Shaw. Prospects for an engineering discipline of software. *IEEE Software*, 7(6):15–24, November 1990.

[Sha93a] Mary Shaw. Procedure calls are the assembly language of system interconnection: Connectors deserve first-class status. In *Proceedings of the Workshop on Studies of Software Design*, May 1993. To be reprinted in [Lam96].

[Sha93b] Mary Shaw. Software architectures for shared information systems. In *Mind Matters: Contributions to Cognitive and Computer Science in Honor of Allen Newell*. Erlbaum, 1993.

[Sha95] Mary Shaw. Beyond objects: A software design paradigm based on process control. *ACM Software Engineering Notes*, 20(1):27–38, January 1995.

[Shn86] Ben Shneiderman. Seven plus or minus two central issues in human-computer interaction. In *Proceedings of CHI '86: Human Factors in Computing Systems*, pp. 343–349. ACM, 1986.

[SHO90] S. Sutton, D. Heimbigner, and L. Osterweil. Language constructs for managing change in process-centered environments. In *Proceedings of ACM SIGSOFT'90: Fourth Symposium on Software Development Environments*, December 1990.

[Sim90] Reid Simmons. Concurrent planning and execution for a walking robot. Technical Report CMU-RI-90-16. Carnegie Mellon University, Robotics Institute, Pittsburgh, Pennsylvania, 1990.

[Sim92] Reid Simmons. Concurrent planning and execution for autonomous robots. *IEEE Control Systems*, (1):46–50, 1992.

[SLF90] Reid Simmons, Long-Ji Lin, and Christopher Fedor. Autonomous task control for mobile robots. In *Proceedings of the 5th IEEE International Symposium on Intelligent Control*, Philadelphia, Pennsylvania, September 1990.

[SN92] Kevin J. Sullivan and David Notkin. Reconciling environment integration and software evolution. *ACM Transactions on Software Engineering and Methodology*, 1(3):229–268, July 1992.

[Spi88] J.M. Spivey. *The Fuzz Manual*. Computing Science Consultancy, 2 Willow Close, Garsington, Oxford OX9 9AN, UK, 1988.

[Spi89a] J.M. Spivey. An introduction to Z and formal specification. *Software Engineering Journal*, 4(1):40–50, January 1989.

[Spi89b] J.M. Spivey. *The Z Notation: A Reference Manual*. Prentice Hall, 1989.

[SS88] Bruce Arne Sherwood and Judith N. Sherwood. The cT language and its uses: A modern programming tool. In *Proceedings of the Conference on Computers in Physics Instruction*. North Carolina State University, August 1988.

[SST86] Steven A. Shafer, Anthony Stentz, and Charles E. Thorpe. An architecture for sensor fursion in a mobile robot. In *Proceedings of the IEEE International Conference on Robotics and Automation*, pp. 2002–2010, San Franciso, California, April 1986.

[Sul86] L.P. Sullivan. Quality function deployment. *Quality Progress*, pp. 39–50, June 1986.

[T+94] Allan Terry et al. Overview of Teknowledge's domain-specific software architecture program. *ACM SIGSOFT Software Engineering Notes*, 19(4):68–76, October 1994.

[Ter92] Michael Terk. A problem-centered approach to creating design environments for facility development. Ph.D. thesis, Civil Engineering Department, Carnegie Mellon University, 1992.

[Tho76] J.W. Thomas. Module interconnection in programming systems supporting abstraction. PhD thesis, Brown University, June 1976.

[THP92] W.F. Tichy, A.N. Habermann, and L. Prechelt, eds. *Proceedings of the Dagstuhl Worshop on Future Software Engineering Directions*, 1992. Reprinted in ACM Software Engineering Notes, January 1993.

[Tic79] Walter F. Tichy. Software development control based on module interconnection. In *Proceedings of the 4th International Conference on Software Engineering*, pp. 29–41, 1979.

[Tor74] Proceedings of Workshop on the Attainment of Reliable Software. University of Toronto, Toronto, Canada, June 1974.

[Tra94] Will Tracz. Collected overview reports from the DSSA project. Loral Federal Systems, Owego, October 1994.

[Ves94] Steve Vestal. Mode changes in real-time architecture description language. In *Proceedings of the Second International Workshop on Configurable Distributed Systems*, March 1994.

[War84] P. Ward. Cruise control for an exercise at the Rocky Mountain Institute for Software Engineering, 1984.

[Wie92] Gio Wiederhold. Mediators in the architecture of future information systems. *IEEE Computer*, 25(3):38–48, March 1992.

[Win94] Jeannette M. Wing. Proceedings of the workshop on interface definition languages. Technical Report CMU-CS-94-WIDL-1. Carnegie Mellon University, Pittsburgh, Pennsylvania, January 1994.

INDEX

A

Abstract data types, 10, 13, 22–23, 35–36, 169
Abstract devices, 106–7
Abstraction, 157–58
  in architectural description languages, 157–58
  hardware levels, 4–5
  historical development, 12–14
  levels, 4–5, 12
  mappings, 186–87
  software levels, 12–15
Active database, 32
Actors, 23
Ada, 157, 163, 168
  adding implicit invocation to, 174–81
ADL. *See* Architecture description languages
ADT. *See* Abstract data types
Aesop, 192–96
Agents, 90–91
Architectural analysis, 155, 158, 211–12
Application interfaces, 105–6
Architectural connection. *See* Connectors
Architecture description languages, 15, 18
  Aesop, 190–204
  UniCon, 183–90
  Wright, 204–12
Architectural design:

automated support for, 192–202
guidance, 97–128
spaces. *See* Design space
using QDS, 116, 120–27
Architectural evolution, 95
Architectural specification, 129–46
  architectural styles, 133–39
  design space, 139–42
  specific systems, 130–33
  theory of architecture, 142
  value of, 129–30
Architectural idioms. *See* Architectural styles
Architectural interaction. *See* Connectors
Architectural patterns. *See* Architectural style
Architectural representation, 196–98. *See also* Architecture description languages
Architectural styles, 2, 15–17, 19–32, 190–92. *See also* Architectural formalism; Architectural description languages
  batch sequential, *See* Batch sequential style
  client-server. *See* Client-server style
  data abstraction. *See* Data abstraction style
  layered. *See* Layered style